Contents

Foreword *vii*

1 The problem of work *1*

2 Visions of alienation *18*

3 Two ethics *36*

4 The nostalgia for permanence *59*

5 The technical environment *80*

6 Anarchism, socialism & work *98*

7 The mystique of creativity *116*

8 Art & work *131*

9 Towards organic living *147*

10 Dangers & contradictions *162*

11 The future of work *181*

Notes *199*

Bibliography *208*

Index *213*

David Meakin

LITERATURE

Man

& CULTURE

IN INDUSTRIAL

Work

SOCIETY

Methuen

First published in 1976
by Methuen & Co Ltd
11 New Fetter Lane, London EC4P 4EE
© *1976 David Meakin*
Printed in Great Britain at the
University Printing House, Cambridge
(*Euan Phillips, University Printer*)

ISBN 0 416 83880 4 (*hardback*)
ISBN 0 416 83890 1 (*paperback*)

Foreword

The emphasis of this book is largely a literary one, although it is
obvious that by the very nature of its subject it must look beyond the
confines normally imposed on literature to involve philosophical, sociological and political considerations. The boundaries are, of course, not
clear at the best of times, and it seems to me that even such a tentative
and imperfect attempt at synthesis might have its place in the context
of a growing realization of the inadequacy of traditional and hermetic
divisions between subjects and disciplines. Many writers themselves defy
classification : are we, to take but one instance, to regard Simone Weil
as a 'literary' figure, a philosopher, a sociologist, or what? The answer,
of course, is : none of these things; to bundle her determinedly into any
one pigeon-hole is to impoverish her, and to perpetuate by a bitter irony
that very fragmentation against which she pitted her life. And the same
is true of William Morris or Albert Camus. The very fact that courses and
journals in the field of European Studies are now proliferating in our
universities is a clear symptom of a certain relaxation of academic
boundaries. Let us hope that some sort of cross-fertilization may result.

The accusation that an enterprise such as this is likely to call forth —
among others, no doubt — is one of dilettantism, and indeed I am well
aware of being something of a dabbler in fields not professionally my
own. Parts of the book will probably appear naïve to experts in the
particular branches of knowledge concerned, and to them I must
apologize for my presumption. Nevertheless, I have written the book in
the hope that it might have some value at least as a hint at what could
be done by others more accomplished in such an art of synthesis. I have

also, I may add, written the book out of more than academic interest, for the issues involved in the whole problem of work and its possible status seem to me to be of major importance to our civilization and culture.

It will be obvious that the aim of this study is not to describe a close and coherent literary 'movement' in the normal sense of the word. What it intends is rather to outline a significant continuum of speculation in the broadest field of literature on this question of the ethical and cultural value of work. 'Movement' would then be a misleading term, as it tends to suggest a conscious and coherent sense of purpose among all concerned, whereas here I am dealing with writers who in some cases (though by no means all) are ignorant of each other's efforts, covering as they do what seems to me a representative selection from several countries. There can be no doubt that Wesker *is* consciously aware of the fact that he 'continues' William Morris in the present age, or that Camus could see the line from Péguy and Sorel, through the French anarcho-syndicalists and later Simone Weil, up to his own speculation on the problem of work. What I am not seeking to prove, however, is any specific influence of Morris on the French writers, or of, say, Péguy and Weil on Wesker. That appears to me to be of comparatively little importance. It does mean, though, that when I am forced for sheer convenience to use the word 'movement' from time to time — although in general I have preferred to refer to a 'tradition' — I do not intend this to be understood in the sense in which one speaks, for instance, of the surrealist movement. I mean rather to denote a recurrent, cultural phenomenon, a current of common preoccupations, a whole pattern of parallel responses to the problem of work and its cultural and ethical status in industrial society, a pattern that does indeed suggest a meaningful continuum. It is this pattern, rather than a systematic exposition of 'influences' (sometimes a rather sterile exercise) that I am anxious to trace.

1 The problem of work

Work is economic necessity, and from the beginning man works in order to survive. The history of man is to a considerable degree the history of forms of work and means of production, and of the associations and relationships created by the work-process. However, the very extent of these relationships in the human world should lead us to suspect at once that work cannot be limited to sheer necessity and physical survival alone. Why does man continue to seek physical work even when he has no pressing need to do so? Why do leisure activities so often take on the character of work — frequently, as in the current 'do-it-yourself' craze, reverting to simple forms of labour corresponding to patterns of work that are rapidly disappearing in a world of increasingly sophisticated technology? Why can we speak of a crisis of conscience in the world of work, a crisis exacerbated rather than allayed by the promise—or threat — of a Leisure-Society, a world where the completeness of automation could practically do away with necessary work altogether for a large part of the population? Why has the potential value and status of work preoccupied so many writers and thinkers, especially since the beginning of what we are accustomed to call the Industrial Revolution, so that we can postulate a continuum of speculation, a tradition?

Clearly, work is an activity that can be invested with something more than survival-value; and today we are accustomed to the notion that work is inextricably linked with our human status, which is also our ethical status; that it is, as the latter-day French marxist, Roger Garaudy, insists, 'the first moral category'.[1] Work — and not least manual work — is an integral part of our humanity and our intelligence. It dictates not only our relationship to nature, to our environment, but thereby also the working and scope of our consciousness itself, for consciousness is born of that active confrontation with nature. Such was the view of work implied by George Orwell when he claimed with characteristic force that 'Above the level of a third- or fourth-grade moron, life has got to be lived largely in terms of effort . . . cease to use your hands and you have lopped off a huge chunk of your consciousness.'[2]

Familiar such views may now be; yet although work has always been the economic mainstay of every civilization and a determining force on relationships and culture generally, we are faced with the phenomenon that it has not had ethical significance for the thinkers of all epochs. It has often been pointed out that if we look back to ancient Greece we find — as we might expect of a society founded on slavery — that Greek thought tends to be disparaging of manual work. In his *Republic*, Plato clearly looks down on smiths, shoemakers and other artisans, 'the meaner sort of people'. The high realm of philosophy is not for them, 'whose souls are maimed and disfigured by their meannesses, as their bodies are by their trades and crafts.'[3] Nothing could be further removed from the earnest attempts of the aged Tolstoy to learn the craft of cobbling, in the hope of capturing an essential truth that he felt would otherwise elude him! We look in vain among the Greeks for that notion of joy or fulfilment in work that we are to find in later epochs. In the philosophy of antiquity, work is discredited above all because it is associated with change and transformation. For the thinkers of that period, the cosmos is fixed and stable in essence, and the world in which we live and move is but its imperfect reflection. All that *changes* is a testimony to the transience and imperfection of that reflection, and is humiliatingly inferior to the perfection of the Idea — that truth which is attainable only through pure contemplation, free from the contingencies of day-to-day living. Any close contact with the changeable world, and in particular any attempt to act physically on that world and, therefore, to effect further change, is at best a degrading necessity, and should be carried out by a slave-population. Slaves there will have to be, according to Aristotle, until the day when work is abolished, 'when the shuttles fly back and forth of themselves . . .' The worst constitution for Aristotle would be one that gave power to the working masses, and 'the perfect constitution will turn no citizen into a working mechanic.'[4]

It is not until the notion of a fixed permanent cosmos yields to philosophies of change and development that work, which is praxis and transformation, can be more highly valued as an ethical activity in its own right. Unworldly as christian values may be (and Christ, the carpenter, downed tools in favour of his mission and drew his disciples away from their crafts), it is the act of Creation that explodes the fixed Greek cosmos, making change part of the nature of the world, and indeed perhaps its highest truth. And thus, too, is postulated a divine archetype for human acts of creation – the Renaissance will make much of this, as man comes to see himself capable of moulding the universe of which he is the temporal master. The notion of man as creator acquires fundamental importance : his work is worthy of equation with the divine act, he is 'a second just creator after Jove'.

Another way in which work has been validated or even spiritualized is by stressing, not its possible creativity, but its status as the fulfilment of duty. Such validation from the outside, irrespective of the nature of the work performed, is what we find in that ascetic concurrence of protestantism and capitalism traced by Max Weber and by R. H. Tawney. Work is God's plan for man, *Beruf* or 'calling' is holy, idleness is among the greatest of sins, and industriousness can be a means to salvation. There is, needless to say, little exhilaration, little joy in this ethos of duty, and we shall meet with very different views of work in due course. For there is more to the ethic of work than this, more than just a grim, moral imperative to do one's earthly duty in pain and suffering. The need to work goes beyond a mere sense of guilt or obligation, deeply entrenched though that same sense may be in our society and our culture.

When Freud, asked what are the things a normal, balanced person should be able to do well, replied : 'Love and work!' he was attributing to work-activity a value that raises it above mere economic necessity, making it a potential means of self-realization, of integration into reality.[5] The ethic he implies is one that partly explains why prisoners, particularly those left unoccupied in prisoner-of-war camps, have so often felt work as a need that strikes deeper roots into the human psyche than survival or duty alone could suggest. The eminent French sociologist, Georges Friedmann, remarks in his important study *Où va le travail humain?* on the striking number of internees during the last war – including those who had not been manual workers in civilian life – who felt the urgent need to work with their hands : 'the ingenuity of some of them, practising on wretched raw materials (bits of wood, scrap iron, tin cans) with rudimentary tools improvised from next to nothing, can only appear astonishing.' As for the intellectuals among them, 'they seemed to take a sort of revenge, thanks to the opportunity of this

enforced leisure, on the professional orientation of their earlier lives.'[6]
In such an environment work appears as a vital element of psychological balance.

For Freud, the vital importance f work is in forging solid links between the individual and reality, and in particular that part of reality which is the human community. In *Civilization and its Discontents* he wrote : 'No other technique for the conduct of life attaches the individual so firmly to reality as laying emphasis on work; for his work at least gives him a secure place in a portion of reality, in the human community.' This was the highest meaning that work acquired for him. But, on a lower level, he also sees in it a therapeutic value, 'purging' energies which if not used in this way – i.e. in the absence of work-activity of any kind – might wreak havoc on our social and psychological equilibrium.

> The possibility it offers of displacing a large amount of libidinal components, whether narcissistic, aggressive or even erotic, on to professional work and on to the human relations connected with it lends it a value by no means second to what it enjoys as something indispensable to the preservation and justification of existence in society.[7]

Work can then be a 'source of special satisfaction', at least if – and the qualification is a significant and far-reaching one – it is freely chosen, if it channels into social directions the elemental urges and instincts of the individual. It follows then that if we are living in an age in which, for reasons that Freud failed to recognize or to examine at all clearly, the whole notion of work is in crisis, a crisis due above all to technological progress, there is surely a possibility that this crisis will also extend to our personal and social balance. If there is, in the industrial world, a grave danger of the devaluation of work, then is not the whole of our life and the values on which we base it thrown into doubt?

The kind of disequilibrium that can result when work loses its adequate meaning as a potential means of self-fulfilment, as a worthwhile channel for the responsible energies of man, may take the form of a disproportionate overloading of other areas of life to make up for what work itself has lost. Thus a team of notable, American psychologists felt able, in 1959, to pose the problem in terms as wide as these :

> One wonders whether the sense of anomie, of the rootlessness and alienation which anthropologists, political scientists and psychiatrists

have found so serious in our world, is not at least in part a consequence of this overloading of interpersonal relationships due to the loss of the direct meaning of work.[8]

To the list of those who have perceived and investigated this sense of 'rootlessness and alienation' we should have to add philosophers and literary figures in general; and the testimony of the latter, who make up in terms of passion and eloquence for what they sometimes lack in practicality and realism will, I hope, appear in the course of this study to be of inestimable value. Of value, that is, if some day our civilization is to modify its direction; and there are many who believe it *must* modify that direction if it is to survive.

In the words of Carl Jung, 'The supreme ideal of man is to fulfil himself as a unique creative individual according to his own innate potentialities and within the limits of reality.' Work can for Jung, as indeed for Freud, constitute a kind of liberation : 'The best liberation is ensured by regular work. Work, nevertheless, is only salutary when it is a free act and has nothing of infantile constraint about it.'[9] The qualification is of course vital. Work is not to be seen as a merely anonymous and in itself insignificant pipe-line for our energies and urges : it must have the qualities, here emphasized by Jung, of freedom (implying choice and responsibility) and creativity. Without these qualities, work no longer satisfies specifically human needs (as distinct from our animal need for survival) — indeed, it negates them. Frustration replaces fulfilment. With this in mind another professional psychologist quotes the writer Albert Camus : 'Without work all life goes rotten. But when work is soulless, life stifles and dies.'[10] And such is the situation that many feel we are in now, in our complex, industrial societies. Camus is one of them, but the perception is as old as the Industrial Revolution itself.

It is obvious that speculation on the problems of work and its possible, but now all too often thwarted, ethical status must become more urgent as the industrial world develops more and more advanced techniques of automation. We are perhaps not far from a time when only a minority of us will need to work, or when many will work for only a couple of hours each day. The quasi-removal of work thus promised will inevitably raise problems, and ultimately they will be ethical ones. What, society will have to ask, were the moral and psychological values which work represented, and can we afford, in human rather than economic terms, to allow those values to lapse for ever? When society asks those questions, though, it will have to ask them in terms of work at its best and more fulfilling; and such, it is often argued, is *not* the dominant mode of work in modern, industrial society. Not *any* kind of work is valuable and satisfying, and it would be manifestly absurd to suggest that the industrial workers who toiled for an eighty-hour week back in the days of Marx's early writings must have been twice as fulfilled as the forty-hour workers of today. To argue thus would be to reduce the ethic of work to an accessory of exploitation (and we shall see presently that some critics have seen it as precisely that, a means of camouflage and of hoodwinking the workers). Long before its possible disappearance, work has been devalued by the development of productive techniques. A significant, latter-day phenomenon is the rise of industrial psychology, and the dramatic increase in the number of studies in what is often described as 'job satisfaction' from about 1930 onwards; all called into being by the profound and often disturbing changes wrought by industrialization on the reality of human work. It is now that the writings of men like William Morris reveal their prophetic quality — and it is now that we have need of their moral urgency and of their revolt. Without that moral urgency, and the concern for social justice, the whole notion of 'job satisfaction' can cover a multitude of confidence tricks.

Clearly there are other valid work-concerns in our society than demands for greater remuneration and better working conditions, vital as these demands undoubtedly are in some cases (and it would be dangerous to forget Brecht's realistic 'First comes grub, morality afterwards!' and to give oneself up to a total, facile moralism, as some writers do). Political movements have sometimes sensed the other concerns at stake — movements such as anarchism, and the revolutionary sydicalism which it influenced, or the Guild Socialism of G. D. H. Cole. The sense of ethical revolt that informs such movements must, however, be set in a wider context — that of the whole questioning of our civilization and its values. It is a questioning that has taken a variety of forms, whether in the protests of Ivan Illich, centring on his condemnation of the ethos of economic growth, his plea for a limitation on technology and for the creation of post-industrial patterns of 'conviviality', or in aspects of the hippy movement and in particular the rural working communes established in the States as a refusal of the dehumanizing power associated with the technical age. In England we have reached the paradoxical state in which guides to non-mechanized subsistence farming may appear (amidst the motor-car advertisements) in the glossy magazines of the affluent, middle class. Whether such nostalgia is becoming a potent force, or whether it is only a passing fashion to be exploited along with the rest, only time will tell.

As a rather different example, we may take the revolt in France in 1968, a revolt which was not exclusively a student matter, and which, as far as the industrial workers of France were concerned, went beyond mere material demands : in its initial stages it was in some respects a revolt against the reality of alienation in work. It is significant that the gaullist government was moved to pacify the rebellious workers not only with offers of wage increases, but also with promises of participation in the running of their factories and other places of work — promises resuscitated, it might be noted, for the purposes of the 1973 legislative elections, for in the meantime they have remained largely unrealized. Unrealized they must remain, too, unless there were to be more far-reaching changes in the social structure than the present leaders of France themselves would care to contemplate. Vague and misleading the promises may have been : but the very fact they were made at all is highly significant in the general context of a rejection of industrial work, the 'refus du travail industriel' so often referred to in France today. What we must understand by it is a refusal of automatic work, of work without initiative or invention, without responsibility and creativity.

Nor is this current of protest without close connection with the fashionable concern for the environment, itself constituting — at its best and most serious — a wave of distrust about the industrial milieu in its more external manifestations. The erosion of the natural environment in favour of a synthetic world where the rhythms natural to man and to rewarding work on his part are fast being replaced by the 'time-and-motion' calculations of maximum productivity at all (human) cost is becoming an ever more acute preoccupation of the modern conscience. The destruction of the natural environment has also its ramifications in the current concern over pollution and the depletion of the natural resources essential to a balanced, human life, a concern that has brought with it yet another wave of distrust of science and the platitudes of progress. This is not to be taken as just another of those periodic reappearances of romanticism : for, perhaps most significantly, even scientists themselves are coming to lend force to this realization, as the recent manifesto, *A Blueprint for Survival*, illustrates, with its radical and idealistic call from a number of eminent scientists for a reversal of the whole current of modern civilization. It is no mere coincidence that a central work of the literary tradition we shall examine, Morris' *News from Nowhere*, unites the problems of work *and* of the environment.

For Morris, indeed, the two questions were merely interdependent aspects of the same; and to restore the cultural and ethical value of work without restoring some sort of 'natural' framework for all activity is unthinkable.

Dated as some aspects of Morris will inevitably appear after almost a century, many of his preoccupations are reflected in the contrast drawn much more recently by Georges Friedmann between the natural milieu and the technical milieu (with the difference that Friedmann is loath to reject the latter out of hand despite all the manifest alienation he sees in it). The natural milieu is that of the pre-industrial forms of work, of the artisan or the peasant, and is first of all characterized by the fact that nothing is interposed between man and the elements, 'he is near to them, things or beings, animals, tools, plants, wind, soil, he is in them.' Friedmann takes the example of a carpenter who, tool in hand, carries out the various operations of his craft from conception to completion : 'Nothing separates him from his materials, from his work. As for the tool, he holds it in his hand, an extension of the hand that knows, adapts and fashions it at will. His tool. An extension of his body, his skill and his art.' The degree of integration — which is the opposite of alienation — went even further in the natural environment, especially for the peasant :

> Was there not a constant circulation between man and that nature of which he was an extension, which he fashioned, and struggled with sometimes in order to dominate her, but without ever moving away or extracting himself from her? A maturing of his emotions, his view of the world, amidst this milieu of elements, of things, of living beings in which his whole life was steeped and whose rhythms it followed? [11]

The result is a more concerete and sentient existence than many of us know today, with a different concept of time and its relationship to work. And a greater *presence* above all : as there is in the natural milieu virtually no means for the transmission of energy, the worker is humanly present in all his tasks. He is present in the choice of materials, the handling of tools; he has no alibi, no way out of a direct confrontation with the world around him, a world of which he feels profoundly a part. In the pre-industrial environment the tool is not yet used to eliminate the human element of production; on the contrary, it serves to humanize production by making it possible for the master craftsman to create a product that is the direct realization of his project, embodying precision, continuity and organic harmony. The tool at this stage is a means of human intervention on nature, and crystallizes what we might term a dialectical relationship with nature, being a means of acknowledging man's bond with, his dependence on nature and simultaneously a means of reproducing nature in the image of human desires and designs.

This active but nonetheless intimate relationship becomes problematic when man moves into a technical environment. Not only is the city-dweller shielded from the elements in the most obvious sense, but in his work the whole concept of tools changes. Initially, it is true, the machine appears as simply an extension of the tool, although moved by energy that is created artificially — but in proportion to its increasing efficiency it becomes a means of avoiding contact with nature. Whereas the pre-industrial tool was a way of *making* contact with nature, and meaningful contact at that. So there has been not only a change of emphasis, and the machine is something other than just a slightly more complicated tool : it is a question of quantitative development becoming, after a certain point, qualitative change. Becoming even, *in extremis*, a sort of ethical negation. The instrument that promises utter mastery all too easily reveals itself as an instrument of slavery; mechanical values tend to replace values of contact, immediacy and involvement; human presence in the act of work (and, therefore, in a large area of life) declines, if not in the conception of a project or design, at least in the mechanical execution of that project or design. This is a far remove from the sort of organic unity between worker and instrument evoked by Marx in a memorable image, at that stage in *Capital* where he describes the artisan structure of the medieval craft guilds :

> Taking the system as a whole, the worker remained connected with the means of production he used, just as a snail is connected with its shell. For this reason there was lacking the primary basis of manufacture, which is that the means of production should acquire an independent existence as capital, an existence confronting that of the worker.[12]

The development into a technical milieu is seen by many observers as a process of uprooting and dehumanizing, giving rise to an undeniable and generalized anxiety, to what Durkheim termed 'anomie' : an absence of laws or meaningful social patterns of behaviour, an absence of adequate values. And what we might call the disqualification of work in an age of mass-production (and this disqualification inevitably goes hand in hand with a certain devaluation of the *products* of work) is central to this modern anguish and sense of rootlessness. It is not for nothing that the search for roots, whether in the work of Tolstoy, Simone Weil or Arnold Wesker, is a recurrent theme in literature that deals with the cultural status of work.

At the heart of the whole problem is obviously the increasing division of labour, whose early stages are analysed in *Capital*. The development of manufacture out of handicraft is there described as a two-fold process : first of all, independent handicrafts may lose their autonomy and become more specialized until they are 'mutually complementary partial operations in the process of the production of one and the same commodity.' Or again, workers involved in a particular craft may divide that craft into its various operations 'which become isolated and independent of one another to such an extent that each is exclusively performed by one particular workman.' In both cases the result is the same in that it removes from the craftsman his high level of initiative and responsibility — and, therefore, makes him less than a craftsman — leaving what Marx calls 'a productive mechanism whose instruments are human beings.'[13]

Now, it is undoubtedly true that this development is in a sense only taking to a further degree the differentiation between occupations that is already found in much earlier and more primitive societies, and which is an essential concomitant of social life. It is equally true that specialization of this kind generally leads to efficiency : if the production of watches were not split into its innumerable separate operations, and were still, as it once was, the responsibility of one artisan, then clearly watches would be scarce items indeed, and only the very rich could afford them. But it is also true that from the point of view of the producer, to step beyond a certain stage in social specialization *can* be humanly dangerous, whatever the compensations in terms of the diffusion of goods may be. Marx himself is quick to point out that 'persistent labour of a uniform kind impairs the intensity and vigour of a man's animal spirits, which find refreshment and stimulus through change of activities.'[14] Efficiency is itself the value which we perhaps most need to question today; it has too long been the driving principle of our civilization, especially in the form of the scientific organization of labour in which it has culminated, that second phase of the Industrial Revolution fathered by Taylor and exemplified by the production line. No doubt the dynamism of production was such that this development might be regarded as inevitable — 'Si Taylor n'avait pas existé, il aurait fallu l'inventer.'[15] Its results are nevertheless a source of anguish in the modern world, and the methods and avowed aims of 'work study' could be interpreted as threatening unforeseen degrees of alienation. The measure of work in the modern, industrial world is modestly but poignantly expressed in the words of a worker's wife, recorded in the researches of R. H. Guest :

> He comes home at night, plops down in a chair, and just sits for about fifteen minutes. I don't know much about what he does in the plant, but it does something to him. Of course, I shouldn't complain. He gets good pay. We've been able to buy a refrigerator and a T.V. set . . .'[16]

Far from providing integration and fulfilment, such work seems rather to isolate the worker, to demoralize him and replace hope for any other kind of satisfaction by resignation to a sort of ersatz fulfilment in the acquisition of consumer goods. This transference of emphasis from creation to consumption is one of the most characteristic features of our civiliation and culture.

Looking back from our vantage-point, it seems ironic that the Industrial Revolution leads to a conscious realization of the ethical value of work in all its fullness — and especially of those qualities enshrined in the artisanate — at the very moment when those same values are seriously threatened and perhaps doomed by the advent of machino-facture. Even Adam Smith, whose *Wealth of Nations* was a milestone in liberal economic thought and who typically tended to demote work to sub-ethical and sub-cultural status by emphasizing its *economic* nature as the source of national wealth, expressed some grave doubts about the human, moral effects of machine production. His famous comment is worth recalling :

> The understandings of the greater part of men are necessarily formed by their ordinary employments. The man whose life is spent in performing a few simple operations of which the effects are always the same or very nearly the same, has no occasion to assert his understanding or to exercise his invention in finding out expedients for removing difficulties that never occur. He naturally loses, therefore, the habit of such exertion and generally becomes as stupid and ignorant as it is possible for a human creature to become.[17]

This perceptive reservation — remarkably prophetic for the year 1776! announces already the dominant theme of that revolt against the despiritualizing force of industrial civilization that we shall trace in the chapters which follow. More systematic, however, is the contrast drawn by Hegel between the highest spiritual and ethical potential of work (a potential revealed by him as by no-one before) and the degradation into which that work is in danger of falling under mechanization.

After the soulless conception of work entertained by liberal economists, Hegel appears as a restorer of ethical value to human activity by his notion of praxis, or creative activity, representing the dialectical reconciliation of object and subject, of man and nature, leading by that very reconciliation to the higher perfection of both. But Hegel, having elevated human effort to this status, also foresees the danger of machinofacture, in so far as it reduces the ideal of intelligent work to 'partial', 'stupid' and 'inhuman' work. Such alienation from value is completed by the domination of money and the profit-motive. The work-world is, therefore, dehumanized, and leaves only a chilling reality summed up in a memorable phrase : 'the autonomous life of what is dead.'[18]

Marx, too, saw in work immense ethical potential : the history of man is the history of his work, he is first and foremost *homo faber*, the tool-maker, and the creative fusion of object and subject through working on the world gives us the true measure of man's greatness and his superiority over all other animals. In his early *Economic and Philosophic Manuscripts*, Marx establishes a fundamental distinction between human and animal production, accepting that animals do produce in the sense that they build nests, dams, etc. Animals produce only under the pressure of immediate need, whereas man can and does produce when free from physical compulsion — and Marx suggests that his highest productions are precisely the most free ones. Whilst an animal identifies directly with its product, man can be freely objective towards his; and this freedom, this objectivity that is his hallmark as *homo faber* allows him access to something quite unknown to animals : beauty, which is inseparable from choice, the choice of forms and criteria suitable not to the mere physical promptings of his own instincts but to the nature of what he produces :

> But an animal only produces what it immediately needs for itself or its young. It produces one-sidedly, whilst man produces universally. It produces only under the domination of immediate physical need, whilst man produces even when he is free from physical need and only truly produces in freedom therefrom. An animal produces only itself, whilst man reproduces the whole of nature. An animal's product belongs immediately to its physical body, whilst man freely confronts his product. An animal forms things in accordance with

the standard and need of the species to which it belongs, whilst man knows how to produce in accordance with the standard of every species, and knows how to apply everywhere the inherent standard to the object. Man therefore also forms things in accordance with the laws of beauty.[19]

It is, therefore, in work that man appears as a free and creative being; and it is there, too, that he appears as a 'species being' — not just as an individual seeking to survive, but as a part of mankind. In every sense, then, work is fundamental to the nature of man's life and embodies his ethical nature and his cultural values. It is indeed the first moral category.

It will be obvious that the nature of work and its status in any given culture affords us an invaluable key to the understanding of that culture as a whole; it is in no case a peripheral, but always a central issue. Industrial civilization, creating forms of work, also creates forms of culture, and it limits our understanding if we utterly dissociate the two. The impoverishment of popular culture is inextricably linked with the impoverishment of work in our society, and if we wish to change the one we must change the other as well.

Industrial society has its own perverse dynamism, of course, and it cannot be shrugged away; Orwell was one who saw the vicious circle — or rather, vicious spiral — of our machine civilization : 'Mechanization leads to the decay of taste, the decay of taste leads to the demand for machine-made articles and hence to more mechanization, and so a vicious circle is established.'[20] There are those, of course, who would deny that taste has declined so completely, and would point to the fact that the industrial world has its own beauties. It would be foolish to deny them : injection-moulded plastics, for instance, *can* result in objects that give a good deal of aesthetic satisfaction as well as being relatively inexpensive and widely diffused. Such rare but happy exceptions do not, however, correspond to any kind of popular culture, and this is precisely why they are so rare, why they are swamped in vulgar and ugly rubbish. For even the best results (in aesthetic terms) of industrial production testify to a frightening, cultural gap : between the creative designer, whose part in the process is long over by the time actual production begins, and the worker, who is generally reduced to little more than a closely calculated series of gestures in a vast productive machine. It is this gap that makes the decay of taste inevitable and deadly.

So again we see that the problems of work and the problems of culture cannot be separated. As Herbert Read once pointed out, if Britain is the country which more than any other shows a profound lack of taste, it is no doubt because Britain was the first country to be industrialized.[21] What we have witnessed, here as elsewhere, is a progressive decline in the organic culture of society, a culture in which work once played a central role, and above all in those popular arts of which William Morris spoke so persuasively.

The earliest societies — and this applies to the pockets of primitivism that have survived — possessed a striking, cultural unity, in which the utilitarian, the religious and the aesthetic were fused into *one* work-activity. If a man worked at carving a totem, this was simultaneously art, worship and economic activity (in the sense that flattery of the gods might favour the hunt, the harvest, or whatever form production might take in that society). Our civilization, on the other hand, has made the separation between these spheres so radical and absolute (especially between 'work' and 'art') that only a general, cultural deprivation can result, whatever we may have gained in terms of *media* for the potential diffusion of a popular culture. Work is relegated to the merely utilitarian, as something done simply in order to earn enough to live or to provide for certain purely material needs of society, whilst art is emasculated by becoming the prerogative of a privileged and educated minority. Fragmentation of this kind is profoundly injurious to the democratic ideal, just as is that division between design and execution at the heart of the modern process of production. For to split apart *homo sapiens* and *homo faber*, knowing and doing, wisdom and work, is not only to do irreparable damage to human integrity, but to prepare the way for a new slave-civilization. The disqualification of work is a threat to democracy : for if men are forced to act as mechanisms in their daily labour, is there not a danger that in time they may lose their independence, their creativity and their sense of responsibility in other aspects of life as well? And what could be a more insidious threat to democracy than that?

Needless to say, the sort of primitive society in which the various realms of human activity were undifferentiated was unlikely to have been profoundly democratic either; any more than was that feudal structure to which, as we shall see, many writers are to look back. For all that the ethic-of-work tradition covers a wide, political spectrum from Right to revolutionary Left, there is, right across this spectrum a common tendency to adopt a backward-looking, 'reactionary' stance that can at times only be called romantic or sentimental. In particular we find a nostalgia for what are assumed to be the unchanging and stable values of a peasant and artisan society preceding the Industrial Revolution, a society founded on certain organic links and structures that have since been burst apart.

Some recent historians such as Peter Laslett (*The World we have lost*) reject the 'catastrophic' vision of the Industrial Revolution as Engels presented it in *The Condition of the Working-Class in England in 1844*. For Laslett, 'One reason for feeling puzzled by our own industrial society is because the historian has never set out to tell us what society was like before industry came.' He rejects the 'Hegelian' or 'Marxist' notion that one epoch must differ fundamentally from its predecessor, and emphasizes the existence of capitalism *before* the nineteenth century, the existence, too, in pre-industrial society of an exploitation and slavery quite as remorseless as those of Blake's or Dickens' England. 'When people could expect to live for only thirty years in all, how must a man have felt when he realized that so much of his adult life, perhaps all, must go in working for his keep and very little else in someone else's family?' Poverty in the pre-industrial age must, he claims, have been particularly harsh, and it extended to 'a good half of all those living.'[22]

Nostalgia is cheap witchcraft, and even cheaper politics; and no doubt there is much truth is Laslett's reaction against idealization of the past. If we turn for a moment from historians to sociologists, we find a parallel reaction in the strictures of Professor Herzberg and his associates :

> Much romantic nonsense has been written about primitive man. A number of social critics have contrasted his presumed close contact with nature, his high level of craftsmanship, and the integration of his work into the aesthetic, religious and social activities of his group with the mad and purposeless frenzy of civilized man, chasing ill-defined goals with a ceaseless round of meaningless activity. Anyone familiar with the first-hand reports of anthropologists would recognize the false emphasis in this picture. Life in primitive socieities is hard and filled with backbreaking toil. There is relatively little opportunity for individual growth and development because of the necessity for constant emphasis on sheer subsistence. In a society which spends 70 or 80 per cent of its labour on the mere growing of food there is relatively little left over for the fullest development of the individual.[23]

Even the authors of that study, though, have to admit the greater cultural integration of earlier communities, to the detriment of our own fragmented age. And the evidence of historians can be invoked here, too. In that debate between the 'catastrophic' and the 'anti-catastrophic' views of the early nineteenth century, between the 'optimists' and the 'pessimists', E. P. Thompson stands up against the recent tendency to play down the destructive impact of industrialization. Whilst admitting that an early pessimist such as Engels undoubtedly *did* idealize pre-industrial weaving communities in order to produce a more dramatic and propagandist contrast with the working conditions of 1844, Thompson shows a proper distrust of certain statistics which have been adduced to demonstrate a rise in the standard of living due to the Industrial Revolution. His point is an important one for our own affluent age as much as for the beginning of the last century: 'It is quite possible for statistical averages and human experiences to run in opposite directions. A *per capita* increase in quantitative factors may take place at the same time as a great qualitative disturbance in people's way of life, traditional relationships, and sanctions.'[24] In the past, the 'pessimists' may well have produced a distortion of the truth; now, however, the all-too-common distortion is that of the 'optimist' who 'muddles over the difficult and painful nature of the change in status from artisan to depressed outworker' with comforting phrases about the reality of exploitation before that period. And Thompson puts his finger on something that Laslett did not take account of, something that concerns us here very directly : 'It is neither poverty nor disease but work itself which casts the blackest shadow over the years of the Industrial Revolution.'[25]

Particularly apposite and well-balanced is the same historian's discussion of the Luddite revolts, that flourished among skilled workmen in particular — croppers, cotton-weavers and framework-knitters — whose artisan traditions and status were undermined by the advent of machinery. Let us not assume that their revolt was purely an economic one : craft pride plays an important role as well, threadbare as the ideals that pride involved may have been. As the tradition declined, so it was 'suffused with nostalgic light'. In their hostility to progress, the Luddites may have invoked the past, looked back to paternalistic structures and old customs now and irrevocably on the dust-heap of history — but is it as simple as that? Cannot this 'looking back', this 'reactionary' vision bear within it the seed of a future and more just world? Speaking of such Luddite demands as the prohibition of shoddy work, Thompson again opens up the debate beyond this particular historical contingency :

All these demands looked forwards, as much as backwards; and they contained within them a shadowy image, not so much of a paternalist, but of a democratic community, in which industrial growth should be regulated according to ethical priorities and the pursuit of profit be subordinated to human needs.'[26]

Equally, in the literary field, the tendency to turn to the past can go beyond mere romantic dreaming to provide at least a valuable foil to inadequacies of present-day society : such inadequacies whose remedy can only be sought in the future, not in the past.

It is strange to reflect that writers who a few years ago appeared impossibly outdated, even weird or cranky for their rejection of technology and the religion of progress, now almost all at once seem relevant again, and no longer such eccentric dreamers. In the crisis of conscience of our developed societies, whose very bases and continued existence have been thrown into doubt by fuel shortages and the findings of scientists, those writers, from William Blake to Arnold Wesker, reveal their seminal power and the startling actuality and urgency of their preoccupations. Among those preoccupations, none is more potentially fertile and far-reaching than the role and status of work. We shall see that it calls into question the basic premises of society, and in particular its present dynamism, the sacrosanct pseudo-value of industrial growth. It is legitimate to speak of a more or less concerted European literary tradition of radical speculation not only on the dangerous aspects of industrialism, but also on the possibility of some sort of salvation through a non-ascetic ethic of creative, fulfilling work. It is an ethic that presupposes revised notions of art, community, of culture in the very widest sense. The quality of this ethic is what we shall try to trace in the chapters that follow.

2 Visions of alienation

Before the positive must come the negative, before the quest for a new ethic and a new culture we must be shown the anti-ethic, the anti-culture, the destruction of old, organic forms of work and life. We have seen it argued that the impact of the Industrial Revolution was in many senses a truly destructive one. This was sensed by literary figures very early, even in the heart of the optimistic eighteenth century. Most of the writers we shall be concerned with fall into the pattern of response initiated back in that age of optimism by Rousseau : Rousseau, very much the lone figure swimming against the intellectual and social current of his century, with his native sympathy for the peasant and artisan classes, his hatred of commerce, large cities, the cult of science, unveiling as no writer before him the extent of man's alienated condition in a society based on inequality and exploitation. He hated, too, the adulteration of the natural milieu through the ugliness of industry such as he saw it as the century advanced and evoked it in a curious and memorable passage of his *Rêveries du promeneur solitaire.* He is contrasting the nascent technical environment with man's harmonious existence in the natural world :

> There, quarries, pits, forges, furnaces, and a whole apparatus of anvils, hammers, smoke and fire take the place of the gentle images of rural work. The gaunt faces of the poor wretches who languish in the vile vapours of the mines, blacksmiths, hideous Cyclops-figures — these are the spectacle that the apparatus of the mines substitutes in the bowels of the earth for that of the greenery and

the flowers, the blue sky and the amorous shepherds and robust labourers on its surface.[1]

Of course, few later writers would go quite as far as Rousseau in his pastoral idealization of the 'amorous shepherds'; but for many the pattern of response is basically similar, and their anguish faced with the world of machines is in essence that of Rousseau with his remarkable vision of coming alienation.

Just as powerful are the visionary depths perceived on the threshold of the nineteenth century by the poet, Hölderlin, who in those wonderful lines of *Der Archipelagus* significantly takes the image of the new factories of the Industrial Revolution to evoke the situation of a humanity estranged from harmony and creativity :

Aber weh! es wandelt in Nacht, es wohnt, wie im Orkus,
Ohne Göttliches unser Geschlecht. Ans eigene Treiben
Sind sie geschmiedet allein, und sich in der tosenden Werkstatt
Höret Jeglicher nur, und viel arbeiten die Wilden
Mit gewaltigem Arm, rastlos, doch immer und immer
Unfruchtbar, wie die Furien, bleibt die Mühe der Armen . . .[2]

[But alas! our generation wanders in night, it lives
As in Orkus, with nothing divine. To their own efforts
Alone are they bound, and each in the loud-roaring workshop
Hears only himself, and grimly they labour, the wild ones,
And mighty their arm, unresting; but for ever and ever
Fruitless, like the Furies, remains the toil of the poor . . .]

Over the literature of work in the nineteenth century broods one image above all — that of the Wheel. We find it already in the description of alienation in Schiller's *Letters on the Aesthetic Education of Man* of 1795 : 'enjoyment is separated from labour, the means from the end, exertion from recompense. Eternally fettered only to a single little fragment of the whole, man fashions himself only as a fragment; ever hearing only the monotonous whirl of the wheel which he turns, he never develops the harmony of his being, and, instead of shaping the humanity that lies in his nature, he becomes a mere imprint of his occupation, his science.'[3] Prophetic words indeed, as Herbert Marcuse has recognized, in the suggestion of a link between mechanism (the wheel), the loss of joy in labour and the disappearance of finality in work, resulting in fragmentation, overspecialization and that same disharmony Hölderlin so deplored.

Prophetic, too, is the vision of Blake, who saw the ugly industrial blight of 'dark Satanic mills' spreading over the face of his Jerusalem; and equally centred on the menacing image of the Wheel are the famous lines from *Vala* in which the poet describes the fall from the arts of life — equated with peasant and artisan activity — to the arts of death. The traditional, wooden water-wheel, itself a product of craftsmanship and integrated into the natural world, is banished and burned, to be replaced by complex mechanism. This mechanism is immediately associated with alienated work and fragmentation :

Then left the sons of Urizen the plow and harrow, the loom,
The hammer and the chisel and the rule and compasses.
They forg'd the sword, the chariot of war, the battle ax,
The trumpet fitted to the battle and the flute of summer,
And all the arts of life they chang'd into the arts of death.
The hour glass contemn'd because its simple workmanship
Was as the workmanship of the plowman, and the water wheel
That raises water into Cisterns, broken and burn'd in fire
Because its workmanship was like the workmanship of the shepherd,
And in their stead intricate wheels invented, Wheel without wheel,
To perplex youth in their outgoings and to bind to labours
Of day and night the myriads of Eternity, that they might file
And polish brass and iron hour after hour, laborious workmanship,
Kept ignorant of the use that they might spend the days of wisdom
In sorrowful drudgery to obtain a scanty pittance of bread,
In ignorance to view a small portion and think that All,
And call it demonstration, blind to all the simple rules of life.[4]

Industrialism is equated with death; and this equation we find again when Blake evokes with intensity the modern, industrial plight of Jerusalem/England :

Upon the dark'ning Thames, across the whole Island westward,
A horrible Shadow of Death among the Furnaces beneath
The pillar of folding smoke . . .[5]

The age is one of mechanical rationalism, when throughout Europe reign supreme the Loom of Locke and the Water-wheel of Newton (here no longer associated with artisanal traditions). Harmony is destroyed by the 'cogs tyrannic' of an extraneous mechanism, and with it disappears the old, concentric order of the world, of Eden :

I turn my eyes to the Schools and Universities of Europe
And there behold the Loom of Locke, whose woof rages dire,
Washed by the Water-wheels of Newton : black the cloth
In heavy wreathes folds over every Nation : cruel Works
Of many Wheels I view, wheel without wheel, with cogs tyrannic
Moving by compulsion each other, not as those in Eden, which,
Wheel within wheel, in freedom revolve in harmony and peace.[6]

Mechanism is seen not as order but — paradoxically — as chaos; not as a regulation of nature but as its destruction; not as an aid to life but as an instrument of death.

So, too, in the work of Carlyle, who in *The Signs of the Times* is already acutely aware of the movement of the age : 'Were we required to characterize this age of ours by any single epithet, we should be tempted to call it, not an Heroical, Devotional, Philosophical, or Moral Age, but above all others, the Mechanical Age.' Achievements there may be, he is quick to admit, in our victories won over rude Nature; loaded with spoils we may be — but at what cost! For mechanism has sunk into the deepest recesses of our being, the internal and spiritual are as much managed by machinery as are the external and physical. So Carlyle perceives 'a mighty change in our whole manner of existence . . . Men are grown mechanical in head and heart, as well as in hand. They have lost faith in individual endeavour, and in natural force, of any kind . . . Their whole efforts, attachments, opinions, turn on mechanism, and are of a mechanical character.'[7]

Society itself, Carlyle argues, has come to be seen as a mere mechanism, and no longer as an organic unit; a mechanism to be regulated — mechanically — by constitutions, associations, the mathematical counting of votes, etc. There can be no doubt about who is the God of this age : 'our true Deity is Mechanism,' Carlyle concludes.[8]

It is this perception that led him to turn back to the Middle Ages as the example of a pre-mechanical society based on living relationships. The contrast he draws between that world and the industrial epoch in *Past and Present* is an important contribution to a potent tradition. Earlier in the century a significant and influential note was struck by Cobbett's highly tendentious *History of the Protestant Reformation*, with its idealization of the Middle Ages serving as a foil to the degradation of the early nineteenth-century present. The same rejection of progress is continued in 1829 in Southey's *Colloquies* and most interestingly is applied specifically to the question of work. The medieval workman is contrasted with his nineteenth-century counterpart, and it is claimed that, whatever the apparent restrictions of feudalism, it is really the latter who is worse off under the system of industrial slavery. Marx and Engels are likewise to set up the qualified example of the Middle Ages as a foil to the atomized nature of a society founded on naked individualism, a society that in its disintegration is the very antithesis of community. Though hardly thinkers to present a rosy vision of the past, they do see that the development from the relatively homogeneous society of that time represents a profound alienation and a brutal uprooting :

> The bourgeoisie, whenever it got the upper hand, put an end to all feudal, patriarchal, idyllic relations, pitilessly tore asunder the motley feudal ties that bound man to his 'natural superiors' and left remaining no other bond between man and man than naked self-interest and callous cash-payment.[9]

The fears of universal mechanism entertained by Blake or Carlyle were not idle fears, as the world of work demonstrates to us. We need only listen to that champion of industrialism, the manufacturer, Ure, praising Arkwright for 'training human beings to renounce their desultory habits of work, and to identify themselves with the unvarying regularity of the complex automaton.' Ure appeared in his *Philosophy of Manufacture* (1835) as the most optimistic of industrial optimists, seeing the factory as a 'vast automaton' where all is 'subordinated to a self-regulated moving force.' Ure noted that the more skilled the workman, the more self-willed he was, and the less suitable to become a component of the mechanical whole; so that manufacturers should aim at replacing such workers by self-regulating automatons. Above all, no irregularities must be tolerated![10] In just the same way Josiah Wedgewood set up as an ideal to 'make such machines of the men as cannot err.'[11]

It is in this context that we must situate Marx's analysis of the alienation of labour as it appears in the *Economic and Philosophical Manuscripts*. Under capitalist, industrial production, a double alienation takes place, operating both in the worker's relationship with his own work-activity as such, and also in his relationship with the actual products of his labour. On the material level the latter estrangement is perhaps the more obvious : whereas the artisan was proud of the product he created, in capitalist industry the products brought into being by the worker's hand become a hostile power, since transformed into capital they become a means of continuing, even intensifying the system in force and thus perpetuating his exploitation. The products of work become essentially *commodities*, their value is an exchange-value, and they are primarily conceived and designed for the circuit Money-Commodity-Money, so that the upshot of the whole productive process is simply the exchange of money for money. How can the worker but be estranged from what he produces if this is its only *raison d'être*?

Instead of that ideal fusion of object and subject which Marx saw as the essence of work's ethical value, capitalist manufacture presents instead the opposition of object and subject, of product and worker, of nature and man. Nature becomes hostile, and is alien to him. This is grave indeed, as man's humanity lies in his free relationship with nature, which he seeks to reproduce and appropriate in his work. Nature is his 'inorganic body' and he must be at one with her if he is to lead a fulfilled life. His natural function of working is potentially the means to his integration with nature, so that the perversion of meaning that work has undergone must be deeply inimical to his spiritual well-being and, in short, to his 'humanity'. Ethically and culturally, his life is in danger of disintegration.

This disintegration spills over into the worker's alienation from his *activity*. The ever greater value put on the world of things, of commodities, leads to a corresponding devaluation of the human world, and a man's work becomes 'an activity which is turned against him, independent of him and not belonging to him.'[12] Instead of being essential to him, his labour has become external, instead of affirming himself in it, he denies himself; so that whereas he should rejoice in his activity, he is unhappy in it, and whereas he should freely develop his mental and physical energies, he 'mortifies his body and ruins his mind.'[13] The development of the means of production and especially of machines has in this context led to an intensified alienation, the worker being reduced to an extension of a machine, and usually regarded as less important than the machine, for he can easily be replaced whereas the machine cannot. In *Capital* Marx writes, 'Whereas simple co-operation leaves the individual's methods of work substantially unaltered, manufacture revolutionizes these methods and cuts at the root of individual labour power. It transforms the worker into a cripple, a monster, by forcing him to develop some highly specialized dexterity at the cost of a world of productive impulses and faculties.'[14] The theme of the 'industrial cripple' is one that we shall see recurring in the literature of alienation.

All these factors combine to reduce the properly human status of work in the modern age; and as a result all the activities of man lose their

character of human culture and become animal. By a perverse kind of
compensation man then tends to exalt those of his activities that are
not work, and that are not uniquely human :

> As a result, therefore, man only feels himself freely active in his
> animal functions — eating, drinking, procreating, or at most in his
> dwelling and in dressing-up, etc.; and in his human functions he no
> longer feels himself to be anything but an animal. What is animal
> becomes human and what is human becomes animal.[15]

Estranged from nature, estranged from himself, man is also alienated
from his fellow-men. For his work has lost its social finality and he no
longer has the impression of working freely with them towards a
common and meaningful goal. The devaluation of work means also the
destruction of community. This sense of a reduction of human life and
a contamination of human relationships generally leads Marx to turn
once again in *Capital* to the contrast between his own age and the
medieval community :

> Whatever view we have of the masks in which the different personal-
> ities strut upon the feudal stage, at any rate the social relations
> between individuals at work appear in their natural guise as personal
> relations, and are not dressed up as social relations between things,
> between the products of labour.[16]

Marx's analysis has great intellectual subtlety, but it is by no means
the last word on the subject; and often Marx is surpassed in eloquence
and the show of passion by more 'literary' figures who argue in images
rather than concepts, complementing, completing and illustrating his
theoretical constructs. They talk, as we see, of the Wheel rather than of
alienation, and in the concreteness of their vision they are led to give
prominence to a feature of the industrial world of which Marx had
little to say in the *Manuscripts* although it did inevitably appear in
Engel's description of the conditions of the Manchester working class.
For the reign of the wheel has brought with it more than the mechanization of all the human areas of life; it has brought ugliness and the
destruction of nature. Far from being just a latter-day intellectual
fashion, the condemnation of such ugliness grows up with the Industrial
Revolution itself. It is there, as we have seen, in Rousseau and Blake; it
is in Cobbett's castigation of the 'great wen' of London, in the evocative
passages of Dickens' *Hard Times* where we read of the soulless quality
of industrial Coketown with its tall chimneys 'out of which interminable

serpents of smoke trailed themselves for ever and ever, and never got uncoiled.'[17] Coketown is a place of machines, of vast buildings that tremble all day long to the relentless motion of the steam-engine pistons, a town in which work itself has become sheer lifeless monotony, where the effort that might have been fulfilment is degraded into hopeless uniformity, into artificial routine.

Of all the prophets of doom, though, who have thundered against the mechanization and the ugliness of the modern world, few have done so with the tragic intensity of feeling that belongs to John Ruskin. There is a typical passage in his essay *Modern Manufacture and Design* in which Ruskin contrasts two visions of an old cottage : one as it had originally been in its pre-industrial setting, with 'the sheep on the far-off wolds shining in the evening sunlight'; and the other as it is now :

There, uninhabited for many and many a year, it had been left in unregarded havoc of ruin; the garden-gate still swung loose to its latch; the roof torn into shapeless rents; the shutters hanging about the windows in rags of rotten wood; before its gate, the stream which had gladdened it now soaking slowly by, black as ebony and thick with curdling scum; the bank above it trodden into unctious, sooty slime : far in front of it, between it and the old hills, the furnaces of the city foaming forth perpetual plague of sulphurous darkness; the volumes of their storm clouds coiling low over a waste of grassless fields, fenced from each other, not by hedges, but by slabs of square stone, like grave-stones, riveted together with iron.[18]

The visionary intensity of this picture is such that it suggests that Ruskin shares a good deal of common ground with the Expressionist writers of Germany whom we shall consider in due course. In such an environment, work must inevitably be bad work, inartistic work, slavery — 'a slavery in our England a thousand times more bitter and more degrading than that of the scourged African, or helot Greek.' Following a pattern that is already becoming familiar, Ruskin sees in the medieval world a damning contrast with the mechanicalness of the industrial nineteenth century — 'and there might be more freedom in England, though her feudal lord's lightest words were worth men's lives, and though the blood of the vexed husbandman dropped in the furrows of her fields, than there is while the animation of her mutitudes is sent like fuel to feed the factory smoke, and the strength of them is given daily to be wasted into the fineness of a web, or racked into the exactness of a line.'[19]

Ruskin carries further Carlyle's hatred of all that is mechanism, whether it appears in the nature of industrial labour itself or in the whole pseudo-science of liberal economics, mechanistic in its premises and based on the inorganic principle of competition as opposed to the organic principle of harmony. What hurts men mortally is to feel 'their whole being sunk into an unrecognized abyss, to be counted off into a heap of mechanism numbered with its wheels, and weighed with its hammer strokes.'[20] And in a suggestive passage of *The Seven Lamps of Architecture* he allies two fundamental images of the literature of industrial alienation — the ugliness of the Furnace and the mechanical-ness of the Wheel — and pleads that they may not be allowed to destroy the humanity in us :

> There is dreaming enough, and earthiness enough, and sensuality enough in human existence, without our turning the few glowing moments of it into mechanism; and since our life must at the best be but a vapour that appears for a little while and then vanishes away, let it at least appear as a cloud in the height of Heaven, not as the thick darkness that broods over the blast of the Furnace, and rolling of the Wheel.

The industrial world besets us with obstacles to our human and artistic fulfilment, with imitation products made of imitation materials, to produce or to contemplate which can only make us 'shallower in our understandings, colder in our hearts, and feebler in our wits.'[21]

A parallel protest against the ugly and the mechanical pervades the work of a writer who must in many ways appear very different — D. H. Lawrence. Raymond Williams has argued convincingly the link between Carlyle and Lawrence; for the latter, too, appears as an anguished prophet of life-destroying mechanization. Distrustful as he was of the whole ethos of progress, Lawrence could see this mechanization under way in all the realms of life, and could, therefore, try to present its impact in terms of human relationships. Hence the intensely pessimistic vision of contemporary society in a novel such as *Lady Chatterley's Lover*, as Lawrence unequivocally pits himself against the process of industrialization : 'The industrial England blots out the agricultural England. One meaning blots out another. The new England blots out the old England. And the continuity is not organic, but mechanical.'[22] Why is it that love — or sex — so often go wrong today? Mellors knows the answer all too clearly, and this is why he has sought work outside the industrial set-up altogether :

It was not woman's fault, nor even love's fault, nor the fault of sex. The fault lay there, out there, in those evil electric lights and diabolical rattlings of engines. There, in the world of the mechanical greedy, greedy mechanism and mechanized greed, sparkling with lights and gushing hot metal and roaring with traffic, there lay the vast evil thing, ready to destroy whatever did not conform. Soon it would destroy the wood, and the bluebells would spring no more. All vulnerable things must perish under the rolling and running of iron.[23]

The mechanical principle that so alienates us from ourselves is embodied in Clifford, crippled and emasculated, in his mechanized wheelchair that does indeed crush the bluebells of the wood beneath its wheels. Resolutely and insensitively 'modern', Clifford espouses the direction of the age in his work, too : his running of the pits has alienation at its very core, for 'the miners were, in a sense, his own men; but he saw them as objects rather than men, parts of the pit rather than parts of life.'[24] Underlying his 'culture' is a cold inhumanity, a negation of human contact in all realms of life and not least in work. His mechanical means of locomotion is a symbol for the cold force he will bring into the world, a force defined in the first version of the novel as 'a new naked will which would *compel* work from men.' Discipline becomes his favourite criterion for work in the pits. 'He was a kind of robot after all . . .'[25]

The same theme, the same vision, appears with force in *Women in Love*. Just as the environment has grown black, ugly and unnatural around the centres of work, so the work itself is contaminated and degraded. This the sculptor, Loerke, sees in that novel, and though Lawrence is far from approving of such a largely repulsive character, his realization is presented with some energy. Loerke, we should remember, is engaged in designing a fine factory, an experiment in the fusion of art and industry, and is naturally much concerned with the degradation of the environment and its effects on the nature of work.

Men will not go on submitting to such intolerable ugliness. In the end it will hurt too much, and they will wither because of it. And this will wither the work as well. They will think the work itself is ugly : the machines, the very acts of labour, whereas the machinery and the acts of labour are extremely, maddeningly beautiful.[26]

This is not the voice of Lawrence, however, for in this novel, too, the spirit of the machine-age is one of the darkest forces at play, the most potent force of disintegration in the modern world. And as for Carlyle, mechanism is equated with chaos — 'the desire for chaos had risen'.[27] It is above all in the character and role of mine-owner, Gerald Crich, that Lawrence embodies his fears about the incompatibility of human fulfilment and involvement in an industrial system and environment. Rejecting the old-fashioned, paternalistic and 'inefficient' attitudes of his father, Gerald reorganizes the pit in function of his own view of the nature of work as something purely mechanical — 'It was mechanical, but then society *was* a mechanism.' By his modernization schemes, Gerald becomes the 'God of the machine', seeing in others only their sheer instrumentality. He is an agent of alienation :

> Everything was run on the most accurate and delicate scientific method, educated and expert men were in control everywhere, the miners were reduced to mere mechanical instruments. They had to work hard, much harder than before, the work was terrible and heart-breaking in its mechanicalness.
> But they submitted to it all. The joy went out of their lives, the hope seemed to perish as they became more and more mechanized.[28]

As they pass Gerald on their way to work there is no authentic relationship, they are to him as minor cogs to the major cog, and appear only as a 'grey-black stream of unemotional acceptance.' Gerald himself is inevitably and deeply contaminated; indeed he more than anyone else exemplifies the fate of the whole race, going 'down the slope of mechanical death.'[29] As a result he is not quite real, unfit, just like the sexless Clifford, for human relationships; unfit above all for love.

In a more Ruskin-like vein, Lawrence also expresses through the sensitive Birkin a certain nostalgia for the artisan values that all this 'foul mechanicalness' has destroyed : hence the significance of the chapter entitled 'A Chair' in which is given the same example of simple but responsible workmanship — a wooden chair — that will later appeal to Arnold Wesker. As Birkin puts it, with vehemence in his sorrow :

> My beloved country — it had something to express even when it made that chair . . . And now we can only fish among the rubbish-heaps for the remnants of their old expression. There is no production is us now, only sordid and foul mechanicalness.[30]

On every front, industrial society stands condemned.

The changes in the means of production hinted at in the Crich mineworks are no mere abstraction, for the world of work was showing that it could advance into spheres of alienation that might even fulfil the most rigorous dreams of Ure or Arkwright, and this through the scientific organization of labour, the Second Industrial Revolution. Henry Ford introduced the production line in Michigan in the year 1913, and announced it with a fervent optimism as 'the modern Messiah'. A Messiah that was soon to triumph as we know, though it brought no salvation; and it was crucified from its earliest days – in the name of human dignity – not only in literature but also in films such as Chaplin's *Modern Times* (where again the cog-wheel plays such a hallucinatory role) or René Clair's *A nous la liberté*. The scientific organization of labour involves going beyond the simple introduction of machines, into the systematic mechanization of the work-process itself, the treatment of the human element of production in terms of pure, mechanical efficiency, to the exclusion of personality, intelligence and initiative.

It is within the frame of this mutation that we can best understand the activist writings of the German Expressionists, Ernst Toller and Georg Kaiser, writings infused with an apocalyptic sense of alienation that centres on the devaluation of work. The modern world they saw as all-debasing, through the loss of creativity and vision in human labour. Evoking the generation of his youth in the second decade of the twentieth century, Toller wrote : 'This world seems to them ripe for destruction, they seek a way out of the dreadful confusion of the age, they seek the activism of the heart, an end to chaos . . .'[31] It is a revolt against the decadence of an age that has forgotten what productivity *should* mean, something qualitative and not just quantitative; the revolt of a generation that had just rediscovered, and for good reason, the poetry of Hölderlin.

One of the starkest warnings made in this period against the dehumanizing of work is to be found in Kaiser's play *Gas* (1920). The play portrays the result of highly perfected industrial techniques, here in the production of gas. From the first stage-direction we know what has happened to the *milieu naturel* – there are the expected clusters of factory chimneys, belching fire and smoke with grim intensity. The paternalistic introduction of profit-sharing into this industry has served to increase effort and output; but this, in the context of highly automated production, leads only to fragmentation and the utmost degree of ethical and cultural deprivation. By the development of extreme specialization, the workers have indeed become industrial cripples, mere hands working levers, eyes watching a dial, or feet operating a pedal, all caught up in the 'monotonous sameness' of mass production. The

depersonalization that results is admirably conveyed by the characteristic techniques of Expressionist drama, a drama that is truly born of the
industrial society : the fact that none of the characters has a proper
name, the 'telegram-style' of the language, together with a total lack of
individuality in speech, the stylized abstraction of the stage-settings, all
contribute to the evocation of a world of utter inhuman efficiency. The
price of this efficiency is explained by the Girl, as she begins to stutter
her way towards some sort of real, human speech :

> I speak of my brother! — I did not know that I had a brother. A man
> went out of the house in the morning and came back in the evening —
> and slept. Or he went in the evening and was back in the morning —
> and slept. One hand was large, the other small. The large hand never
> slept. It moved constantly to and fro — day and night. It fed on him
> and grew out of his whole strength. This hand was the man! Where
> was my brother then? Who played by my side — and built sand-
> castles with his two hands? He rushed to work. Work needed only
> one hand from him — that pressed and raised the lever —minute by
> minute up and down — counted to the second![32]

There *are* unforeseen breakdowns in the mechanical system, breakdowns
that are beyond the explanation of mere science and that are introduced
by Kaiser to demonstrate the limitations of science, the prime importance of the irrational side of man's nature. In the second part of the play,
a change in shift arrangements, breaking a tyrannically rigorous routine,
allows the eruption of real thought for the first time in years. The
workers crowd into the hall of the factory, and actually start to look at
each other and at themselves as individual human beings. Realizing that
they are all uniformly dressed in grey, the women pull the cloths from
their heads and shake their hair free. But though there is a momentary
promise of utopia, a visionary dream of regeneration by a return to a
rural, non-industrial community, the dream comes to nothing : the
insane dynamism of technical progress proves too powerful, and the
workers themselves too conditioned by it. The play ends in universal
destruction through the massive unleashing of the latest scientific
'advance' — poison gas.

The same themes, without quite the cosmic breadth of Kaiser's
despair, recur in Toller's factory dramas. *Man and the Masses* (*Masse
Mensch*) turns on the sin of capitalist society against *homo faber* :

> Who robbed our brothers of their human face,

> Who forced them into mechanicalness
> Reduced them to mere pistons on machines?[33]

The heroine of the play calls out for a return to creative work, but somehow within the context of the improved, modern techniques of production – and that semi-mystical vagueness that is characteristic of Expressionism, abetted by typical stammering, ecstatic utterances, allows Toller to be no more precise than that. So, too, in the same author's drama of the Luddite revolts, *The Machine-Wreckers* (*Die Maschinenstürmer*) we find the usual criticism of the nascent industrial society. The villain of the piece is here the factory-owner, Ure, whom we have met already; he and the system he supremely represents are accused by the hero, Jimmy Cobbet, of turning workers into wares, into mere, insensate things, incapable of any immediate response to life. The weavers ask to be allowed to create as they created before the machines arrived. Yet *can* the clock be turned back to a pre-industrial, artisan structure, the author's spokesman asks doubtfully – and Toller's reading of Marx (such as it was) prompts him to add : is it really desirable?[34]

We must not think that the largely despairing vision of these plays was only typical Expressionist exaggeration and grim caricature, as Toller himself later discovered on visiting a Ford factory during his travels in America in the late twenties : for him the experience of the new 'rationalization of labour' was a frightening realization of the nightmares of Expressionism, mechanization carried to the point 'where man sinks to the level of a lifeless hammer or lever.'[35] Many other writers were similarly affected – in France the novelist, Céline, was to include in that devastating panorama of human degradation that is his *Voyage au bout de la nuit* (1932) a description of work in the Ford plant at Detroit, of which he had first-hand experience. His 'hero', who applies for a job there is told at the medical examination that his studies and intelligence will be of no use to him in that environment, that they are indeed a liability :

> You haven't come here to think, but to carry out the gestures that you will be ordered to perform . . . We don't need people with imagination in our factory. It's chimpanzees we need . . . Another piece of advice : never talk to us about your intelligence again! All the thinking will be done for you, pal! You can take my word for it.

This advice turns out to be accurate. The work is inhuman in its obedience to the rhythms, not of man, but of machines. The only thing of importance is 'the deafening continuity of the thousands and thousands of machines that commanded the men.' It is a grim and powerful picture of alienation, and plays an important role in Céline's nihilistic vision of the world.[36]

The phenomenon of an ever greater division between thought and labour necessarily implies a social division between thinkers and workers. This is the dangerous tendency that Aldous Huxley satirized in his *Brave New World*, with its warning of the dire consequences of dividing the world biologically into the separate species of *homo sapiens* and *homo faber*, producing a hierarchical slave-civilization in which the lower orders are bred to be subnormal to fit them for the infinitely repetitive tasks of the technical environment. The same tendency had already been prophesied, however, some time before, and carried to the outer limits of fantasy by H. G. Wells. In *The First Men on the Moon* Wells suggests the ultimate stage of that social specialization, and working within his science-fiction genre can portray extremes in the formation of 'industrial cripples' that even the Expressionists cannot match. However, his portrayal and his prediction contain a certain ambiguity of attitude that we do not find in, say, Georg Kaiser. It is both for this extremeness and for this ambiguity that we shall consider Wells' vision in some detail.

In *The Time-Machine* Wells had shown a simple though extreme division of society into workers and non-workers, and suggested the disastrous consequences of the separation of work and 'culture'. His description of the moon-civilization, however, shows a much greater degree of specialization, as we see from Cavor's message on the extreme division of labour among the Selenites, a message notable for its tone of enthusiasm. It is a society based on a fixed and calculated hierarchy, where each knows his place and is born to it; moreover, 'the elaborate discipline of training and education and surgery he undergoes fits him at last so completely to it that he has neither ideas nor organs for any purpose beyond it.' Nor do the moon-inhabitants, whose guiding principle is efficiency, ever doubt that this *should* be so. Take the example of the mathematician — over-developed mathematically but crippled in every other respect :

> If, for example, a Selenite is destined to be a mathematician, his teachers and trainers set out at once to that end. They check any incipient disposition to other pursuits, they encourage his mathe-

matical bias with a perfect psychological skill. His brain grows, or at least the mathematical faculties of his brain grow, and the rest of him only so much as is necessary to sustain this essential part of him . . . His brain grows continually larger, at least as far as the portions engaging in mathematics are concerned; they bulge ever larger and seem to suck all life and vigour from the rest of his frame. His limbs shrivel, his heart and digestive organs diminish, his insect face is hidden under its bulging contours. The faculty of laughter, save for the sudden discovery of some paradox, is lost to him; his deepest emotion is the resolution of a novel computation. And so he attains his end.[37]

Such big-headed Selenites are, of course, the aristocracy of this society, headed by the Grand Lunar, 'that marvellous gigantic ganglion', and they are carried about by specialized bearers — muscles without brain — and attended by whole retinues of other creatures formed entirely to their one function, whether they be swift messengers 'with spider-like legs and "hands" for grasping parachutes' or attendants with enormously developed vocal cords for communication purposes. Such attendants have no other purpose but to serve, their very subordination is their *raison d'être* : 'Apart from their controlling intelligence, these subordinates are as inert and helpless as umbrellas in a stand. They exist only in relation to the orders they have to obey, the duties they have to perform.'[38] Clearly there is a total incompatibility between extreme specialization in work and any kind of democratic ideal.

Equally, the mooncalf-minders have no other thought but the discharging of their duty. At the basis of the whole social set-up lies a *mechanical* principle : 'And so it is with all sorts and conditions of Selenites — each is a perfect unit in a world machine.' Most of the animated cogs of this machine observed by the fascinated Cavor are of the 'operative class'; and in their case the figurative term 'machine hand' has become something more than a mere figure, for they are made up of little else but 'huge single or paired bunches of three, or five, or seven digits for clawing, lifting, guiding, the rest of them no more than subordinate appendages to these important parts.' Like fantastic anticipatory caricatures of the workers who will be evoked in *Gas*, some of these work-creatures have huge ears, others huge noses (for delicate chemical operations), whilst 'others again have flat feet for treadles with ankylosed joints; and others — who I have been told are glass-blowers — seem mere lung-bellows.' All of them are put to sleep in the intervals when they are not needed for work; what else, indeed, could they do but sleep?

Of course, behind any such mechanical system of subordination lies a structure of coercion, with a lunar police as purpose-designed to its task as any of its charges are to theirs, 'to rule over these things and order any erring tendency there might be in some aberrant natures.'[39]

The method of producing operatives is particularly frightening : they are confined in jars with only their fore-limbs protruding, and their 'hand' is fed and stimulated by injection while the rest of their body is systematically starved. 'A highly developed system of technical education' Cavor calls it. Yet even he, for all his uncritical enthusiasm for this technological 'rationality', has doubts at this point, doubts which contain a neat, ironic thrust at our own society, which is not yet that of the Selenites. 'That wretched-looking hand sticking out of its jar seemed to appeal for lost possibilities; it haunts me still, although, of course, it is really in the end a far more humane proceeding than our earthly method of leaving children to grow into human beings, and then making machines of them.'[40] The uneasy ambivalence in Wells' attitude throughout comes from his own 'progressive-optimistic' outlook, his fundamental faith in science and some kind of rational order that he is – to a large degree – satirizing in this novel. Wells, indeed, despite the warning of alienation he has presented to us, makes no contribution to the positive aspect of that tradition we are investigating, for he attributes to human work no particular cultural or ethical potential at all. He has, indeed, considerable regard for the Wheel, for the 'civilizing' power of the machine, and he unsatirically affirms it in *A Modern Utopia*; for him, it is not the advances of science and technology that are wrong, it is men themselves. He shows clearly where *his* priorities lie : 'Science stands, a competent servant, behind her wrangling under-bred masters, holding out resources, devices, and remedies they are too stupid to use.' Not surprisingly, we find that Wells is hostile to the ethic of work, preferring as he does the sort of hierarchy he caricatured in his lunar fantasy, with a culture-bearing leisure class – 'A certain pro-portion of men at ease is good for the world . . .' His attitude to work is nearer to that of the Greeks than to that of most of the writers we shall look at; and typically he mocks William Morris and the 'outright Return-to-Nature Utopians' for their belief that work may be made a joy.[41]

With Wells we might contrast another writer who yet shares his faith in scientific and technological progress, Émile Zola. Zola's positivistic optimism is, as we shall see, countered by a nostalgia for personal, artisanal values in work centring on the basic equation work : happiness. Wells might argue, or rather Cavor might argue that his mooncalf-minders carry out their work 'in perfect happiness', but there it is only the mechanical satisfaction of an extremely limited intelligence, it is nothing but the automatic response to a total mental and physical programming. Happiness hardly seems a suitable word in the context; but for Zola, as for Ruskin or Morris, it is to have a different resonance altogether, and this resonance, this moral vibrancy that is all too lacking in Wells comes from the positive search for an ethic of work fitted to the modern world and its problems. It is a quest to be carried on with greater and greater urgency as man becomes ever more inextricably a part of the increasingly technical world he has created, and which by its dynamism too often seems to be moulding *him* — in its own image — and in the process destroying all human value in the acts of work. So it comes about that, by reaction, happiness and efficiency are seen as incompatible concepts. Happiness (in the highest sense of an ever-broadening fulfilment) is a human value; efficiency is a mechanical value. Only a dehumanized world can prevail if efficiency is exalted as the supreme criterion in society. Professor Herzberg tells of an experiment in which C. Agyris, professor of industrial relations at Yale, caused a number of mental patients of sub-normal intelligence to be employed in routine, highly repetitive tasks, in single-operation jobs on a production line. The first striking result of this experiment was that production went up by some four hundred per cent, which more than suggests a correlation between efficiency and sub-normality![42] The experiment only confirms what so many writers have sensed, from Blake onwards : that there is a hiatus, even a contradiction, between mechanical and human potentialities. It is in the light of this contradiction that we can see the importance of the search for human values in work, for an ethic of fulfilment that might one day form the centre of a radically new culture.

3 Two ethics

Many writers, we find, are to look back in their revolt against the industrial world to a part-idealized, medieval period when work, as embodied in particular in the building of the Gothic cathedrals, might in a vision rose-tinted by romantic nostalgia be seen as responsible, creative labour and as such ample fulfilment for a man. Even if such attractiveness in work ever really did exist in the medieval world, its days were numbered; and the threat has been seen to come from the twin forces of capitalism and protestantism, which together imposed on the world a very different notion of work, its nature and its role in man's life. The result is to be a clash between two ethics, a clash that is still directly and urgently relevant to our present society, our present morality and indeed our whole way of life.

Generally speaking, if we follow the analyses of Weber and Tawney, the development of protestant ideas of work marks a move away from the medieval view that labour is morally superior to trade, trade being close to usury and, therefore, to sin. This progression is usually presented as crystallizing, in two major phases, around the figures of Luther and subsequently Calvin.

Luther saw idleness as a sin; the exercise of one's profession takes on for him a spiritual significance as the means of serving God in this world. Weber summarizes his teaching on the subject :

> Christians should earn their living in the sweat of their brow . . . Like Melanchthon, Luther thought that the most admirable life was that of the peasant, for it was least touched by the corroding spirit of

commercial calculation . . . The labour of the craftsman is honourable, for he serves the community in his calling; the honest smith or shoe-maker is a priest.[1]

The widespread acceptance of this notion of a religious value in work may be sensed from the diffusion of puritan, edifying works such as *Navigation Spiritualized*, *Husbandry Spiritualized*, or *The Religious Weaver*. This marks a great step towards removing the distinction between 'other-wordly' piety and everyday activity; but it is a severe ethic rather than an ethic of joy. The value attributed to work comes from the outside, as the earnest fulfilment of duty, rather than from the inside as delight, fusion with nature or creativity.

If this joylessness is true of Luther's view of work, it is all the more so of Calvin's. Whereas Luther, closer in this respect to medieval catholicism, still distrusted trade for profit and the whole commercial ethos, the change in emphasis that is calvinism may to a degree be seen as the spiritual counterpart of capitalism, Profit is now added to industriousness, if not as a means at least as a *sign* of salvation : zeal in acquisition cannot actually win grace, but it is a tangible indication to others that one is among the elect, and that one is following God's plan for man in this world. The ethic here implied is clearly one of business circles rather than an ethic of free, creative craftsmanship such as many writers, fundamentally opposed to the capitalist organization of work, will seek to propagate. The profits of trade – and here for Ruskin or William Morris is the fatal step from which our ethical and aesthetic decline must be traced – are put on the same level of respectability as the earnings of the labourer or craftsman. The rigid and disciplined severity of this attitude has further connotations, suggested by Adriano Tilgher :

Intermittent occasional work will not do. It must be methodical, disciplined, rational, uniform, and hence specialized work. To select a calling and follow it with all one's conscience is a religious duty. Calvinism thus lays the foundation of the tremendous discipline of the modern factory founded on the division of labour – very differ-ent from the easy-going ways of the independent artisan.[2]

The ethic of industriousness prepares the way for industry.

This interpretation of the impact of protestantism on the attitude to work is further borne out by E. P. Thompson's analysis of the historical function of Methodism, which he sees as essentially a means of aiding adaptation from the old artisanal and 'free' modes of work to the new and mechanical world of the factory, and it comes as no surprise to find that this particular branch of protestantism was upheld and supported by a number of the foremost manufacturers of the early nineteenth century. Methodism, in other words, might be said to have had the function of instilling into the popular consciousness what Ure called the 'patterns of obedience'. Crucifixion on 'the daily Cross of toil' — a common theme of Methodist hymns — thus becomes a religious duty that parallels the mortification of Christ. A grim duty, of course, but then man is not made for joy, nor should he seek his fulfilment in that direction.[3]

The protestant ethic has indeed become part of our consciousness, and we shall not escape from it easily, it surrounds us with a thousand guilts and a thousand ambitions. But there is the possibility of a very different ethic of work, and one that bears a much less stern and rigidly industrious face. If we seek a total contrast to the puritan ethic, we can do worse than to invoke the curious figure of Charles Fourier, that early nineteenth-century visionary who has exercised a protracted influence on writers and thinkers even up to the present day. For beneath the wild play of Fourier's uninhibited fantasy lay a startlingly different concept of work, one that gave human labour ethical value whilst freeing it from the repressive ethos of duty. In short, Fourier's vision was one of work as potential joy, as fulfilment that could be *immediate*, and not *mediated* by religious faith.

Fourier, too, is a rebel against modern civilization, as the title of one of his last works suggests : *La fausse industrie morcelée, répugnante, mensongère . . . Mosaïque des faux progrès, des ridicules et cercles vicieux de la Civilisation . . .* In his visionary Phalanstery, or working community, there is, it is true, a departure from traditional, artisan values; in fact a complex division of labour replaces those values and the methods they presupposed, but unlike in the present organization of labour this division does not lead to a diminution of personality. This is because Fourier bases the economic life of his community on the ability to change frequently from one job to another, so that in an average day a person would be involved in some eight occupations, covering areas such as gardening, forestry, harvesting, manufacturing, etc. This principle of variety or diversity is the fulfilment of what Fourier sees as a fundamental passion of man — the 'butterfly' — which is thwarted in the present age. Once this passion is fulfilled, however, work loses all repressive or ascetic character and becomes joy. Fourier then has great importance in the formation of a non-ascetic ethic of work, although it is true that his emphasis on *partial* work, on carrying out only a specialized part of any given task, will not be shared by many who follow his lead. It is noteworthy that he takes his examples from the realm of horticulture rather than manufacture, for the division of tasks in an industrial context can present a very different picture from apportioning of partial jobs in a garden, and demands a higher and more limiting degree of specialization, even of continuity and repetition, that must finally destroy that very ideal of diversity and change. It is experience of the extreme division of labour in such industrial contexts that will in later writers lead to a revolt against the division of labour as such.

By presenting work not only as the ethical basis of his society but also as a fulfilment of natural, human passions, Fourier contrasts with the more ascetic approach of his contemporary, Robert Owen. In the Phalanstery, even the dirty work that is necessary in society, by being given over to errant bands of children who would be regarded as the knights-errant of the new world, is to become a natural function – for do children not like and seek out dirty occupations quite spontaneously? Domestic labour, too, is to become joy and fulfilment when it tumbles over into instinctual gratification and into art : gastronomy is to give way to gastrosophy, meals will run to thirty or forty dishes and will represent the summit of the scientific achievement of that community. Cooks in the state of Harmony will not only be esteemed scientists, but also 'pivots of education and enjoyments.'[4]

In order to achieve this state, education must become a vital field of reform. Children will begin to go into workshops from the age of three, and certain useful work might even be pleasurably done from the age of two! The combination of productive work and education reflects Fourier's desire to do away with the distinction between manual and intellectual work, and to strive throughout for some kind of organic and integrated personality centred on fulfilment in work. It is symptomatic of his idealism that he once stated that even Nero would have been an inoffensive, integrated and useful member of society if his education had not sought to repress his natural instincts, and if he had instead been placed in the butchery group of a harmonious society from the age of three![5]

Fourier's greatest limitation (absurd mysticism apart!) lies in his failure to foresee and take account of the problems posed by industrialism. This is especially so as he repeatedly insists that his future society will not only be harmonious, but also highly productive. It is obviously one thing to discuss labour in the context of gardening, quite another in terms of factory production. Be that as it may, his notion of pleasure and fulfilment is potentially a great seminal force for the future, for a future vastly different from anything Calvin could have imagined. This is why, in recent years, Fourier has been cited with enthusiasm by that prophet of cultural revolution, Herbert Marcuse. Marcuse does criticize the French utopian writer in his important *Eros and Civilization* for retaining repressive elements in his blueprint for the organization of work and society — a serious and unresolved contradiction since 'work as free play cannot be subject to administration; only alienated labour can be organized and administered by rational routine.' In other words Fourier presents the contradiction of a repressively disciplined and time-tabled, social organization that would contain a liberated, psychological attitude towards work — a manifest impossibility, and the measure of Fourier's utopianism. Nevertheless, he remains for Marcuse the writer who has come closest to understanding and persuading that the salvation of man comes from transforming labour into pleasure, or to put it in Freudian vocabulary, 'the possibility of "attractive labor" (*travail attrayant*) derives above all from the release of libidinal forces.'[6]

Although we have seen that Freud saw work as of great importance in man's social life, he did tend to associate it often with pain, repression and unhappiness, writing for instance in *Civilization and its Discontents* : 'And yet, as a path to happiness, work is not highly prized by men. They do not strive after it as they do after other possibilities of satisfaction. The great majority of people only work under the stress of necessity, and this natural human aversion to work raises most difficult social problems.'[7] In a sense, then, there is a parallel to be drawn between Freud's view of work and the ascetic, protestant ethic. This is apparent in Marcuse's summary:

Civilization is first of all progress in *work* — that is, work for the procurement and augmentation of the necessities of life. This work is normally without satisfaction in itself; to Freud it is unpleasurable, painful. In Freud's metapsychology there is no room for an original 'instinct of workmanship', 'mastery instinct', etc. The instinctual syndrome 'unhappiness and work' recurs throughout Freud's writings, and his interpretation of the Prometheus myth is centred on the connection between curbing of sexual passion and civilized work. The basic work in civilization is non-libidinal, is labor; labor is 'unpleasantness', and such unpleasantness has to be enforced.[8]

A view more different from that of Fourier could hardly be imagined. The change in human make-up implicit in 'civilization' meant for Freud a necessary move from the dominance of the pleasure-principle (primary, instinctual gratification) to that of the reality-principle, from immediate satisfaction to the delay of satisfaction, from pleasure to the restraint of pleasure, from joy to toil, from receptiveness to productiveness. The result is that during work, pleasure is suspended and the instincts, whose basic demands are incompatible with the social reality, 'have to undergo a repressive regimentation.'[9] The value of productivity then becomes the predominant value of our culture, resulting in all kinds of alienations and repressions, in a split between social and individual needs. Productivity runs counter to the instinctual pleasure-principle, and worst of all tends to become an end in itself.

Not that *all* work need be repressive : we have seen that Freud himself acknowledged that work can involve a 'considerable discharge of libidinal component impulses'; and Marcuse is careful to draw the essential distinction, unfortunately overlooked by Freud, between *alienated* work, which by its nature is repressive of libidinal expression and human potentialities in general, and *non-alienated* work, which may involve 'erotic' fulfilment in the widest sense of the word, i.e. satisfaction of the basic life-impulses. This is the crux of the distinction between these two ethics of work : there is a repressive ethic that relates to alienated labour (and the so-called protestant ethic would be a part of this) and a potentially very different, life-enhancing ethic relating to non-alienated work, compatible with happiness and liberty. The former makes a cult of productivity and efficiency, the latter is concerned less with quantity than with the quality of life itself. The tragedy is that in a society based on economic competition it is the former ethos that predominates. Marcuse is one who hopes for a swing towards the latter, the discovery of a new, non-repressive reality principle — 'the liberation of Eros could create new and durable work-relations.' It is in this context that he invokes the example of Fourier and his non-ascetic vision of a working society.

In the more specifically literary field, the distinction between the two ethics may be illustrated, though not in absolutely antithetical terms, by a contrast between Carlyle and Ruskin. We know that the two have, of course, much in common in their vision of alienation, and both are attracted by the Middle Ages. Their emphasis, however, is not quite the same. In *Past and Present*, Carlyle uses his evocation of twelfth-century St Edmundsbury as a foil to the modern age, and a condemnation of it. With infinite nostalgia he looks back to the pre-industrial time when the world 'was a world, and not a void infinite of grey haze', when the streams and rivers were still pure and 'no Steam-Demon has yet risen smoking into being' to create monstrous, pitchy cities throughout the land. Carlyle sees the fearsome decline from that rosy past into the modern age as the result of man's loss of religious feeling : the mystical aspirations basic to man's nature have been ousted by crass commercialism, and this loss and decline crystallize in modern man's growing away from the notion of work as an ethical force. After all, what is true work, he asks, but religion? And he adopts the motto of the old Monks – *laborare est orare.* All true work is sacred, it has something divine in it; wide as the earth, 'it has its summit in Heaven.' Sweat of the brow is to be equated with the highest heroism, with martyrdom, with that 'agony of bloody sweat' men have called divine.[10]

Carlyle does see that work gives us the value and the measure of a man; for indeed we have no knowledge but that we get by working, 'the rest is yet all a hypothesis of knowledge, a thing to be argued of in schools, a thing floating in the clouds, in endless logic-vortices . . .'[11] Work leads inevitably to truth, to Nature's laws and regulations. So it is that the worker, however humble in appearance, may be regarded as the mysterious possessor of some deeper insight than the superficially brilliant and 'knowledgeable' intellectual. There is, though, a significant condescension in his portrait of the poor labourer (such as we sometimes sense in D. H. Lawrence) : he, the Man of Practice, is 'thick-skinned, seemingly opaque', 'almost stupid'. But who will win in the confrontation of such a seeming dullard and the light, adroit Man of Theory?

> The clowdy-browed, thick-soled, opaque Practicality, with no logic utterance, in silence mainly, with here or there a mere grunt or growl, has in him what transcends all logic utterance : a Congruity with the Unuttered! The Speakable, which lies atop, as a superficial film, or outer skin, is his or is not his; but the Doable, which reaches down to the world's centre, you find him there![12]

For Carlyle, this is a working planet, not an idle one, and nature's basic law is one of labour, so that liberty can never be freedom *from* work but freedom *for* work, to find what sort of work a man is apt for, and then to do it.

Unfortunately the spirit of good and conscientious work has been undermined by the commercial spirit : trading and selling become more important than making, just as the London hatter 'instead of making better felt-hats than another, mounts a huge lath-and-plaster Hat, seven feet high, upon wheels; sends a man to drive it through the streets; hoping to be saved *thereby*.'[13] In Carlyle's eyes, however, the commercial spirit is not alone to blame, but with it the (utilitarian) happiness-principle. It is a principle he deplores, for he equates work with industriousness, pain and heroic endeavour : work alone is noble and dignified, but all dignity involves pain, for 'a life of ease is not for any man, nor for any god. The life of all gods figures itself to us as a Sublime Sadness, – earnestness of Infinite Battle against Infinite Labour. Our highest religion is named the "Worship of Sorrow".'[14]

It is true that Carlyle does reach beyond this stern and repressive ethic of duty; he argues that not only does man create order in external nature through work, but within himself attains harmony and equilibrium :

> Consider how, even in the meanest sorts of Labour, the whole soul of a man is composed into a kind of real harmony, the instant he sets himself to work! Doubt, Desire, Sorrow, Remorse, Indignation, Despair itself, all these lie beleaguering the soul of the poor day-worker, as of every man : but he bends himself with free valour against his task, and all these are stilled, all these shrink murmuring far off into their caves. The man is now a man. The blessed glow of Labour is in him, is it not as purifying fire, wherein all poison is burnt up, and of sour smoke itself there is made bright blessed flame![15]

Let us not, however, overlook the significance of the phrase 'even in the meanest sorts of Labour . . .' Carlyle fails characteristically to distinguish between alienated and non-alienated work, even though he does have, as we have seen, an overall vision of mechanical alienation in modern society. For him, 'all work, even cotton-spinning is noble.' Even commercial work, work at making money, has the possibility of nobility in it. So, too, Carlyle ultimately accepts industrialism, accepts machines as the basis of the modern world, declaring the epic of our times to be 'Tools and the Man'. He integrates into his world the 'cunning mechanisms and tall chimney-steeples' – at least if they can be cleaned of soot and sedition![16] The implications of his largely ascetic and repressive ethic of work here become apparent. What he upholds is a static hierarchy in which work must be accepted as a

destiny or a duty rather than sought as a joy. There is, above all, no
aesthetic dimension in his view of work, no hint of the possible equation
of work and art.

It is here that the contrast with Ruskin becomes clear. Ruskin sees
no such latent poetry in industrialism, and refuses Carlyle's integration
into an alienated society. His writings emphasize the importance of
happiness in work, lost in the modern world; for enjoyment is the
sign and precondition of all good work. The value he attributes to
human labour is, therefore, internal, not transcendental and external.
This emphasis gives Ruskin an importance at least equal to that of
Marx in the formation of a non-ascetic ethic of work. William Morris
was to have no doubts about the vital role of Ruskin's indictment of
modern civilization and the work-values he set up in contrast to it :
of that key chapter 'Of the Nature of Gothic' in the older writer's *The
Stones of Venice*, Morris wrote that it was 'one of the very few necessary
and inevitable utterances of the century', commenting from his own
time on what a dull place the world would have been twenty years ago
had it not been for Ruskin.[17] Nor is his influence to stop short at the
end of the nineteenth century : in 1934 we find Eric Gill devoting an
essay to Ruskin, showing how central that writer is in the formation
of his own ideas, and indeed he returns constantly to the opinion that
'industry without art is brutality.' It is hardly surprising, either, to
come across enthusiastic praise of 'the great, still neglected Ruskin'
in one of the lectures collected in Arnold Wesker's *Fears of Fragmentation.*

That chapter which so impressed Morris and which, it might be said,
formed the basis of his thought and art, is the one in which Ruskin
forcefully argues that the special significance of medieval architecture
was a direct result and symptom of the status of the workman under
the 'pre-commercial' regime of feudalism. Opposing puritanism, which
he sees as the destruction of art and the artistic spirit, he presents work
as being potentially not painful, not ascetic, but fulfilment in happiness,
therefore having the qualities of art. The medieval workman, argues
Ruskin, lending his eloquence to the creation of a potent myth — was
free *in his work*, however rigid the social hierarchy in which he
laboured; and this freedom in work made him into an artist. Those
sometimes crudely but always vitally carved goblins and gargoyles of
the Gothic cathedrals are testimonies to 'the life and liberty of every
workman who struck the stone; such as no laws, no charter, no
charities can secure; but which it must be the first aim of all Europe at

this day to regain for her children.'[18] The medieval worker had that
happiness that men can only know when they are not reduced to
machines, when they are conscious and creative, when their work is not
ruled by the inhuman principle of perfection. Designer and 'hand',
Ruskin argues, should never be separated — one man's thoughts should
not be carried out by another's manual dexterity : 'Now it is only by
labour that thought can be made healthy, and only by thought that
labour can be made happy, and the two cannot be separated with
impunity.'[19] The architect should at all costs work in the mason's yard
with his men. It is to encourage a modern and most insidious slave-trade
to buy anything that is produced without invention and pleasure having
some part in its making.

In *The Seven Lamps of Architecture* Ruskin had already established
his criterion quite clearly, and in its simplicity it admirably characterizes his ethic :

> I believe the right question to ask, respecting all ornament, is simply
> this : was it done with enjoyment — was the carver happy while he
> was about it? It may be the hardest work possible, and the harder
> because so much pleasure was taken in it; but it must have been
> happy, too, or it will not be living.[20]

Good work must be joyous expression, not stern repression; it must
have a strong instinctual or libidinal content. All other work is alienation,
and we should do what we can to be rid of it. The only salvation for
civilization lies in a return to the Gothic principles, a revival of the ideal
of pleasurable craftsmanship. To this end Ruskin was to found his
Guild of St George, an enclave of medievalism within late nineteenth-
century England, feudal in most of its principles including its modes of
production — 'But there shall not be on St George's estate a single thing
in the house which the boys don't know how to make, nor a single
dish on the table which the girls will not know how to cook.'[21]

Just as Ruskin was led from his initial, aesthetic insights to an
increasing concern with socio-political questions, so, too, was William
Morris; but while his aesthetic starting-point was very much the same
as that of the older writer, his political conclusions were to be largely
different. Philip Henderson has rightly spoken of this pioneer socialist's
attempt to combine Ruskin and Marx, and has pointed out that this
attempt can only result in grave contradictions. The undoubted
presence of such contradictions should not blind us, however, to the
very real importance of Morris' protest against the modern world.

Raymond Williams has aptly called him a 'pivotal figure' of our age; and surely as our awareness grows of what we have done to our environment and to our work, he will be increasingly recognized as such. A Janus-figure he may be, looking simultaneously backwards and forwards, yet the simple, moral force of his protest and ideals has something irresistible about it. Irresistible partly because of the compulsive unity of all his work : it is not for nothing that the period when he was most prolific as a designer of wallpapers, textiles and carpets was also a highpoint in the intensity of his political activity and his speech-making tours throughout the country. As craftsman, artist, poet, socialist he is always the *same* Morris with the one central and unifying preoccupation — work.

Immediately the contrast with Carlyle imposes itself, and the clash between two conceptions of work becomes yet more apparent. For Morris, far from sharing Carlyle's view of labour as virtue through suffering, with all its overtones of Calvinist rigour, agrees with Ruskin that work is potential happiness, and perhaps the greatest and most permanent happiness known to man. And this in turn colours his own particular vision of the Middle Ages, as he describes it in *The Art of the People* : the history of that period was not really as it is taught, he stresses, and the essential fact is not to be found in the succession of kings and battles but in the daily reality of rewarding work :

> Not every day, you may be sure, was a day of slaughter and tumult, though the histories read almost as if it were so; but every day the hammer clinked on the anvil, and the chisel played about the oak-beam, and never without some beauty being born of it, and consequently some human happiness.[22]

Pleasure, not pain, in daily labour is something that 'nature cries out for as its due' — and Morris shows how far he stands from the Carlyle position in the original title of the essay quoted above : *Labour and Pleasure versus Labour and Sorrow.* Inheriting much of Ruskin's uncritical admiration of the medieval guilds of craftsmen — and anticipating the Guild Socialism of G. D. H. Cole and others — Morris enthuses over the medieval workman's imagined freedom of hand and mind, 'subordinated to the co-operative harmony which made the freedom possible.'[23] The result was, once again, Gothic, and Morris dwells especially on architecture not only because he had studied it early in his career, but because it was a tangible result of what was best in the feudal system according to his own optimistic interpretation of

it : co-operative creation in the production of a work of art, of a focus
of culture, which in theory at least belonged to the whole community,
i.e. the great cathedrals or the humble, local churches. An image,
indeed, of the 'co-operative harmony' Morris dreams of in the future and
which he is to body forth in the charming, utopian romance, *News from
Nowhere*. The comparative harmony of a society based on mutual moral
obligation and on pre-industrial modes of production was translated
spontaneously into aesthetic values and experiences we have all but lost
sight of today :

> The special beauty of medieval buildings, which after a long period
> of neglect and ignorance has forced itself on the attention of our
> time, should surely now be recognized by all intelligent persons as
> the outcome of the conditions of the society of that epoch, a thing
> impossible of reproduction under the modern system of capitalist
> and wage-earner . . . The whole surface of a medieval building shows
> intelligent, free, and therefore pleasurable work on the part of the
> actual workman, while that of the modern building has nothing in
> it more than toil done against the grain under the threat of
> starvation.[24]

In time, of course, the medieval society of status had to give rise to
the modern society of contract. Morris is realistic enough, moreover,
to see and admit that that development, whatever man may seem to
have lost by it, was a necessary and inevitable one. We had, alas, to
move away from the time when the 'mystery and wonder of handicrafts' was universally acknowledged as a matter of course, when
'imagination and fancy mingled with all things made by man.'[25]
Historically necessary the evolution may have been, but Morris' regret,
his sense of loss is what strikes the reader of his work most forcibly,
even bearing in mind his balanced criticism of the not-to-be-mourned,
political servitude of the feudal system. In the essay *Gothic Architecture*
he describes the fall from medieval craft-consciousness to the allied
pests of Commercialism and Bureaucracy which he compares to the
Black Death:

> By that time Europe had begun to transform the great army of
> artist-craftsmen, who had produced the beauty of her cities, her
> churches, manor-houses and cottages, into an enormous stock of
> human machines, who had little chance of earning a bare livelihood
> if they lingered over their toil to think of what they were doing :

who were not asked to think, paid to think, or allowed to think.[26]

Morris does realize that what he calls the Century of Commerce (i.e. his own) has had a positive aspect in the gaining of a certain political freedom and in the erosion of prejudice; but he insists that we cannot equally call it the Century of Education, though some of his contemporaries claimed it as such — for after school, are not the great majority degraded into mechanical life, doing work that is not fit to develop them either physically or mentally? This constitutes a sane contradiction of Carlyle's facile belief that labour of *any* kind mystically leads to true knowledge and insight. It also points the way towards the view of Simone Weil and others — that work itself should ideally be a means and a source of education; a view anticipated already, as we know, by Fourier and subsequently by Marx.

Nothing proves this decadence of the modern age more than the products of modern work : thousands of useless articles, created as mere counters of the competitive market, the 'commodities' of Marx's analysis. The cheapness of goods forced on the consumer can produce only one thing — a cheapness of life. What could be more different, Morris pleads, from the production of goods in medieval Europe, where the beauty of things made was inseparable from the vital pleasure of making them, and a function of the aesthetic freedom of the responsible craftsman:

> The medieval craftsman was free on his work, therefore he made it
> as amusing to himself as he could; and it was his pleasure and not
> his pain that made all things beautiful that were made, and lavished
> treasures of human hope and thought on everything that man made,
> from a cathedral to a porridge-pot.[27]

If this value is to be rediscovered, then Marx's 'struggle with nature' must become quite definitely a pleasure; only if work could be the joy of our lives might our relationship with nature become a truly fertile and harmonious one. This means a radical change in society : only through the overcoming of capitalism and the recreation of community could that invaluable joy in work become feasible for society in general. It was a joy that Morris at least knew as an individual in real first-hand terms, and not as a ready-made and condescending moral concept *à l'usage des intellectuels*. As an exemplary figure he acquires much of his force from his own cultivation of a whole series of varied crafts, all pursued with the same professional conscience and concern for excellence. His designs for wallpaper and textiles have kept an astonishing freshness about them; he became expert in tapestry-weaving, even, at Kelmscott House, having a loom set up in his bedroom and beginning work on it sometimes as early as five o'clock in the morning! With the same thoroughness he turned his hand to carpets and rugs and investigated the half-lost craft of dyeing. To which we might add his earlier modelling in clay, carving, illumination and embroidery; and finally, of course, his study of typography, resulting in the Kelmscott Press with its aim of making books physically and tangibly things of beauty and fine workmanship. Through this latter activity Morris put into practice the belief of his friend, the veteran anarchist, Kropotkin, that the intellectual who wrote books should also, as a necessary counterbalance and completion of this, learn the manual trade of producing them as objects.

By such activity Morris recognizes in actual terms, as Carlyle had recognized it in a theoretical way, that the scope of the intellect alone is limited – 'pure' intellectualism is deprivation. Hence in the future society of *News from Nowhere*, we learn that 'early bookishness' is not encouraged – a far more vital role in the education of children is played by 'genuinely amusing work, like housebuilding and street-paving, and gardening.'[28] Once again, we note the insistence on pleasure. The result is a world from which idleness has disappeared, or where if it should abnormally appear a short course of aperient medicine quickly carries it off. Morris creates a delightful though also (as he doubtless knew) all too incredible world where work *is* a joy; a constantly sunlit world in which men and women pursue a whole variety of trades, boatmen one day, makers of ornaments in metal the next, and where all happily fall to at harvest-time to work in the fields. It is a universe of great physical as well as moral beauty, for not only are the rivers clean and pure, the skies unpolluted by the belching smoke-stacks of Morris' day, but the fortunate inhabitants, too, of this fairy-tale kingdom of the twenty-first century give by their appearance a striking impression of youth and harmony – a harmony resulting directly from happiness and fulfilment in work. The fond dream created in *News* is the characteristic answer of Morris' imagination to the plea uttered in his poem *The Pilgrims of Hope* in which the narrator, sensing his own alienation from his craft,

I take up fear with my chisel, fear lies twixt me and my plane, cries out:

> Shall the sun arise some morning and see men falling to work,
> Smiling and loving their lives? [29]

For this is the essence, the pivot of any meaningful change in society;
for what is revolution to achieve, on what are future values to be based,
if not on our day-to-day activities, our work?

> I say, as we turn away from the flagstaff where the new banner has
> been just run up; as we depart, our ears yet ringing with the blare of
> the heralds' trumpets that have proclaimed the new order of things,
> what shall we turn to then, what *must* we turn to then?
> To what else, save to our work, our daily labour? [30]

In his elaboration of this ethic of pleasure, Morris, we might note,
explicitly invokes Fourier : the narrator asks the old man in *News* what
could possibly be the reward of labour in a society without money?
and receives the reply, 'Fourier, whom all men laughed at, understood
the matter better.'[31] *News from Nowhere* was clearly written as a foil
to the ugliness and joylessness of the modern world and its work, a
foil in particular to that England which, Morris complained, had of late
been too much occupied with the counting-house and not enough with
the workshop. After all, he admitted readily that, apart from his
constant desire to produce things of beauty, the chief passion of his
life was always the hatred of modern civilization.

It is worth remarking, however, that the non-ascetic ethic of work,
which entails placing work at the very centre of culture, is not always
to be associated with yearning medievalism and rejection of the modern
world. Fourier, after all, was himself no medievalist, and neither was
the most important French writer to be directly influenced by Fourier,
Émile Zola. Zola, trained as an engineer, differs profoundly from
Ruskin or Morris in welcoming the technological possibilities of his
century; but just as much as the English writers he sees work as the
pivot of human life and all values to be derived from life. Having
emphasized in his earlier works the alienating effects of poverty and
wretched living and working conditions, he turns in the later, prophetic
novels to a positive exaltation of work. In *Paris* he shows Pierre, the
disillusioned priest, emerging from his despair and torment through the
discovery of a new, earthly faith as he is drawn into the industrious,
Froment family-circle : the microcosm of a happy and integrated
working community.

> And for the first time, amidst the torment that oppressed him, he

glimpsed the necessity of work, a fatality that appeared also as health and strength. There he at last discovered a solid footing, in the effort that upholds and saves. Was it the first glimmer of a new faith?[32]

Indeed it was, and by the end of the novel Pierre has come to see work as — ideally — the fulfilment of passion. It is, we should note, engineering work of a thoroughly modern kind, for Guillaume Froment, after some vicissitudes, brings forth as the fruit of his much-praised labour . . . a combustion engine. The salvation of the world is for Zola very much bound up with the progress of technology.

So, too, in the utopian *Travail* of 1901, which with heavy-handed emphasis presents work as one of the Gospels of Zola's lay religion. Like many of those we are dealing with, it is a work as interesting in its contradictions as in its immediate propositions. In a sense, it is because these contradictions exist that Zola can be counted as a true contributor to the current of speculation we are examining. For were many of his beliefs not grounded in positivism, in a faith in scientific progress which obviously must appear quite inimical to a Morris or a Ruskin? And yet there are, in *Travail*, definite points of contact with those writers; overall, the novel may be seen as the attempted but pathetically unsuccessful synthesis of faith in science on the one hand and the familiar view of work as potential happiness and morality on the other. As Fourier had done with rather more fantasy, Zola tries to blend scientism and messianism; and in so doing he bases the whole of his ideal society on his understanding of Fourier's theory of work, of the passions, of education, and so on. The vital turning-point in the novel is when the central character, Luc Froment, after experiencing some of the miseries of the industrial organization of labour in and around an iron foundry, spends the night in a room lined with the books of the great social prophets according to Zola, 'all the apostles of the new gospel' — Fourier, Saint-Simon, Proudhon, Cabet . . . but not a mention of Marx! Here Luc reads a summary of Fourier's doctrine, dwelling particularly on his hopes for work, the ideal of 'oeuvrer dans la joie'. In Zola's eyes this was the ultimate stroke of genius : 'Work restored to honour, become a public function, the pride, the health, the gaiety, the very law of life. To reorganize the whole of society, all that was necessary was to reorganize work . . .'[33]

Labour, Zola's hero learns, should be a 'fête', and it is to fulfilling this promise that he devotes his life, becoming eventually the paternalistic head of a Fourierist community whose example will spread, by a mysterious and apparently irresistible contagion, throughout the land and even beyond. Luc has been left in no doubt about the urgent need for this change : he is supposed to know already the reality of labour, being not only an engineer but also, we are told, a man who has felt the need to learn a manual trade as well, working as a mason in Paris. On arriving at the ironworks at the beginning of the novel he soon sees what manual labour so often means by the beginning of the twentieth century : 'everywhere was the filth of joyless, careless work.'[34] These two attributes of industrial work are, of course, inseparable, lack of care implies lack of joy, and vice versa. By way of contrast to the ideal, the kind of degradation that such alienation can produce is typified in two ways in the figures of the workers, Ragu and Fortuné. The name of the latter is pure irony — never was a child less fortunate than this victim of the division of labour, reduced to mental and physical deformity by his 'rôle de machine, aux gestes éternellement semblables'. His life in fact has become mechanism, for Zola believes with Morris and others that the mode of work determines the content and value of life. And this is Fortuné's work, as he remains motionless for hours on end, living only by an automatic gesture of his hand :

> The lever over to the right to make the hammer fall, over to the left to raise it again, and that was all, and the whole thought of the child was contained in that, in that tiny space. For a moment, in the bright glow of the sparks, he could be seen, so frail and slight, with his pale face, his discoloured hair, his vague eyes — the eyes of a wretched being whose brutish unattractive work, bereft of free choice, stunted his physical and moral growth.[35]

The other example of degradation is the brutal Ragu, not himself an automaton but hating his work and anything but conscientious at it; 'mauvais ouvrier' is what he is called throughout. He is in Zola's eyes a typical product of the present organization of labour, having no ambition in life but that of some day possessing the means to idleness. The very idea of work has become tainted for him, and this is presented as being the origin of all his vices, his cruelty and his crimes. If degrading work is bad and dehumanizing, so is no work at all : this is demonstrated through the figures of the idle capitalist, Boisgelin, and his dissolute mistress. He is to end up as a vague-eyed, open-mouthed idiot, a wretched and barely animate shadow of a man, haunting the outer fringes of the happy work-community created by Froment; whilst his mistress, whose force is spent in destruction and not in creation, finally destroys herself and her husband as well.

In antithesis to Ragu stands not only Luc Froment but more directly the 'bon ouvrier', Bonnaire, with his 'fine equilibrium of the laborious and healthy man.'[36] Even under the old system Bonnaire, as an exceptionally skilled workman, has a rare degree of responsibility in the tasks he performs as master puddler; the work of such a man in its natural skill and dexterity may be something of beauty, and the reader senses at once the delight of Zola in the acts of work well done as Luc watches the master founder pouring out the molten metal 'with precise, light gestures, of a simple beauty.'[37] Amid the shower of sparks he appears to Luc — and to Zola — as a maker of stars, a creator of worlds.

Bonnaire has the special quality for Zola of being both a good worker and a revolutionary, a man with strong, craft pride who is yet not afraid of the right kind of change. The same can not be said of another conscientious workman in *Travail*, old Morfain, the traditionalist whose family has looked after the antiquated furnace for three generations and who takes considerable pride in his arduous and unrewarding task. There is once again a loving description of the acts of labour as Morfain skilfully clears the blocked furnace and draws off a good casting; he even sleeps by the furnace that night to make sure that all is well, and as he works he is seen as 'one of the obscure heroes of labour entering suddenly into glory.'[38] Morfain's pride in his efforts is, however, more akin to the attitudes suggested by Carlyle than those of Morris : his dignity is of a stoic variety, the pride of continuous, painful effort, 'the ancient nobility of deadly toil', rather than the joy of the craftsman. Joylessness, indeed, is one of his chief characteristics, together with a passive acceptance of his lot. This is why Zola, for all that is admirable in Morfain, must go beyond him, and reveal his inadequacies. There is no revolt in Morfain, no wider view for the future, he has never considered going on strike in order to change the nature of work, and he has in him none of the lighter spirit of Luc's community; he fears change, fears the new machinery, seeing all his honour in the hand-to-hand struggle with nature, with the flame of the primitive furnace. Zola feels he has to put him in an increasingly critical light as the novel proceeds and as he stubbornly refuses all improvement and finally commits suicide when his old job is rendered unnecessary by the new electric furnaces. Too much about him belongs to the alienated past; there is no place for his ethic of suffering in the liberated community of joyous work.

Zola agrees with all our writers that idleness alone is without hope or salvation — at best it may be regarded as a disease, a result of those internal disorders so easily cured in *News from Nowhere*. Laziness is an unnatural state, argues a doctor in *Travail*, and so combats the representative of what Zola presents as the christian viewpoint, the Abbé Marle, who can only see work as the expiation of original sin, as a punishment to be born. For Zola, on the other hand, work is the natural activity of man, and laziness is death; work is the first principle of happiness in a future society of fulfilled individuals. The most rapturous expression of this faith comes, rather significantly, from a character who is not himself a routine worker but — like the novelist himself — an original mind, an inventor. This is Jordan, who is to perfect the machinery that will help liberate work in the community and who devotes his whole life to this end. Work is his *raison d'être*, and despite his frail, physical constitution such constant effort is described as the necessary and natural play of his limbs and organs; it is not for nothing that he lives, like Luc and Bonnaire, to a quite incredibly old age. Not only is work the principle of life in general, it is also in itself a political constitution, claims Jordan somewhat vaguely : the meaning is presumably that no other political constitution is needed than the simple organization of work on a free, communal basis. Work, then, has clearly a redemptive power for a corrupt world, and it is described in highly-charged religious terminology by Jordan :

> I would that the religion of work were at last founded, the hosanna to work the saviour, the one truth, health, joy and sovereign peace.[39]

So it is that when the community is founded and develops, Zola stresses that despite mechanization — and there are terrible vaguenesses and contradictions here to be examined later — no end to labour is envisaged even in the remotest future. 'L'éternel travail futur' will continue to be the law of life and society. By the time we reach the end of the novel, labour has become a pleasure and a recreation thanks to obedience to Fourier's ideas of diversity. By a beautifully utopian paradox, 'progress' brings in fact a move away from the factory structure and back to an artisanal one. The new generation seems to favour a form of free domestic industry, 'the small-scale worker at home, free, master of what he makes', each house becoming a family workshop. 'A whole people of artisans' is coming into being. After all the trumpeting about technological progress, the development of the City has led to a rediscovery of and a return to the old, pre-industrial modes of production.[40]

The two ethics we have defined are not always (as the example of Carlyle suggested) absolutely separable. Although there is, for instance, no real asceticism in Morris' vision, there are a number of writers of a more religious frame of mind who have their place in the tradition, and in them we often find a curious mixture of both currents. Tolstoy, to take the most notable example (and we shall return to him in the next chapter) sought something more than just a Morris-like pleasure in his dilettante, cobbling activities or the physical exertion of mowing, carting manure and building in which he liked to indulge on his estate. It was also the path of righteousness, and the first teaching of the Gospels in Tolstoy's reading of them : 'In the sweat of thy brow shalt thou eat bread.' 'Bread-labour', i.e. that work which is absolutely essential to the sustaining of life, is to be 'the remedy which will save the human race' (as he wrote in his essay *The Triumph of Labour*). This it will be in two senses : first of all because man can only be really happy and contented when performing his share of useful labour, and secondly because this alone is the means to spiritual salvation. Bread-labour will give back true understanding – that intelligence that goes beyond the intellect – to those who have lost it by their withdrawal from 'the natural line of mankind', will bring them to harmony with the laws of God and nature, those allied forces that have assigned to all men some 'undoubtedly useful and joyous occupation'. Tolstoy's idea was that man has four essential types of activity : that of his muscles, hard labour; that of his fingers, skilful handicraft; that of his intellect; and that involved in the commerce with other men. Every man's day should be organized so that he does all four in the course of it. Only by accepting this can we see 'the curse lifted which in our imagination is laid on work; and all labour becomes joyful'.[41] Tolstoy's cult of work might be seen as a synthesis of the two very different approaches we have traced in this chapter. Paradoxically, it is at once immediate pleasure and fulfilment, and yet mortification of the flesh. The paradox is characteristic of mysticism in its mixture of pleasure and pain.

So, too, we find a similar complexity in the writings of Simone Weil, a union of the ascetic and the joy-in-work currents, the transcendental and the intrinsic validation of work. She is to see the factory as ideally a place where one should make 'a hard and painful, but nonetheless joyful contact with life.'[42] At times she seems essentially concerned with the possibility of direct satisfaction from work, at others she emphasizes the suffering necessary for a truly spiritual life – the purpose of manual labour being to bring about direct contact with God.

It is certainly true that the figure of the happy and fulfilled artisan plays less of a role in her writings than in the work of such as Morris. Weil's thought is closely paralleled by that of the catholic artist, Eric Gill : for him, too, the working life is the truly contemplative life, and in the light of this belief he himself tried to set up a religious, working community, a latter-day version of the Brotherhood that Morris and his friends had once dreamed of in Oxford. Work is a means to culture, but even more, for Gill, it is sacred : so the Leisure State is to be rejected as the grand climax of the industrial world, the result of all its vices — the way of life it promises is 'clean contrary to the nature of this physical world, to man's physical nature, and to the nature of his desires.' To labour is to pray, he repeats — or at least it *was* so in pre-industrial times when food, clothing, furniture and houses were all humanly made by hand, 'and were often actually and always potentially works of love, of prayer, of contemplation.'[43] As in the case of Weil, though, this Morris-like note is supplemented by the ascetic concept of the ethical fulfilment to be found in pain — when, he adds, that same pain is the necessary companion of good work. The result is claimed to be a form of holiness comparable to the agony (cf. Carlyle's 'agony of bloody sweat') of martyrdom! In his case, too, the two ethics shade into each other in a sometimes problematic fashion.

Finally we must consider the possibility of a different kind of transcendental or external validation of human work, quite outside the religious sphere but in some ways analogous to it. This is what we have when a *cause* — such as that of 'building socialism' in the first enthusiastic years of the USSR — is seen as giving to work its ethical content and its justification. This moral impetus through collective aspiration and idealism is reflected in a good deal of Soviet writing during the twenties and thirties. Understandably, it had, too, its echoes in western literature. Thus, to take one prestigious example, the transformation and moral fulfilment of the character Hemmelrich in the epilogue to André Malraux's *La Condition humaine*. In the past, Hemmelrich has always been an embittered and pathetic figure, working without knowing why; he flees, however, to the USSR, takes a job as a fitter in an electricity generating plant, and at the end of the novel can say, 'It's the first time in my life that I'm working and knowing why, not just waiting patiently to die.' And the character who reports this statement remembers the marxist teaching of Gisors, one of the central figures of that novel :

A civilization is transformed when its most painful element — humiliation for the slave, work for the modern worker — becomes all at once a value, when it is no longer a question of escaping from that humiliation, but of seeing in it one's salvation; no longer of escaping from that work, but finding in it one's reason for living. The factory, which is still only a sort of church of the catacombs, must become what the cathedral once was . . .[44]

It is interesting to see Malraux taking up in this context the image of the cathedral which played such a part in the thought of Ruskin or Morris; as a tangible symbol of collective aspiration it is also to recur in Arnold Wesker's *Their Very Own and Golden City*.

No doubt such aspiration can be a moral value, even in the context of fragmented labour-processes, by the predominance of an authentic finality in the ideal of an ethical community sustained by such labour. This is borne out by a report on the *Communauté de travail Boimondau*, an institution that grew out of the more radical aspirations of the French Resistance movement of the last war : one of its members, quoted by Friedmann, wrote, 'However fragmentary his job, the man in the community knows that the operation he performs contributes to the greatness and solidity of his business, his enterprise, of the corporate group of which he is a member . . . Joy in industrial work is possible, but on condition that the means of production are collectively owned.'[45]

However, just as the same spokesman was later forced to admit that idealism was foundering against the necessity for an increasingly scientific organization of work-processes, so, too, the Soviet example had already lost much of its appeal in this respect. Lenin himself had shared and reiterated Marx's views on the need to re-humanize work; but he was aware that post-revolutionary Russia presented the curious situation of a proletarian State in which the proletariat itself, given the sheer numerical predominance of the peasantry, was in the minority. He thought that at all costs, especially in view of the added urgency created by foreign intervention, Russia had no alternative but to industrialize as quickly and as efficiently as possible. The result was inevitably a reproduction of many of the vices of the period of capitalist accumulation in western Europe, that very period which Marx had condemned for its degradation of man as a working being. Whilst 'official' literature was to continue to exalt all necessary work in the name of the collective goal, disillusionment was not slow to set in. On a visit to a Soviet institute for work-study, Ernst Toller was dismayed at the 'scientific' regulation of work in the sole name of efficiency — the same faults he and his colleagues had been so sensitive to in the capitalist world were all too clearly reappearing here.[46] Under Stalin, such vices were to be intensified beyond all necessity and work estranged from any immediate sense of finality. No more damning confirmation of this need be sought than the measures of constraint and repression imposed on Russian workers in the thirties, the institution of punishments for non-punctuality or absenteeism, laws forbidding the mobility of workers. The very existence of coercion and of labour camps was eloquent proof that the effort to make work itself the basis of human freedom and dignity had been shelved for an indefinite period. The external work-ethic waned, and the intrinsic work-ethic had never been created. We can understand, perhaps, why a disillusionment with 'change' of this kind tended to throw writers over to an emphasis on tradition, on permanence, on roots. But then that emphasis had always been a part of the moral and cultural speculation with which we are concerned.

4 The nostalgia for permanence

A number of themes are closely interlinked in the movement of thought with which we are concerned. In the current of speculation on the ethical and cultural status of work there is often a strong element of tradition-alism, a nostalgia for permanence in the face of a fast-changing environment that seems to have lost its human dimension; and closely allied with this is the concern for rooted existence in opposition to that alienating character of lifeless mechanism. There is a delight in demon-strating that just such a rooted existence inevitably means health, moral and psychological equilibrium. These themes fuse, of course, with that of joy and fulfilment in work, especially work in the natural *milieu*. A few examples will carry us up to the present day, when that nostalgia — and with some cause — is more acute than ever.

Carlyle, for his part, devoted a whole chapter of *Past and Present* to the subject of 'Permanence', and his sentiment may be summarized in the statement : 'Permanence, persistence is the first condition of all fruitfulness in the ways of men.'[1] The point was to be illustrated in novelistic form by George Eliot at her most didactic.

Already a nostalgic light suffuses the world of her *Adam Bede* (1858). Adam is the ideal of the sort of craftsman George Eliot saw to be dis-appearing, and she sets her story some sixty years earlier; the emotional framework is one of looking backward to a vanishing way of life. As such a craftsman, Adam is no genius, no superman, but for all that :

> He was not an average man. Yet such men as he are reared here and there in every generation of our peasant artisans — with an inheritance

of affections nurtured by a simple family life of common need and common industry, and an inheritance of faculties trained in skilful courageous labour; they make their way upward, rarely as geniuses, most commonly as painstaking honest men, with the skill and conscience to do well the tasks that lie before them. Their lives have no discernable echo beyond the neighbourhood where they dwelt, but you are almost sure to find there some good piece of road, some building, some application of mineral produce, some improvement in farming practice, some reform of parish abuses, with which their names are connected by one or two generations after them.[2]

In old age such men are the most respected members of the community, occupying a place of honour and telling their children 'how pleased they were when they first earned their twopence a day.'

Adam himself stands out as an exemplary figure first of all by his quality as a workman. Not for nothing is the first chapter entitled 'The Workshop', and we are introduced immediately to the carpentry in progress there, the making of doors and window-frames, the carving of a wooden mantelpiece. As soon as the clock strikes six, all the other workmen throw down their tools at once, leaving screws half driven in, gestures of labour half-completed, reaching for their coats even before the chimes have died away. Adam, who has gone on with his work, is indignant : 'Look here now! I can't abide to see men throw away their tool i' that way, the minute the clock begins to strike, as if they took no pleasure i' their work, and was afraid o' doing a stroke too much.'[3]

Not only is good carpentry 'God's will', but earthly salvation as well. After the grief of his father's death, and none too happy in love either, Adam awakens the next day with the coffin to make. The prospect of work restores a sense of balance, and he is

eager to begin the new day, and subdue sadness by his strong will and strong arm ...

'There's nothing but what's bearable as long as a man can work,' he said to himself : 'the natur' o' things doesn't change, though it seems as if one's own life was nothing but change. The square o' four is sixteen, and you must lengthen your lever in proportion to your weight, is as true when a man's miserable as when he's happy; and the best o' working is, it gives you a grip hold o' things outside your own lot.'[4]

The sentiments here are important and typical : amidst the flux of human life, work and its stable laws establish permanence, fixity. The work-world at its best is a rooted world, and rooted in unchanging truths that are the truths of nature. So it is that the sound of hammers at work can draw Adam out of the most sombre preoccupations, it is to him like the sound of an orchestra to the musician and produces that same harmonizing effect that Carlyle had noted : 'the strong fibres begin their accustomed thrill, and what was a moment before joy, vexation, or ambition, begins its change into energy. All passion becomes strength when it has an outlet from the narrow limits of our personal lot in the labour of our right arm, the cunning of our right hand, or the still, creative activity of our thought.'[5] Thwarted in his love for the frivolous Hetty, Adam falls back on his work, and is thankful that sadness has not spoiled his skill nor his taste for the craft. 'Since I've been spared that, I've no right to grumble. When a man's got his limbs whole, he can bear a smart cut or two.'[6] Once again, work appears as the anchor-point in a man's life, and the key to equilibrium.

There is a similar respect for work, and a certain nostalgia for permanence outside history, in the Wessex novels of Thomas Hardy. Hardy was preoccupied by the problem of *déracinement*, the sometimes demoralizing and even tragic effects of uprooting individuals from the old traditions that had given their ancestors stability and a sense of gravity in the world. Yet with Hardy the problem is more complex : for he does not idealize the traditional milieu, seeing as he does the cruelty, superstition and the terrible limitations that rootedness can imply. Nature, he knows, can also be destructive. This is why he is to sympathize so much in his later novels with the characters who strive beyond their milieu : yet if he is a man of progress, Hardy is a tragic one. It is this complex balance in his works that gives them their special fascination, and it has understandably produced controversy among critics. Thus Merryn Williams has recently accused Irving Howe and others of distorting Hardy by their own 'romantic view of the old rural England', particularly in interpreting novels such as *Tess of the D'Urbervilles* or *Jude the Obscure*. For Hardy was aware of conflicts and contradictions *within* rural society before the full advent of industrialization, argues Williams. This is true; and yet with qualification Hardy does belong to the tradition we are tracing. Nostalgia for permanence has a place in his view of the world, and his estimation of work is a high one indeed. As Irving Howe puts it, 'He felt that working with one's hands had both aesthetic propriety and redemptive value, that there is health in a life close to the earth . . .'[7] The same critic makes the point that Hardy defines his characters through the work they do or fail to do; and it is good work consistently done that gives them solidity, density and stability. With this point of view Merryn Williams cannot disagree, affirming that 'the great dividing line between Hardy's authentic and inauthentic characters is determined by their various approaches to work.'[8] Idleness, there is no doubt, is seen as a bad quality, and one that is destructive of all equilibrium (as in the case of Eustacia Vye in *Return of the Native*). Acting, as opposed to working, becomes associated with inauthenticity.

In the earlier novels the issues are relatively simple. Like Adam Bede, Gabriel Oak in *Far from the Madding Crowd* retains his integrity and equilibrium after being rejected by his beloved Bathsheba by devoting himself conscientiously to his tasks as shepherd and subsequently as farm bailiff. The most persistent images that the reader retains of Gabriel are, for example, those of his saving the ricks from a violent storm by his thatching – and at the same time saving himself, for this occurs at one of the saddest moments of his life. We understand his craftsman's incredulity and incomprehension when he learns that Bathsheba's other disappointed suitor, the farmer, Boldwood, has totally neglected to protect *his* corn, despite the clear warnings of bad weather. Boldwood's neglect of his work is a symptom and an essential part of his general disintegration, the loss of integrity which culminates in his moral collapse and murder of Bathsheba's husband at the end of the novel.

Of particular significance in the book are scenes such as the sheep-shearing in the Great Barn, an ancient medieval edifice such as Morris himself loved, and described by Hardy, the admirer of Gothic, in loving detail, with its arches of stone, its natural grandeur and beauty. A fit setting indeed for work well and pleasurably done, work which itself is presented as part of the seasonal rhythm of nature – 'the barn was natural to the shearers, and the shearers were in harmony with the barn.'[9] We find a similar feeling in the descriptions of Giles' craft of woodsman in *The Woodlanders*, with 'his marvellous power of making trees grow.'[10] The novel presents us with the picture of a dedicated and conscientious work-life amid the natural environment, and Hardy pays tribute to the subtle hand of Giles whose very work is directly concerned with the establishment of roots.

More complex is the role played by work in *Tess of the D'Urbervilles*. Tess, basically innocent girl that she is, with her healthy capacity for hard work, is particularly contrasted with the idle and dissolute Alec D'Urberville who seduces and ruins her. After their first affair, and the

death of their child, Tess goes off to the Talbothays dairy farm, and
what takes place in the idyllic pages that describe her stay there is a
story of regeneration and stabilization through 'natural' work. The idyll
of this work-a-day world would be complete were it not for the fact that
the man she falls in love with there is a characteristic Hardy hybrid.
Angel Clare has broken away from the pattern of his ecclesiastical
parents, he has realized the value of work on the land and set about
learning it with a will; but though he is favourably contrasted with his
hide-bound, 'well-educated' brothers he is still an intellectual, a slave
of abstract, inhuman principle and the consciousness of social conven-
tion. He is shown as lacking the fundamental and unalterable good
sense of a Gabriel Oak, and eventually he fails in his work as he fails in
life generally. What amounts really to his betrayal of Tess leads to the
next episode in her working life; but what a contrast with the dairy!
She moves to Flintcombe-Ash, to work barren land in an impersonal
framework; here the figures of the labourers stooping over their arduous
tasks suggest not harmony so much as 'a mechanical regularity', rural
paternalism gives way to a more modern and anonymous form of
economic exploitation. True, nature itself is harsh, desolate and cruel
here, and the work of digging up swedes in the driving rain can be
nothing but miserable. A further form of wretchedness appears, though,
in the famous passage in which Hardy introduces the threshing-machine,
'the red tyrant that the women had come to serve', and which converts
work into toil by destroying any natural rhythms there may be in that
work. Especially striking is the portrait of the engine-man, a dark figure
not organically of the agricultural world at all, but now taking it over.
He represents the rootless, industrial era :

> While they uncovered the sheaves he stood apathetic beside his
> portable repository of force, round whose hot blackness the morning
> air quivered. He had nothing to do with preparatory labour. His fire
> was waiting, incandescent, his steam was at high pressure, in a few
> seconds he could make the long strap move at an invisible velocity.
> Beyond its extent the environment might be corn, straw, or chaos;
> it was all the same to him.[11]

It is not work such as this that can save Tess now.

If we have to beware of oversimplifying issues in *Tess*, this is all the
more true of *Jude the Obscure*. A prey to what Hardy calls 'the modern
vice of unrest', Jude is yet clearly admired for his striving beyond the
narrow world into which he is born. Again, the subtlety of Hardy lies

in his seeing the value of roots and permanence whilst also being fully aware of the narrowness, the frustration and ignorance they can imply. In any case, the rural world of Jude's childhood is already caught up in a state of flux — 'Many of the thatched and dormered dwelling-houses had been pulled down of late years, and many trees felled on the green.' The quaint old church has gone, and in its place a tall, new building with no organic relationship with the milieu, 'unfamiliar to English eyes, had been erected on a new piece of ground by a certain obliterator of historic records who had run down from London and back in a day.' The obliterated graves — a Ruskinian note — now have only a paltry and impermanent, industrial consecration, 'commemorated by nine-penny cast-iron crosses warranted to last five years.'[12]

Whereas Jude's first occupation of bird-scaring is seen as being of very little value to him, for it is narrow and uninspiring work indeed, his exercise of the craft of stone-mason in Christminster is a different matter. Hard and exploited as the work is, the stone-yard is seen at once as a 'centre of regeneration'.[13] Jude is a true craftsman with a comprehensive skill, and this phenomenon Hardy relates to his rural origin, contrasting him with the fragmented, industrialized city work-man :

> He was a handy man at his trade, an all-round man, as artisans in country towns are apt to be. In London the man who carves the boss or knob of leafage declines to cut the fragment of moulding which merges in that leafage, as if it were a degradation to do the second half of one whole.[14]

Jude is authentic in this work, unlike his beloved Sue, whose profession of designing church texts is hypocritical : this, as Williams has remarked, is symptomatic of her irresponsibility in life as a whole. Jude even feels for a moment that his carving is just as worthy an occupation as 'that dignified by the name of scholarly study' after which he hankers so throughout the novel. But striving and unrest prove stronger than the appeal of the work, and even carry Jude into a loss of faith in work generally as he sinks to bread-baking and utters a statement full of despair : 'But one can work, and despise what one does.'[15] It is a sign that tragedy is close at hand.

All that remains at the end is Jude's ideal, valuable but unfulfilled — and still awaiting realization today. Merryn Williams summarizes it with sensitivity : 'It is an ideal of a society of integrated human beings, in which spirit and flesh, intellectual and physical labour, can be fused into a harmonious whole.'[16]

Less subtle in some ways, and characteristically more dogmatic, is Tolstoy. Greatly influenced by Rousseau's vehement denunciation of what we call 'civilization', Tolstoy was led to the sort of hefty indictment of modern society that we find in *Resurrection* and the essay *What Then Must We Do*? It is an unnatural society, one that brings out only the worst in man. Why do we have criminals? Because, he replies in the novel, we create them with our perverted institutions, amongst which modern industry has, of course, pride of place; and it is interesting to see in what company industrial institutions are placed by Tolstoy : 'factories, foundries, work-shops, public-houses, gin-shops, brothels'![17] Instead of seeking to regulate these we should destroy them. Away with telephones, motor-cars, railways, factory-made cloth, if to produce them ninety-nine per cent of the people have to remain in slavery. To eliminate them would be no real privation : 'Truly enlightened people will always agree to go back to riding on horses and using pack-horses, or even to tilling the earth with sticks and with their own hands.'[18] Backed by the mighty optimism of this belief, Tolstoy shared Morris's conviction that the way to a true community was not, as the positivistic, Saint-Simonian school thought, through increased production of goods, but through a simplification of life and the return to a rooted work-existence. Only in this way could the chief evils of luxury, idleness, and all the attendant vices be finally banished. Carrying distrust of the intellect, of positivist 'reason' and the faith in science even further than most other writers, Tolstoy could see only 'poverty of thought' in the sciences. The real truth is to be found elsewhere — and where but in work rooted in the *milieu naturel*, and especially in the earth? This indeed is where Tolstoy found it, as he tells in his Confession : 'But the life of all the toiling folk, of all humanity which was creating life, rose before me in its true significance. I came to understand that this is life itself, and that the meaning given to this life is truth, and I accepted it.'[19] As in the case of Morris, this was to be no mere intellectual concept : Tolstoy worked in the fields with the peasants, until he felt himself too old to do so; he applied himself with some persistence to the self-imposed task of learning the cobbler's art, and although he apparently had less aptitude for this sort of thing than Morris had — his shoes were pretty awful! — he certainly idealized the craft. 'How like a light morally splendid in his dirty, dark corner,' he wrote of the poor cobbler who tried to teach him.[20] It was the same craft that was to become the subject of a whole novel in the following century : Charles-Louis Philippe's *Charles*

Blanchard, in which, in a similar way, the humble artisan's shop is seen
as a repository of some great moral truth : 'The shop was full of this
truth, it was full of truth. One plied one's craft there because one
simply must ply a craft.'[21]

The theme of work as a force for joy and health appears early in
Tolstoy's fiction : in *The Cossacks*, we have Olenin, tired of life in
Moscow, discovering the life of the Caucasian peasants and, in particular,
of the girl, Maryana. Her simple work-a-day life, with all its implications
of pleasure and permanence is described with obvious enthusiasm :

> Early in the morning, at the first glow of dawn, she sprang up,
> washed her face in cool water, muffled herself up in her kerchief,
> and ran off barefoot after the cattle. Then, after hastily getting on
> her shoes and her beshmet, she took some bread in her bundle,
> hitched up the oxen, and went off to the garden for the day's work.
> There she took only a brief hour for rest; she spent her time in
> cutting off the clusters of grapes and in lugging the baskets, and then,
> at eventide, cheerful and unwearied, pulling the oxen by a cord and
> guiding them by a long branch, she would return to the village.[22]

The result of all this is that Maryana is 'full of glowing life', a state
which only natural work, subject to the rhythms of seasonal change
and repetition, can ensure. This is a lesson that Tolstoy teaches with a
much increased, moral emphasis in *Anna Karenina*. In contrast with
the tragic story of Anna herself we have the relative fulfilment of Levin,
the figure into whom Tolstoy put more of himself than he did into any
other of his fictional characters. Levin expresses his revulsion at the
artificiality of city life by withdrawing to his country estate. On his
first appearance in the novel we are told how he looks scornfully at the
white, carefully manicured hands of the bureaucrat, Grinevich, hands
that clearly have never done any necessary work. When he subsequently
goes to dine with his friend, Oblonsky, he expresses a preference for
bread and cheese over the oysters he is obliged to eat, and wonders at
the city habit of consuming finicky, complicated foods in order to make
meals last as long as possible, whereas in the country 'we try to get over
our meals as quickly as we can, so as to be able to get on with our work.'[23]
Unlike his bored acquaintances in Moscow, he has a fundamental, moral
equilibrium that is all the more sure for not being the result of superficial ratiocination. Returning home to his estate after being rejected by
Kitty, with a wound in his heart that seems incurable, he throws
himself into work. His life is busy and full despite his loneliness, and

this saves him from going to pieces. 'Time and work told,' the author remarks. The task of supervising the farm cannot satisfy him, he wants to labour directly with the peasants whose work seems to him to express a 'joy of living' : 'it struck him that it depended on himself to change his wearisome, idle, and artificial personal life for that pure, delightful life of common toil.'[24] Such joy and peace he, too, finds in that memorable incident when he spends the whole day mowing with his employees; not only does he discover simple truths, such as how good water can taste from a rusty cup after such great exertion, but he experiences the pleasure of letting his most natural instincts and rhythms take over in the work itself :

> The longer Levin went on mowing, the oftener he experienced those moments of oblivion when his arms no longer seemed to swing the scythe, but the scythe itself his whole body, so conscious and full of life; and as if by magic, regularly and definitely without a thought being given to it, the work accomplished itself of its own accord. These were blessed moments.[25]

It is because of such activity that Levin can never become a tragic figure. Work gives him a stability that he tries to explain to his uncomprehending, intellectual brother, telling him 'what a remedy it is for every kind of folly.' He will enrich medicine with a new term, he adds : *Arbeitskur* (work-therapy)![26] And thanks to this fundamental sanity and stability that he owes to the permanence of the natural world, he is protected from such aberrations as enthusing over the war at the end of the novel; nor does he commit suicide at the height of his religious crisis, for resolute work again quietens his anguish. We know that he will go on in his fundamentally conservative manner, trying, as he says, to live as his father and grandfathers lived before him.

Other christian writers, sometimes with their nostalgia for medieval structures of life predating the atomization of the bourgeois-capitalist world, equally stress the importance of permanence and the role of work within that permanence. We might take the example of Charles Péguy, poet, mystic and 'socialist' of a kind, imbued with a sense of tradition and continuity. He described his socialism in the retrospective *Notre Jeunesse* as having been a doctrine of 'the restoration of work', an attempt to find again the ethos and forms of work that reigned before they were destroyed by what Péguy always called the 'bourgeois' contamination of acquisitiveness and self-seeking.[27] Men's roots were once in work, he says; but there are no roots in money. In *L'Argent*,

one of his last works before his death in 1914, he idealized the attitude
to work in some indeterminate past when labour had its own honour,
'the same as that which in the Middle Ages ruled hand and heart.' Men
used to sing at their work, he claims :

> Whether people can believe it or not, . . . we have known workers
> who wanted to work. People thought only of working. We have
> known workers who in the morning thought only of working. They
> got up in the morning, and at what an hour! and they sang at the
> idea that they were off to work . . . Work was their very joy, and the
> profound root of their being. And their reason for being.[28]

Never would they have imagined the idea of voluntarily *not* working,
adds Péguy with horror! He himself was always proud of being of
peasant stock and the son of a woman who earned her living by recaning
chairs; and again and again he stresses his imagined closeness to the
'people'. As much as Ruskin or Morris, he passionately believed in the
moral, as well as the aesthetic value of work well done. Back in that
once-stable past, he claimed, it was instinctively recognized :

> A chair spindle had to be well made. That was understood. It was
> vital. It didn't have to be well made for the wages or in exchange
> for the wages. It didn't have to be well made for the boss or for the
> connoisseurs or for the boss's customers. It had to be well made in
> itself, in its very being . . . Every hidden part, in the chair, was just
> as perfectly made as those parts that showed. It was the very same
> principle as that of the cathedrals.[29]

Péguy himself tried to perpetuate the tradition by turning to the craft
of book-printing, learning typography and the allied skills. The old
spirit was not really dead, he thought : the workers are still unhappy
when they aren't at their jobs — and he introduces the concept of race
that haunts his writings, asserting that the spirit of the 'race laborieuse'
will out. Their hands itch, anxious to work.[30]

For Péguy, strike action is part of that bourgeois contamination and
uprooting that has destroyed work-traditions generally, and he remains
hostile and uncomprehending before it, thus giving his socialism a
curious cast indeed. It is clear that he is tragically unaware of the
problems posed by the development of modern industry and the
extreme division of labour. There are, it is true, sudden insights in his
last works, as when, having defined the present apparent dislike of work
as 'the deepest flaw, the central flaw of the modern world', he goes on

to say that the reason for it lies in modern industrial conditions, which correspond to a sort of terrestrial version of Hell — 'there is no place of perdition better designed, better equipped, better fitted out, so to speak . . . there is no tool of perdition more purpose-built than the modern workshop.'[31] Such glimpses are rare, though, and the outright and facile moralism of his rejection of strike action, based as it is on the vaguest of nostalgias, can suggest only lack of awareness or sheer irresponsibility. The former, no doubt, for Péguy always spoke in terms of the age-old peasant and artisan classes he fondly imagined himself close to, and never of the industrial proletariat of his own age. No wonder he felt isolated in his time, and was so fond of complaining that the world had changed more in the last thirty years than in the previous two thousand!

Simone Weil, though she has a great many similarities to Péguy, is different in this respect : she knew what industrial work was like, and could see the further developments in 'rationalization' that had taken place since his death. She, indeed, took her deep commitment to the question of work to the extent of taking an unskilled factory job for a year : in 1934—5 she worked first at the Alsthom electrical works, then at the Forges de Basse-Indre, and finally at Renault. During this period she learned a great deal about what work could become in a dehumanized environment, and she expressed what she learned in the famous *La Condition ouvrière*. Like Marx before she sees — and actually experiences — that for the individual worker in such a milieu his labour has the character of necessity but not of finality, for the end is not *willed* by him, indeed the end is often unknown to him. The work is carried out in response only to an immediate need, and not for a moral aim, a good — 'à cause d'un besoin, non en vue d'un bien.'[32] The only rewards to be expected from such work are the most unnatural of stimuli, a sordid money-lust implanted in the heart of the working class by an inhuman system : this is what we have instead of real satisfaction, instead of simple moral incentives such as praise, thanks, or the sense of doing something worthwhile.

A further and more general alienation, however, is the vast problem of uprootedness with which Simone Weil was much proccupied and to which she devoted her book *L'Enracinement*. This uprootedness she attributes to 'modern civilization with its poisons'.[33] It is a vice that is not restricted to factories and urban civilization generally, but has infected the rural world as well. The result is a fundamentally unnatural situation, for 'it is against nature that the earth should be cultivated by uprooted beings.'[34] The vital task of the age is the restoration of roots, and this means, as for Péguy, the restoration of work as the spiritual centre of life. In *L'Enracinement* she notes, 'Our age has as its special mission, its vocation, the constitution of a civilization founded on the spirituality of work.'[35] For this task she saw premonitory hints in Rousseau, Proudhon, Tolstoy, Marx and the papal encyclicals. The list bears witness to Weil's eclectic spirit; and indeed she expressed the hope that the search for this spirituality would unite marxists and christians in a common ideal.

Unlike her fellow-christian, Péguy, though, she does not reject strike action as merely a symptom of the modern state of flux, far from it : apropos of a strike of metal-workers in 1936 she writes that as long as the action is carried out not *only* for more money it can be for the moral good of the participants, and can even represent a kind of salvation, 'le salut de l'âme'. During the dispute and the occupation of the factory she sees workers becoming men again in a pure joy quite independent of material demands. Owing to the occupation the factory becomes a place of life for once, and not just a place of work artificially and absolutely separate from the private sphere. The strike, in other words, offered a hint, a promise, of what a man's relationship with his work could become if industry were organized in a very different way and according to very different principles.[36]

Above all, Simone Weil conceives of work as a means of 'getting directly to grips with the world', in both an immediate, physical *and* a spiritual sense. Like Carlyle she sees work as a deep mysterious contact with the basic, inexpressible realities; and this 'getting to grips with the world' means also grasping the fixity and permanence of the world. For she, too, is deeply distrustful of philosophies and ideologies of change and flux, and in particular of any facile doctrine of 'progress'. Hence her indictment of the eighteenth-century *Encyclopédistes*, flower of the French Enlightenment, 'all uprooted intellectuals, all obsessed by the idea of progress.'[37] The scientism with which that ideology is associated is seen as one of the most potentially destructive aberrations of the modern intellect, its logical culmination being in totalitarianism, the exaltation of science and 'inevitable' historical movement over all static and permanent humanistic concepts. The reasons for her fears we may appreciate more in due course after looking at the totalitarian, technological world of Ernst Jünger. For the moment we can say that it is in her criticism of the nihilistic potential of mechanical, historical determinism — which she saw in fascism and also, not in Marx himself but certainly in debased varieties of contemporary 'marxism' – that the real affinity between Simone Weil and Albert Camus is most obvious.

For the nostalgia for permanence has nothing inherently christian about it. It can be shared by writers of such a 'pagan' sensibility as Camus, or the regional novelist of Provence, Jean Giono; and for both of them the link between permanence, equilibrium and valid work is a vital one.

Camus made no secret of his enthusiasm over the writings and spirit of Simone Weil. He planned a preface for *L'Enracinement* in which he expressed admiration for the way she had understood and laid bare the malady of the age. Surely, he suggests, no real rebirth of values in Europe can fail to take note of the needs she defined in that work. In another text devoted to *L'Enracinement* he dwells particularly on the valid 'traditionalism' of Weil : such traditionalism, indeed, lay close to his own anxieties in the post-war period. In *L'Homme révolté* he is led to present Hegelianism and its ideological offshoots as the source of all the nihilism he perceives in the modern world, creating a universe of mere flux and consequently anguish. Historical *movement* has become the focal point of man's existence, and the result is a loss of roots and a negation of culture. In the somewhat imprecise manner characteristic of much of his thought he states in his notebook : 'German philosophy has placed a movement in the things of reason and the universe – whereas the Ancients placed fixity there. We can only go beyond German philosophy – and save mankind – by defining what is fixed and what is mobile . . .'[38] Elsewhere, especially in the essays of the collection, *L'Été*, he expresses his nostalgia for the permanence of the natural world, in a prose vibrant with the luminous sense of immediate life, his 'vraie patrie', and complains, in *L'Exil d'Hélène*, of the current disrespect for unchanging, natural beauty that is all too characteristic of an age that seems to have time only for what is relative, moving and impermanent. 'Deliberately, the world has been amputated of all that gives it permanence : nature, the sea, hills, evening meditations.' Hegel he criticizes in the same essay for having exalted the modern city as the realm of self-discovery, the terrain on which the mind can become aware of itself, and he links this with a disappearance of natural landscapes from great European literature since Dostoevsky.[39]

It is this concern that explains the recurrence in Camus' work of certain key images of the natural world, especially the sun and the sea (as in the famous passage in *La Peste* where the narrator escapes a while from the contingencies of the world of historical struggle by going to bathe in the sea; in a way he is charging his spiritual batteries). In the play, *L'État de siège*, the sea and the whole sensual world of fruits and sunshine is lyrically associated with the freedom that the town has lost by the arrival of the totalitarian plague and to which it constantly aspires. Moreover, the semi-mystical concept of 'la pensée de midi', the myth of a mediterranean culture at the end of *L'Homme révolté* is based on this same search for a permanent area of experience and identity, connected once again with the image of sunlight.

The same nostalgia for permanence is perceptible when Camus turns to the specific and related problem of work, as, notably, in his short story, *Les Muets*, from *L'Exil et le royaume*, where he evokes in some detail the craft of cask-making. Significantly enough, the story opens with the sea, which throughout is a sort of backdrop to the story itself. As the cask-makers − true and skilled craftsmen − begin work again after a protracted strike, there is a suggestion of pleasure in the work itself, despite all the bitterness of their lost cause. There is a reawakening in the familiar smell of wood-chips, the feel of the tools and so on :

> The smell of the burnt wood-chips began to fill the hangar. Yvars, planing to size the staves cut by Esposito, recognized the old scent and his heart eased a little. They all worked in silence, but a warmth, a kind of life reawakened gradually in the workshop. Through the big windows, a fresh light filled the hangar. The smoke lent a bluish tinge to the golden atmosphere. Yvars even heard an insect buzzing near him.[40]

The pleasure, though, is overshadowed by a pervasive sadness at the sense that the artisan way of life and work is doomed by forces of change : great industrially-produced tanks are taking over from casks, and there is nothing that anyone can do about it. All the skill will inevitably go to waste. There is a further sense of loss, too, in the sense Yvars has of approaching old age; for he is already past his prime, and his attitude towards his work can turn to one of bitterness : 'Where muscular effort is required, work can finally become a curse, it precedes death . . . His son wanted to be a teacher, and he was right; those who made speeches about manual work didn't know what they were talking about.'[41] By dramatizing his character's mind in this way, Camus manages to give us a subtle evocation of a man's relationship with his work in difficult circumstances. Sometimes the pain prevails, but we remember the work and Camus' knowledge of it.

Like Péguy, Camus tried his hand at printing and took pride in it, especially under the special exigence of clandestinity imposed by the occupation; and he was always anxious to stress his own closeness to the working class where his own origins lay. In a well-known speech at the *Bourse du Travail* at Saint-Étienne, Camus declared that the authentic source of revolt — the source from which, he claims, revolution has become dangerously estranged — is work; and the true ally of the committed intellectual is the worker himself.

In the same way, the confusion of bourgeois intellectuals stems from the fact that the double mystification, i.e. the bourgeois and the pseudo-revolutionary, has separated them from their only source of authenticity, the work and the suffering of all, has cut them off from their only natural allies, the workers.[42]

In one of the essays of *L'Été*, Camus lyrically unites his preoccupations in the call for a new Prometheus : 'Yes, all we need is an evening in Provence, a perfect hill, the smell of salt, to see that everything is still to be done. We have to reinvent fire, to reinstall crafts if the body's hunger is to be appeased.'[43] The permanent beauty of Provence and the special satisfaction of work rooted in such a milieu is the theme to which Jean Giono's writings are devoted. The humblest, rural craftsmen are his heroes — shepherds, potters, conscientious agricultural workers or the men who look after springs and fountains. All of them are shown to have a deep and stable culture, and a profound respect for the natural world that gives them equilibrium and health. Even men of the cities can respond to the simple words of nature, and can sense that the work they do is unnatural —

The world! we weren't created for the office, for the factory, for the underground, for the bus; our mission is not to make cars, planes, cannons, tractors, locomotives; our goal is not to sit in an armchair and buy all the corn in the world by sending messages along transatlantic cables. That isn't why our thumbs can face our other fingers.[44]

For Giono, time is not linear, as our false civilization has tried to convince us; it should not be thought of as a long progression towards a distant goal. Time is cyclical, and the form of our days is circular, 'that form of all static and eternal things'. Hence the title *Rondeur des jours* given to one of his typical collections of essays and stories. He shares Camus' distrust of living for the future, and celebrates the present with

a primitivism that at its worst is sentimental, at its best movingly
sensual.

In novels such as *Regain* and *Un de Baumugnes* Giono shows how
deeply attached men may become to the earth they work, and how that
attachment can spontaneously feed their humanity and their psychological balance. And yet careful work can have a similar value in a very
different milieu, as far removed from Giono's Haute-Provence as could
be : in that most unnatural and alienated environment of prison- and
labour-camps created by Alexander Solzhenitsyn. In that grim
'concentrationary universe' to which the Russian writer testifies, work
— careful, painstaking work or elemental, physical effort — stands out
as a value that even the most deprived can cling on to. It is one stable
thing amidst so much dehumanizing flux and uncertainty, and an
essential repository of that uniquely human spirit of perserverance that
is quietly exalted in the pages of *The First Circle.* Solzhenitsyn creates
figures such as the prisoner, Popatov, who lavishes a world of care on a
plastic cigarette-case he has made with his own hands and who, we are
told, had weathered three grim years in a German POW camp 'thanks
to his extraordinary skill in making attractive lighters, cigarette-cases
and holders out of rubbish, and without tools of any sort.'[45] Any kind
of meticulous work can become a source of value and inner balance —
even darning : as one inmate insists, 'Darning, to be any good, must be
done conscientiously. God save us from a formalistic approach. Don't
hurry it, do it carefully stitch by stitch and go over it twice.'[46] When
the well-to-do diplomat, Volodin, is arrested at the end of the novel,
and subjected to humiliations he had never even dreamt of before, he
finds a kind of peace in an occupation he has certainly never had to try
in the past — sewing buttons on his tunic. His unhurried absorption in
the task is enough to take away his fear and desperation for a while.
Even one of the prison warders reverts in the evening to the craft he
once learned, tailoring, and which has now become his secret hobby
and the one significant centre of a life that is professionally absurd.
'After his duty in the prison corridor with its crazy, feverish atmosphere,
he was calmed by the rustling cloth, the soft pliant folds and the
innocuousness of the work.'[47] Physical effort has its part to play, too.
A life of physical labour is shown to have contributed not a little to the
fundamental good sense of the prison handy-man, with his natural
craftsman's ability to do things with his hands; and one of the central
figures of the same novel, the prisoner, Nerzhin, seeks to emulate him
in this by volunteering with a fellow-inmate to saw wood for the kitchen.

They stand to gain nothing from this apart from the innate value in the act of work itself, to which they devote 'that especial zeal and enjoyment that go with a job unforced by compulsion or need.' The steady rhythm of the sawing, as they become better and better at it, calms their thoughts and brings them a kind of peace.[48]

In an open 'Letter to the Soviet Leaders' published in March 1974, Solzhenitsyn has explicitly stated his adherence to a certain ideal of permanence and stability. He, too, castigates 'the murky whirlwind of progressive ideology' which swept in on Russia from the industrialized west, and which 'has tormented and ravaged our soul quite enough.' Given that modern urban life is 'utterly unnatural', the only hope lies in a cultivation of small-scale technology, eliminating the destructive cult of economic growth, and leading to a stable economy on a human scale. The result of this will inevitably be 'an increase, not a reduction, in manual labour.'[49]

Many writers have brought their own type of moral fervour and intransigence to the quest for a culture and an ethic that would blend work, happiness, fulfilment and a sense of permanence. The quest is still with us, of course, and never perhaps has the problem been so widely recognized in all its ramifications, including the whole question of how long we dare go on destroying what is left of the natural environment − and the work-patterns and rhythms that were part of it − and still remain fully human. The most explicit latter-day expression of this in literature has, I suppose, been the work of Arnold Wesker. Wesker, in fact, helps prove the validity of talking of an ethic-of-work tradition at all by resuming the characteristics and themes we have so far seen to be typical of it.

Central to his work, as in the case of Simone Weil, is the exposition of the evils of *déracinement* and the plea for the necessity of roots. Hence, of course, the title of one of his best-known plays, *Roots*. This itself is part of the indictment of an unnatural and stifling world, an indictment vehemently expressed by one of his characters, Ada, in the first part of his Trilogy, *Chicken Soup with Barley*; reacting against the decay of socialist ideals, against inter-left squabbles, Party tags and the 'clap-trap' of threepenny pamphlets that destroy all vestiges of real communal feeling, she cries out :

> The only rotten society is an industrial society. It makes a man stand on his head and then convinces him he is good-looking. I'll tell you something. It wasn't the Trotskyists or the Social Democrats who

did the damage. It was progress! There! Progress! And nobody dared fight progress.

She turns on Harry, her ineffectual, communist father, to declare that he and his ideals have failed because of communism's fatal acceptance of the progress-idea, its wish not to abolish the industrial world but to win and exploit it.

> No, you did not want to do away with the jungle, I suppose. You have *never* cried against the jungle of an industrial society. You've never wanted to destroy its *values* – simply to own them yourselves. It only seemed a crime to you that a man spent all his working hours in front of a machine because he did not own that machine. Heavens! the glory of owning a machine! [50]

Much of the dullness of life comes from a loss of contact, in politics and in life generally, with work and its specific nature and demands. The result is a society that Wesker, drawing on his own work-experience, presents in microcosm in his play *The Kitchen.* The busy restaurant kitchen is, as Kenneth Tynan remarks, 'a metaphor for the dehumanizing world of commercialism and mass-production. *The Kitchen* achieves something that few playwrights have ever attempted : it dramatizes work.' Not rewarding work, however; the men are forced to seek what little satisfaction they can *outside* their work, whether in building a portable radio or dreaming of working in a place where they will be able to create masterpieces – moussaka instead of the eternal chips. The fragile, human relationships in this place of work prove no match for the false and unnatural rhythms imposed by the peak period rush : bickering and dehumanization are the inevitable result. This is not work capable of creating what Saint-Exupéry once called 'un noeud de relations'. On the contrary, the most horrible thing about it is the realization of just how superficial is the men's involvement with it as living, human beings : as one of the main characters, Peter, explains eloquently enough in his broken English :

> It'll go on when we die, think about that. We work here eight hours a day, and yet – it's nothing. We take nothing. Here – the kitchen, here – you. You and the kitchen. And the kitchen don't mean nothing to you and you don't mean to the kitchen nothing. [51]

When Peter finally revolts out of sheer frustration, the boss Marango simply cannot understand : after all, he pays them, doesn't he? 'I give work, I pay well, yes? . . . He works, he eats, I give him money. This is life, isn't it?'[52] What is there more? he ends up crying in incomprehension. What there is more — and what he has never been able to provide — is of course real, rewarding work.

The attempt to find such work, and with it to find roots and permanence, is embodied in the story of Dave and Ida in the Trilogy. In the final part, *I'm Talking About Jerusalem*, Wesker shows their efforts to opt out of the jungle of industrial society, as they move to a remote corner of Norfolk, in the midst of fields. They have indeed, as one cynical observer remarks, 'gone back to William Morris'; and they protest vigorously against the accusation that they have deserted socialism in favour of the ivory tower, replying that they simply want to *live* their socialism, and not just talk and conceptualize about it. Clearly socialism is for them, as it was for Péguy, a philosophy of the 'restoration of work'.

A decisive experience for Dave has been the revelation he experienced in Ceylon, outside the industrial scene altogether. It is a capital revelation, and we must quote it in full :

Being a carpenter I used to watch the local carpenters at work. They used to make their own tools and sometimes they'd show me. They'd sit out on the beach fashioning the boats or outside their houses planing and chiselling away at their timber, and they let me sit with them once they knew I was also building boats. And you know, one day, as I watched, I made a discovery — the sort of discovery you discover two or three times in a life-time. I discovered an old truth : that a man is made to work and that when he works he's giving away something of himself, something very precious.[53]

What Dave describes here is the rediscovery of what Friedmann calls the *milieu naturel*, with the vision of the Sinhalese artisans working in the strikingly natural setting of the beach or within the domestic framework. Far from having a complex and impersonal machinery of production interposed between them and what they produce, they, in fact, make for themselves, and, therefore, 'humanize', the tools of their craft.

Thus inspired, Dave is making furniture by hand, in a barn just at the back of the house; and what Wesker is particularly good at, expressing the sheer pleasure of making things, can be fully indulged here. It is a pleasure we find throughout his work, whether it be in the real home-baked loaf in *Roots*, or the apple strudel in his later, non-

naturalistic play, *The Four Seasons* (1966). In the summer section of
this work, Adam makes an apple strudel for his Beatrice; and whereas
she, with uncomprehending condescension, sees in this elaborate process
only his delight in 'small things', he regards the whole operation as a
'miracle'. The stage-directions at this point are extremely, lovingly
detailed, and Wesker adds a long note for the actor, which begins : 'The
process of making apple strudel is a very dramatic one.'[54] So why should
actors not learn to cook as they learn to fence? Ought they not to learn
the gestures of work as well as those of play? And Wesker makes as
precise as possible the 'beautiful' gestures required for this particular
work. It is such love of the acts of labour that is so infectious and
sympathetic in the writings of this playwright, and nowhere more so
than in Dave's enthusiasm over the hand-made chair in *Jerusalem*, a
chair that really 'looks as though it's sitting down' — a sure sign of true
craftsmanship, a sign that it genuinely *works* as a chair. We can understand after this Dave's disappointment when his young apprentice tells
him that he wants to leave in order to go into industry for the 'easy'
money, whether it means reducing his work to mere machine-minding
or no. Desperately, Dave tries to dissuade him by dwelling on the
human value of that vital making of things, with its sense of responsibility
and freedom :

> Sammy, remember that chair? Remember what you said about it? It
> looks as though it's sitting down, you said. That's poetry, boy, poetry!
> No, not poetry, what am I talking about. Er — it's — it's — O Jesus
> how do you start explaining this thing. Look, Sammy, look at this
> rack you made for your chisels. Not an ordinary rack, not just bits
> of wood nailed together, but a special one with dove-tail joints here
> and a mortise and tenon joint there, and look what you put on the
> side, remember you wanted to decorate it, so you used my carving
> tools and you worked out a design. For no reason at all you worked
> out a design on an ordinary chisel rack. But there was a reason really,
> wasn't there?[55]

The desperation, as we might expect, eventually spills over into his own
life, for the sheer force of economics makes him, too, compromise,
leaving his Norfolk retreat for a more modern workshop in London.
People are just unable or unwilling to pay for careful handiwork. Dave
knows he is the odd man out in a world committed to industrialism,
and a sense of defeat hangs heavily over the end of the play.

What, it would seem, but pessimism could be the end result of such a late flowering of the tradition we have followed through from the beginning of the nineteenth century? Perhaps we are too grown up for utopias — and the technical environment presses too hard upon us. But we are undoubtedly sadder for our wisdom.

5 The technical environment

Whilst we can establish the common elements in all the diverse writers who partake of the quest for an alternative culture based on the morality of work, whilst we can define a movement of sorts, or at least a tradition in the succession of their writings, they none the less appear still, taken individually, as lonely voices crying in the wilderness of an alien, industrial society. They are often well aware, like Wesker's hero in *I'm Talking About Jerusalem*, that they *are* odd men out, swimming against the tide of history. Their almost total unanimity in rejecting the reality or validity of 'progress' as the nineteenth century understood it, in calling for some kind of 'simplification of life' is really an expression of a certain sense of helplessness and anguish.

It is true that even among those who attribute a high degree of ethical value to work there are those who, whilst standing in many respects as the conscience of their respective ages, yet remain very much *of* their age. Such is the case of both Carlyle and Zola, who both welcome the potential of machines if not their contemporary application and the ugliness it has produced. Carlyle does so because he subscribes fundamentally to a highly successful, bourgeois-calvinist world-view even though he protests, as we have seen, against features of the age from within that world-view; Zola, because of a dogged faith in science, presupposing an acceptance of technical progress and an optimism that largely releases him, too, from anguish. Such faith, acceptance and optimism are, however, far from typical of the tradition in general.

We have seen the picture Hardy presents of the intrusion of an impersonal and monstrous machine into the agricultural scene. Tolstoy, for his part, turning his back on the modern world with religious intransigence, rejected out of hand the real utility of machinery in the rural environment. And it is machines and their possible role that constitute one of the chief bones of contention in this movement of revolt.

For Ruskin, it was above all an aesthetic question and a problem of equilibrium. 'Industry without art is brutality,' he asserted, and his statement is echoed nearer our own time by Eric Gill. Gill points out the dangers of living by science alone, for its application converts the human activity of making things for human use ('the normal occupation of human beings') into a purely quantitative exercise that is abnormal and subhuman. Scientific industry has, he claims, created ten miseries and pains for every one it has alleviated; that 'constant potentiality' of labour, holiness, is in scientific industrialism 'ruled out from the life and the work.'[1] He adds, though, that the present degradation of life is the result not of machines as such but of the rise of the merchant class following on the decay of the medieval conception of life. It may be naïve to dissociate the development of the early bourgeoisie as a social force and the eventual growth of machinofacture, but certainly William Morris, too, saw the essential agent of corruption to be not the machines themselves but a civilization founded on commerce. He did not oppose machines (though on more than one occasion he affirmed that he had no great fondness for them) so much as the mechanical principle in life, the proliferation of cheapness and ugliness for profit : 'it is the allowing of machines to be our masters and not our servants that so injures the beauty of life nowadays.'[2]

The same attitude is shared by Toller, the heroine of whose play, *Man and the Masses*, expresses the hope that industrialism, despite its inauspicious beginning, may lead to a fulfilled future of some kind in the long run.

> Let factories be servants
> Of decent living
> And let the soul of man
> Conquer the factories.

Her attitude has the virtue of a certain realism — the movement of technology, whether we can legitimately call it 'progress' or not, is hardly to be undone completely or reversed :

> For see, this is the twentieth century;

The case is judged, is settled.
Machines can never be undone.[3]

The debate is given a sharper edge in *The Machine-Wreckers*, and as the title suggests is one of the main themes of that play. Unlike the negative Ned Lud, Jimmy Cobbett (Toller's mouthpiece in this work) recognizes that 'the machine is our inevitable fate.' The Luddites have picked a scapegoat, not the true enemy of their best interests, namely the employers and their economic system — 'there are other enemies, mightier than the structures of iron, bolts, cables and wood we call machines.'[4] The weavers ask for their old work back; but was it really much more than forced labour (*Frondienst*) anyway? When the rebels break into the factory to wreak vengeance on the machines, the engineer pleads that these same technical achievements may be a form of salvation, created by the mind of man and to be controlled by the mind of man. One of the rebels, however, is actually killed by a machine, whilst another goes mad and prophesies the total automation of mankind, the death of the soul, and totally mechanized war. Although Jimmy condemns them for the form their rebellion has taken, his optimism about the future role of machinery fails to dispel the dark sense of tragic foreboding that is created by the ending of the play. The grim prophecy dominates, despite Toller's attempts to integrate the machine into his vision of life. One feels rather that in the attempt he was trying to be something that did not come naturally to him — a good marxist. For all the intellectual and ideological ratification of the machine, affectively it is rejected, together with many of the 'nihilistic' tendencies of modern civilization.

The pious hope that Morris entertained was that eventually people would realize the limitations of machines, and wherever possible would go back to handicrafts out of sheer preference. Perhaps the elaboration of machinery, he hoped, would lead in time to a simplification of life, which in turn will produce a voluntary restriction of the use of machinery. We can only conclude that Morris was blinding himself to the dynamism, the self-generating quality of the technical world, and to the hold (less obvious, to be sure, in his own day than it is now) that a consumer civilization acquires over its members.

Certainly, as he says in *The Aims of Art*, he can see the utility of machines for grinding corn, etc., leaving man free to think or to 'carve the handle of his knife.'[5] It is all a question of application and degree, and he definitely admits approval of *real*, labour-saving machinery (as distinct from machinery that only 'saves' labour so that it can be used for tending other machinery). After all, there are machines and machines, and he looks forward to the day when men will turn from the production of cannons and such 'to the invention of machines for performing such labour as is revolting and destructive of self-respect to the men who now have to do it by hand.'[6] Ultimately Morris recognizes that man is a slave to the machine only because he is at present a slave to the system of large-scale production for profit. So it is that for all his avowed hatred of modern civilization he will be able to go on to envisage, in an essay of that name, *A factory as it might be*; just as Simone Weil, for all her distrust of science, is not to unrealistically propose, in her plan for *enracinement*, the complete abolition of machinery. It is a different kind of machinery she will envisage, and like Morris she presupposes a different organization of society and its productive forces.

It is true that machines are very little in evidence in *News from Nowhere* and its peaceful rural setting. Although we hear vague hints of perfected machinery performing certain essential operations, we are told less about that than about the Banded-Workshops that have replaced factories, and which are 'places where people collect who want to work together' but which are not powered or automated but given over exclusively to the collective practice of handicrafts. Whereas in the 'old world', we are told, the so-called labour-saving machinery had only the effect of producing more useless pieces of work for the world market, thereby ultimately increasing the burden of labour as well as rendering it less human, in this utopia all irksome tasks are performed by refined machinery (carefully camouflaged it would seem!) whilst anything that can be done by hand with pleasure *is* done by hand. Technology has lost its destructive dynamism because economic competition has been eliminated – this is the essence of the 'humanity regained' of *News from Nowhere*. The nature of Morris's own tastes and fancies self-indulgently dresses the liberation up in fourteenth-century clothes : the pattern of life in this England of the twenty-first century is strikingly medieval. The buildings are 'quaint and fanciful', railways have been abolished, and rowing-boat would appear to be the standard means of communication. Far from having given in to a dynamic technology, the countryside has reasserted its rights – a process of decentralization has led the population from the cities back to the villages which, with the familiar reference, 'were more populous than they had been since the fourteenth century.'[7] *News* is a dream, of course, and not a literal blueprint for the future; Morris himself knew all too well that 'the stream of civilization is against us, and we cannot battle against it.'[8] In that dream, however, he does express what for him was an ideal — a natural, rural and highly individualized society on which industrialism never impinges, where technology, if there is any, is carefully hidden away while it does its work. We may well see in this 'hidden technology' a certain form of romantic dishonesty, an attempt to take the advantages of technology without accepting the cultural transformations that go hand in hand with it. Less unkindly, we could call it an unresolved contradiction in Morris' vision of the world.

If by way of contrast we turn to Zola, we find that, far from being discreetly camouflaged, the machines are proudly exhibited in all their splendour : after all, is it not through the advanced technological innovations introduced by the inventor, Jordan, that the City spreads and flourishes? Industrialism is by no means condemned in itself; indeed, Zola's faith in progress prompts him to assert that 'tomorrow iron would finally become the source of justice and peace, once science had definitively conquered it.'[9] Science, Luc believes, is the greatest of revolutionaries. Due homage is rendered to the machine through certain curious incidents in the book, such as the wedding celebration that takes place within the foundry itself amidst the resplendent machines, garlanded with flowers and standing clean and powerful, 'd'une beauté souveraine', as the festive party dances around them. The colossal presses and mighty power-hammers seem to look on benevolently from under their décor of branches and flowers . . .[10]

As another curious and rather unfortunate note, Zola comments that the bread in the harmonious city of *Travail* is so good that one can tell at once that it is kneaded and baked by careful machines. It is an example of the writer's faith in technology that must, to the modern consumer of packaged horrors, seem incredibly over-optimistic![11] More seriously, Zola runs himself into contradictions — very different in nature from those of Morris but at least as grave — with regard to his ethic of work on the one hand and his persistent faith in science and progress on the other. For as the novel and its utopia develop, we find that manual work is increasingly taken over by a proliferation of ingenious mechanisms in home and factory alike. At the centre of these modifications stand the new, electric furnaces which replace the old, awkward and temperamental ones. Three children, we are told, can work them — each sitting with his finger on a button to control one of the essential operations of the plant. Suddenly we find ourselves (thankfully, perhaps) out of the arduous hell of the old means of production, but apparently in the new, polished and flameless hell of push-button and fragmented labour. Machines now do almost all the work, we are told, they are become the friend and ally of man, his 'liberator, toiling for man while he rested.'[12] Does this not run counter to the ethic of work elaborated, as we have seen, in this same novel? Does it not negate the author's ethic of creativity and initiative? Certainly Zola does seem to sense this dilemma, and his unconvincing response to the problem resides firstly in the strict limitation of the hours spent on automatic and almost totally mechanized labour, and secondly in the break-up of the factory system for operations other than the initial production of basic materials such as iron. It is in this way that Zola can postulate a return to the responsibility of the home-based artisan, though this development itself is a result of technological progress, each house being equipped with new, electric tools. The superficial attractiveness of this solution does not hide its vagueness; the contradiction is far from resolved.

One way of avoiding such contradictions would, of course, be to drop the ethic of pleasurable work and all its cultural connotations and to greet every aspect of technological civilization with open arms. Few indeed are the writers who are prepared to do this, and it is precisely the refusal of those we are mainly dealing with that constitutes the greatest unity of their disparate writings. Perhaps it is Morris, once again, who best sums up the general attitude : machinery, he says in *The Revival of Handicrafts*, may be indispensable as an instrument for forcing better material conditions of life on us – but as a condition of life in itself it is 'altogether an evil'. 'To me', he wrote, 'it is inconceivable that machine-production will develop into mere infinity of machinery, or life wholly lapse into a disregard of life as it passes.'[13] One writer, however, did face up to the possibility – for him a certainty – of a 'mere infinity of machinery' and the concomitant loss of life as we have known it. This was the German writer, Ernst Jünger, whose vision of present and future projected in the notorious *The Worker* (*Der Arbeiter*) of 1932 provides a startling illustration of what the more gentle souls with whom we have so far been concerned reject – that total automation of humanity glimpsed with terror in *The Machine-Wreckers*. Jünger shows us the culture of industrial society carried to its logical conclusion, and his prophecy, therefore, has great value whatever we may think of his own explicit evaluation of that culture.

In one undoubtedly powerful but thoroughly unpleasant passage of his long essay, Jünger mocks at the 'snivelling artists' who play Don

Quixote against the modern world, who try to lead the spirit away from that 'hard and pure realm' in which the great decisions are to be carried out; and vengefully he prophesies — with horrible foresight — the persecution of such sentimental *Artistentum* by the new youth of Germany.[14] His own attitude, the acceptance and affirmation of the technical milieu in its most absolute form, he characterized as 'heroic realism'. Through this 'realism' Jünger is to face up to and ultimately welcome all the elements of the ideology of technological progress that Herbert Marcuse has since condemned :

> However, intensified progress seems to be bound up with intensified unfreedom. Throughout the world of industrial civilization, the domination of man by man is growing in scope and efficiency. Nor does this trend appear as an incidental, transitory regression on the road to progress. Concentration camps, mass exterminations, world wars, and atom bombs are no 'relapse into barbarism' but the unrepressed implementation of the achievements of modern science, technology and domination.[15]

In *The Worker*, imbued as the essay is with the desire for a strong hierarchic State based on obedience, Jünger shows just how much at one his thought was — in this period anyway — with a certain Nazi ideology, an ideology to which he was one of the most intellectually prestigious contributors. Jünger's own particular response to the questions posed by the development of industrial society had begun long before : when as a youth he fled from a comfortable home in bourgeois society to join the foreign legion, and then, more emphatically, after his engagement in the first world war, an experience that remains central to his work in the decades that follow. What he sensed was the bankruptcy of bourgeois society and civilization, and his reaction has a truly Nietzschean vehemence and scorn about it. 'Bourgeois' is, however, not primarily an economic or sociological category for Jünger, but a moral and psychological one. The bourgeois, regarded as the outgrowth of the Enlightenment, is defined as the man who 'acknowledges security as the highest value and determines his way of life in the light of this realization.'[16] He is by nature opposed to adventure and the irrational, wishing only to convince himself and the whole world that there exists nothing dangerous at all, and that an economic law safely rules the world and its history. The result is a world where the exceptional man (that figure so distrusted by William Morris) is stranded like Baudelaire's albatross, and where the highest embodiment of energy, the warrior, is out of place 'because the life of grocers fills him with repulsion.'[17] This aristocratic scorn and cult of energy give the tone for Jünger's hatred of the bourgeois order, and his portrayal of it is permeated with a sense of decay, as he evokes 'the face of late democracy, on which betrayal and impotence have left their marks', and 'the atmosphere of the swamp that can only be purified by explosions'.[18] If these statements seem to have an anarchist ring to them, it becomes immediately obvious in the further stages of Jünger's argument that he stands at the opposite pole to every genuine anarchist ideal.

'Whole cities are overshadowed by a mood of putrefaction,' he claims; such is the fate of a civilization that converts everything to the abstract and enervated level of ideas and concepts, and flounders between the poles of sentimentality and self-satisfied 'reason'. Europe is still covered to this day, Jünger claims in 1932, with the pale wash of bourgeois ideology, an ideology that owes its success to date to its ability to fuse all opposites and energetic conflicts into a pacific whole based on compromise. Its days are numbered, however, as the Great War has taught us, and this is the colossal importance of that holocaust : it has shown up the bourgeois-enlightenment fraud as the hollow sham it is, and not least it has exploded the myth of humanistic progress. Not only because it was a war — there had been many before and the bourgeois world-view had assimilated *them* — but because of the new kind of war it was, one that heralded a new kind of society and a new culture.

Up to this point, Jünger has expressed much of the critique of a 'decadent' society that we have seen to recur in ethic-of-work writers. It is when we move on to the grim 'positive' aspect of his attitude that he appears as a striking and instructive contrast. He places no hope in socialism, of course, claiming to regard capitalism and socialism as twin branches of the same outdated enlightenment-individualistic tree. Instead he looks to what he calls the 'elemental' which is associated first and foremost with that realm of danger the bourgeois fears. 'Reason' is merely a rampart against naked, creature life, based on energy, and the exploitation of this defence is what distinguishes the bourgeois radically from such elemental figures as the artist, the sailor, the hunter, the criminal, the warrior — and the 'Worker'! The revelatory nature of the War lay for Jünger in its brutal reassertion of the elemental (expressed in his early work *In Storms of Steel* (*In Stahlgewittern*)). Those lessons of war are not to be unlearned. The value he read into the figure of the front-line soldier is to be continued in the figure of the Worker, and it is not accidental that the comparison between Warrior and Worker recurs throughout the later essay. 'It is only from the consciousness of a warlike attitude that it is possible to accord to the things around us their true value,' he comments in his usual frighteningly abstract style.[19] The world of the Worker is set against the 'dusty old rights and insipid pleasures' of the past, against sordid vote-catching and the retailers of freedom who can see totalities only in terms of the sum of constituent parts, can only see numbers rather than the spirit (an attack on democracy, of course) : suddenly they are disturbed by a vague intimation of a new greatness, a new concept of life that is that of the Worker and his universe.

Before going any further we must define what Jünger means by the 'Worker'. Just as he declines to use the term 'bourgeois' in a strict sociological sense, so, too, he presents the Worker not as a member of a separate and defined class or social group, but as the symbolic type (*Gestalt*) of a new man and a new society. To underline this special usage I have given the word a capital letter throughout this discussion. The Worker is both the representative of the naked elemental force that Jünger had revelled in back in 1914 and also the embodiment of the new, modern dominance of technology. Here we see the profound difference between Jünger and, say, Lawrence : whereas for the latter technology and the elemental were opposed forces, leading to a revolt against the one in favour of the other, for Jünger they are one and the same, technology is the modern form of the elemental. The Worker and his civilization are the logical culmination of what the move into a truly technical environment is irresistibly leading us towards. And although Jünger claims neutrality and objectivity in his portrayal of this process, declaring that his aim is to see and describe lucidly and not to pass value judgements, it is immediately obvious that *The Worker* stands as an affirmation of the process, a conscious acquiescence. We have comments such as this : 'There is no way out, no sideways or backwards; the main issue is to heighten the growth and speed of the processes in which we are involved.'[20] This is the lucid acceptance that Jünger calls his 'heroic realism'. Certainly he does not flinch from any aspect of technological civilization; what he accepts and even welcomes, though, can only appear highly disturbing and repugnant to most of us.

Again we must return to the War as a turning-point. For 1914–18, releasing the 'elemental', also for the first time channelled that force through such highly technical tools and organization; and as such its

creation was not just an old army with new weapons but the beginnings
of a radically new type of man. The highly technical army is 'the warlike expression in which the symbolic figure of the Worker appears.'[21]
In concrete terms, the clatter of Manchester's weaving-looms and the
rattle of Langemarck's machine-guns are, according to Jünger, both of
them the signs and ciphers of a new language we must not shrink from,
but master! We can best see the concordance between the new techniques
and the new type of mankind if we consider the changes in the figure
and psychology of the soldier. The old artillery man was an artisan still,
but during the course of the War this type becomes impossible, unthinkable. The battle-field acquires a *total* character, ruled by scientific
calculation, created by steel, gas and other modern means. Taking yet
another military image, Jünger describes technical progress as the
'mobilization' of the world, heading towards the ultimate state of
'total mobilization'. Here all the qualities of highly organized precision
war will become the characteristics of life itself, which will be measured
and controlled with unheard-of exactness thanks to advanced clocks
and measuring apparatus. There is small hope, according to Jünger, for
the natural rhythms and human time that more nostalgic writers wish
to salvage! A static and highly ordered universe is to replace the
anarchic, individualistic one of the past, a universe of 'closed totality',
with no divergent elements, no individual manifestations of any kind.

In this world, everything will be work — 'a peculiar identity of work
and being' is what he envisages.

> Work, therefore, is not just activity. It is the expression of a certain
> mode of being that seeks to fulfil its realm, its time, its regularity.
> That is why it knows no opposite outside itself; it is like fire,
> devouring everything that burns . . . The realm of work is unlimited,
> just as the working day spans the whole twenty-four hours.[22]

There will simply be no condition that is not part of the work-totality.
Is this tendency not already under way, Jünger asks, particularly in the
so-called leisure pursuits of the present? Sport, for example, has
obvious work-character, and all other pleasures are merely counter-
weights *within* the context of work, and not at all the opposite of work.
'Work is the tempo of the fist, of thought, of the heart, of life by day
and night, science, love, art, faith, cult, war; work is the vibration of
the atom and the force that moves stars and suns.'[23] A pure work-world
awaits us — and all we must do, it seems, is to abandon our individuality
and prepare the new language of work (nothing to do with the old

artisan concept, of course — William Morris will be of no help; anyway his books will have been burned at an early stage!), a language that will be applicable to all things. It is in Jünger's acquiescent vision of the disappearance of the individual in all its forms that his thesis, whatever 'realism' it may involve, appears at its most antipathetic.

New social structures are emerging in which masses are no longer seen as collections of individuals, but in terms of 'streams and chains of faces flashing hurriedly by, or in ant-like columns whose advance is no longer ruled by whim, but by an automatic discipline.' [24] Modern war, once again, offers a parallel in the appearance of the anonymous phenomenon of the 'unknown soldier' who recurs throughout Jünger's essay. He draws a psychological contrast between, on the one hand, the soldiers at the beginning of the War, going gloriously over the top with the enthusiasm of their individual sacrifice but being mown down by technical means; and, on the other, a new type called into being by the very fact that 'the feelings of the heart and the systems of the mind are refutable, whereas an object is irrefutable — and such an object is the machine-gun.' [25] The new type already began to appear during the War, displaying as one of its chief characteristics 'an extreme, cool-headed and, as it were, mechanical coldness, thanks to which the heroic consciousness has learned to treat the body as a mere instrument, and to force from it, even beyond the limits of the instinct of self-preservation a whole series of complicated achievements.' [26] So, too, this transform-ation has been reflected in physical, facial changes : man's expression has lost in individuality and variety, the face has become more metallic, as if galvanized on the surface, the bone-structure is more apparent, the traits are tense and sparse. Such is the face of a new man in a new land-scape. The type replaces the 'humanistic' individual, and is directed more and more exclusively by the sole principle of *efficiency*.

Such is the process that is now extending to the whole of society, and it may be seen with particular clarity in industrial work, which is at the heart of the whole transformation. We may perceive it in the growing uniformity in jobs which, Jünger claims, already exists even under the guise of modern work-specialization : a total and uniform work-character invades all spheres. Would a complete stranger to our civilization distinguish easily between work in a modern, well-equipped photographic studio and work in an equally modern and well-equipped clinic for internal disorders? Would he distinguish between a battle-field and an industrial estate? Showing quite clearly that he accepts all the depersonalization of modern industry, Jünger goes on to assert that the very concept of personal achievement in work is undergoing a striking change, whereby the centre of gravity of man's activity is shifting from the individual work-character (exemplified in the artisan structure) to the total work-character. It is because of this change that all attempts to strengthen the individual work-consciousness within the modern factory have been doomed to failure. History and technology are against them. We must simply realize that the necessity of a stereotyped activity (regularly pressing a lever etc.) can never be justified in terms of the joy or satisfaction of the individual. Jünger's conclusion is not that such organization of work is therefore dangerous or downright bad, but that the individual and his sentimental, artisanal values are utterly out-of-date![27]

Frightening indeed is the picture Jünger paints for us of a phenomenon he traces throughout the whole of society and its activities, leading us inexorably towards a new life-style under the sign of complete efficiency. Just as the military have adopted a uniform that is purely functional and no longer decorative, so we are heading for a general 'work-uniform' for all, one that will stress, of course, the type rather than individuality. The dominant reproductive art of our culture is no longer painting, which stressed that same individuality, but – again thanks to technical advances – photography, which brings out uniformity in portraits and once more emphasizes the type. So, too, the cinema, particularly with its mechanical repetition of identical performances, is taking over from the theatre, and provides a new kind of 'star' of a much more stereotyped nature. Moreover, does not man appear in films as a toy of technical objects, constantly assailed by cars, locomotives and mechanisms generally? Together with the evolution of the human physiognomy towards what is described as a 'metallic' uniformity for men, a 'cosmetic' uniformity for women, goes the significantly increasing role of *masks* in our society and its work; gas-masks distributed to whole nations, masks for high altitudes, protective masks for work where there is danger from rays, explosions or poisoning. This is a sign-post for the days to come : Jünger sees a great future for masks.

'The end justifies the means' – such might be Jünger's motto, and given his avowed desire for a strong, totalitarian State, the rest follows logically : the total, technical milieu, the decline of individualism, the ideal of complete obedience, of optimum, automatic productivity, the reduction of people to types and forces, the constitution of 'a race of the highest uniformity', and the vision of total mobilization. The latter is defined in these terms :

The object of total mobilization is the transformation of life into energy, as manifested, as far as the economy, the technical sphere and communications are concerned, in the hum of spinning wheels [im Schwirren der Räder], and where the battlefield is concerned, in fire and movement.[28]

This vision of total mobilization — and indeed so much of the spirit that infuses Jünger's essay — had already been expressed in both theoretical and artistic form earlier in the century by the Futurist movement, which grew up in Italy under the leadership of Marinetti. Futurism, too, welcomed the machine-age with open arms, and equated it with the elemental, with what Marinetti called in the Manifesto of 1909 'the enthusiastic fervour of the primordial elements'.[29] Famous enough is his statement from that same provocative document that a racing-car is more beautiful than the *Victory of Samothrace*. There have been enough human figures in art, and, above all, enough nudes : the beauty of speed is the new beauty, and with it goes an exaltation of mechanical efficiency, of industrialism. Straight lines in art are to be preferred to curves. The spirit of the movement and its artistic productions is vividly summarized in this first Manifesto :

We will sing of great crowds excited by work, by pleasure and by riot; we will sing of the multicoloured, polyphonic tides of revolution in the modern capitals; we will sing of the vibrant nightly fervour of arsenals and shipyards blazing with violent electric moons; greedy railway stations that devour smoke-plumed serpents; factories hung on clouds by the crooked lines of their smoke; bridges that stride the rivers like giant gymnasts, flashing in the sun with a glitter of knives; adventurous steamers that sniff the horizon; deep-chested locomotives whose wheels paw the track like the hooves of enormous steel horses bridled by tubing; and the sleek flight of planes whose propellers chatter in the wind like banners and seem to cheer like an enthusiastic crowd.[30]

Music, too, Luigi Russolo insists in a later document, is to be in tune with the mechanical bustle of city life, with 'the palpitation of valves, the coming and going of pistons, the howl of mechanical saws, the jolting of a tram on its rails'.[31]

Futurism, then, is 'grounded in the complete renewal of human sensibility brought about by the great discoveries of science.' Violence, cruelty and injustice are all to be accepted as part of this new sensibility.

War is glorified as an expression of the modern spirit, it is 'the world's only hygiene' and stands as the supreme example of that fusion of technology and instinct that Jünger will exalt in such a disturbingly inhuman way. Marinetti speaks in 1913 of 'a fusion of instinct with the efficiency of motors and conquered forces.'[32] As in the case of Jünger, the cult of energy, of technology, of conquest and heroism, of militaristic patriotism, feeds into a most inhuman and bellicose fascism.

All that the Futurists acknowledge and accept is, of course, the very opposite of the desire for a non-ascetic morality of work as we have understood it; it negates, too, all the allied, cultural preoccupations implied by that desire, and not least the concern for a 'natural environment'. The world of Jünger and the Futurists is a world without roots, and nothing typifies this better than Antonio Sant'Elia's *Manifesto of Futurist Architecture* of 1914, where all 'traditionalist cowardice' is scorned, all fixity, all attachment to the past. After all, movement is the essence of the new life and the new aesthetic, and 'the fundamental characteristics of Futurist architecture will be its impermanence and transience. Things will endure less than us. Every generation must build its own city.'[33] Men are become artificial, what they need is an artificial environment. So, too, in his vision of total, gleaming, mechanical efficiency, Jünger envisages the disappearance of the natural milieu, the abolition of all distinction between town and country – to the detriment of the latter. By his negation, Jünger makes obvious the importance and relevance of environmentalism to the ethic-of-work tradition. He himself can have no time for that ethic : he says quite definitely, and without a trace of anguish, that part of the process of transformation he foresees is a radical change in the meaning of the word 'work', whereby it will no longer be a moral concept at all. And if it were possible to evolve a morality of work it would not be in the usual sense but directly opposed to it : concepts drawn from work, and particularly efficiency, would be applied to morality, not moral concepts to the idea and reality of work.

Twelve years before the appearance of *Der Arbeiter*, Georg Kaiser had expressed his horror at the advent of just such a world of 'total mobilization' and had painted, with anything but acceptance, the completely technical environment. With specific reference to war, Kaiser wrote a story, *Leutnant Welzeck*, which portrays a vision and a mentality closely akin to that urged by Jünger – except that the machine-dominated landscape of total war is clearly rejected as abhorrent. Above all, however, it is in *Gas* that he exposes the horrors of a world in which efficiency does govern morality. What has happened by the beginning of the play is that, due to the incentive of a profit-sharing scheme, a Jüngerian situation has been reached, a vast factory in which everything is geared to maximum productivity. This is suggested by a conversation between the Scribe and the visiting White Gentleman (who is a harbinger of coming disaster) in Kaiser's usual telegram-style :

> *Scribe* : Coal and water-power are redundant. The new energy moves millions of new machines with mighty impulse. We create it. Our gas feeds the technical progress of the world!
>
> *White Gentleman* (at the window) : Day and night — fire and smoke?
>
> *Scribe* : The extreme possibility of our productivity is attained!
>
> *White Gentleman* : Because poverty is abolished?
>
> *Scribe* : Our mighty effort creates!
>
> *White Gentleman* : Because the profits are shared out?
>
> *Scribe* : Gas!
>
> *White Gentleman* : And what if the gas should one day . . .
>
> *Scribe* : The work cannot pause for an hour. We are working for ourselves, no longer for another's pocket. No slacking and no strikes. Uninterrupted the work drives on.[34]

When in the course of the play the Engineer talks the rebellious workers into rejecting their newly-discovered aspiration to a truly human life, his arguments have a Futurist ring — a more emotive anticipation of Jünger's colder reasoning : 'Your achievement creates the miracle in steel. Power drives on machines, which you work. — Gas!! — — Your energy hastens on the railways, thundering your triumph over bridges that you rivet fast! . . . You are conquerors — of all-powerful achievement in your work — You create gas! Such is your mastery (*Herrschaft*), founded on shift after shift.'[35] We might note that the full title of Jünger's essay is to be *Der Arbeiter. Herrschaft und Gestalt*. The theme of domination was likewise prominent in the Futurist Manifestos.

After the workers agree to renounce their humanity, the second part of the play (*Gas II*) takes the vision of 'total mobilization' even further; and once again in anticipation of Jünger's thesis that this is allied with the situation of total war. The Blue Figures, at war with the Yellow Figures, are seen (in uniform, of course) sitting stiffly at desks where lights flash on and off to indicate the level of productivity and the state of the war — the two elements have now become inseparable. Language is now completely functional and factual : something like the new

language, presumably, that Jünger is to look forward to. A crisis in the
permanent war situation leads to orders from the Blue Figures demanding
optimum, mechanical efficiency from the workers : 'Increase in productivity of gas without regard for man, woman, or child. No more shifts —
shift merges into shift without release . . .'[36] When eventually the
Yellow enemies take over after a second attempt to liberate the workers
(foiled once again by the technology-mad Engineer) we find that but
for their colour they are identical to their predecessors. They sit down
at the control desks with the same rigid posture, they carry out the
same stereotyped gestures, utter the same functional phrases. The war
continues. The logical conclusion of science and technology, if left to
their own inhuman dynamism, is the negation of human fulfilment :
such is Kaiser's thesis, and unlike Jünger he is filled with horror at the
prospect.

The kind of fulfilment that Kaiser envisaged could lie only in the
diversity of human occupations and responses, and this is precisely what
Jünger, from the standpoint of efficiency, says is on the way out. His is
the ideological justification of the production-line and all its evils. It is
a Jüngerian conception of the world that Lawrence is criticizing in the
figure of Gerald Crich in *Women in Love* — Gerald for whom total
mobilization is the apotheosis of the will to power : 'the very expression
of his will, the incarnation of his power, a great and perfect machine, a
system, an activity of pure order, pure mechanical repetition, repetition
ad infinitum.' Ultimately he would like to extend over the whole earth
a technically perfect and mechanical system : 'It would need a marvellous adjustment of myriad instruments, human, animal, metallic,
kynetic, dynamic, a marvellous casting of myriad tiny wholes into one
great perfect entirety.'[37] A man with such aspirations is bound to be
incapable of genuine, human relationships.

In reaction against this spectre of efficiency and uniformity, the
writers who reject the industrial world insist deliberately on individual
diversity. One of the most emphasized features of Péguy's youthful
utopia is that 'men will burst forth in unexpected varieties.'[38] Even
more markedly, any sense of uniformity was quite absent from Morris'
utopia — on the contrary, it is the individual traits, foibles, eccentricities
and quirks of character that were particularly brought to light. No
doubt this is linked with the kind of work at the centre of people's
lives : whereas for Jünger it is highly automated and fragmented
participation in a corporate form of production, for Péguy or Morris it
is artisan production with all its implications of individual initiative,

responsibility, and self-imposed time-scales and rhythms, though set in a milieu of spontaneous co-operation.

Jünger, of course, scorned their outlook, their romanticism, their all too facile nostalgia for a pre-industrial primitivism. Yet it is not only among them that hostility to the technical environment is to be found. George Orwell, who was more than a little suspicious of Morris' faith in what we might call the 'withering away of machinery', and who did not want to be seen as a backward-looking figure, could propose only the most grudging and limited resignation to technology : 'The machine has got to be accepted, but it is probably better to accept it as one accepts a drug — that is, grudgingly and suspiciously. Like a drug, the machine is useful, dangerous and habit-forming.' There is no doubt, though, that Orwell sees the full extent of the danger inherent in the terrible dynamism of mechanical efficiency. 'The process of mechaniz-ation has itself become a machine, a huge glittering vehicle whirling us we are not certain where, but probably towards the padded Wells-world and the brain in the bottle.'[39]

This is what awaits us if we let efficiency continue to be a dominant value of our civilization. Efficiency is the characteristic value of a joyless machine-world; it is, as we have said, a mechanical and not a human quality. This is why it is important, even in the midst of a world whose workings are so far removed from his own, that we remember Ruskin and his hatred of the rule of efficiency. Indeed, it is hardly going too far to say that Ruskin, approaching the world from art as he did, based his whole concept of good, humanly valuable work on the criterion of inefficiency. Only slave-civilizations rely on perfection of execution, as in Greek architecture where simple and limited tasks had to be carried out meticulously, without individuality or imagination. Christianity, on the other hand, admitted imperfection by reason of its stress on the unique and inviolable worth of each individual soul : hence the special human quality of Gothic. So in work generally the cult of perfection (or to use the modern term, efficiency) destroys that 'thoughtfulness' in the worker which for Ruskin was all-important and which we must encourage at all costs, 'whatever faults and errors we are obliged to take with it.' It is all a question of which priorities we choose, human or mechanical, in the work we give a man to do — 'ten to one he makes a mistake in the first touch he gives to his work as a thinking being. But you have made a man of him for all that. He was only a machine before, an animated tool.'[40] Are we to be tools or men in our work? The question Ruskin poses is hopefully not without relevance even to a world where so much work inevitably depends much more on precision than on imagination. These are the consequences of making the wrong answer to that question :

> The eye of the soul must be bent upon the finger-point, and the soul's force must fill all the invisible nerves that guide it, ten hours a day, that it may not err from its steely precision, and so soul and sight be worn away, and the whole human being be lost at last — a heap of sawdust, so far as its intellectual work in this world is concerned.[41]

The language may have dated, but dare we deny, in our production-line civilization, that the thought is prophetic?

6 Anarchism, socialism & work

Herbert Marcuse has remarked that ideology, far from disappearing from the modern world, is now contained and expressed more absolutely than ever within the process of production itself; industrial culture is, therefore, inherently ideological in its imposition of certain organized patterns of life on a society conditioned by advanced technology. The result he sees – in his *One-Dimensional Man* – as a more or less subtle totalitarianism.[1] Jünger, as we have seen, conceptualized this ideology in a particularly naked, brutal and (in a sense) honest form. Equally there is, of course, ideology in the refusal of blind, industrial dynamism, and one of the peculiar characteristics of this ideology is the tendency to look simultaneously backwards and forwards, showing nostalgia for earlier patterns of working life and yet aspiring towards a more just and harmonious society in the future. Hence that basic duality in Zola's utopia whereby he looks forward to an egalitarian community such as has never existed, yet at the same time has to hark back to an earlier, artisanal form of production.

In some cases this duality could lead to a mixture of radical social thought on the one hand and extremely reactionary politics on the other : Ruskin is the obvious example of this, and indeed there is a curious ambivalence lurking within the common cult of the medieval organization of labour. As Margaret Grennan points out in her study of William Morris :

> It is the dichotomy found in revolutionary Spain where the ideal of medieval economy and the communal life of the medieval Spanish

village fed the Carlist hopes, but the same ideal served — and again
this is characteristic of the movement that included Morris and
Carlyle — as the rallying-point for the anarchists.[2]

Her perception is directly relevant to us here. Whilst it is true that
certain of the major writers of the tradition could be accused of
reactionary or repressive politics, and whilst there is a danger of the
exploitation of the ethic of work by fascism and the extreme Right in
general (as we shall see in a later chapter), it is more immediately
apparent that many of them do show a distinct affinity with, and often
an explicit sympathy for, elements of anarchist thought. It is certainly
striking that all of them, from Carlyle to Wesker, are profoundly distrustful of the vaunted paraphernalia of bourgeois democracy, and they
refuse to see the ballot-box as an adequate guarantee of a fulfilled life;
for fulfilment lies elsewhere.

It might be argued that socialism in general begins from a great respect
for human work — and indeed we do find this respect in the works of
utopian socialists such as Morelly and Babeuf in the eighteenth century,
just as we find it in the highest theoretical terms, as we have seen, in
Marx. Yet there is a significant difference in emphasis, if not in direction,
between anarchism and marxism; it is a difference that James Joll
summarizes as a distinction between Marx and the father of anarchism,
Proudhon.

> If for Marx the proletariat was to be the class destined by the
> immutable laws of history to triumph, for Proudhon the proletar-
> iat was to be the class whose toil and sufferings were to make possible
> a new moral as well as a new social order. The sense of the dignity
> of labour, and the necessity of preserving it from the degradation
> imposed by machines and the exploitation imposed by the capitalist
> system, runs through all Proudhon's work, and this idea of the
> worker's duty to himself and his mission to the world is the basis of
> all subsequent anarchist thought.[3]

Many writers, indeed, feel emotionally closer to Proudhon than to
Marx, less clear and complete though some of the former's analyses and
theories may be. Proudhon was very much aware of his own artisan/
peasant background, and was himself a trained printer. He, too, thought
that fundamental to any truly ethical society were the virtues embodied
in craftsmanship, pride in a task well and conscientiously done, in
closeness to the earth and a life of hard, physical effort. The whole

point of working-class revolution was for Proudhon to re-establish these virtues, for 'work is the first attribute, the essential characteristic of man.'[4] Only the working class has kept any semblance of contact with the qualities that have the power to regenerate society, and to save it from its decadence and self-seeking corruption. For it is a society — and this is to be an important theme — that has lost its organic nature (replaced by the mere mechanical juxtaposition of individuals and institutions), that very organic nature that was an essential condition of its functioning as an ethical unit.

The anarchist, Kropotkin, was equally to think that labour has intrinsic value, whilst Bakunin describes work in his *Revolutionary Catechism* as the basis of dignity and of all human rights : only through free and intelligent work can man conquer his own humanity and create out of indifferent nature a true civilization. We must remember, too, that anarchism has always exercised its greatest appeal among the peasantry or among artisans and skilled workers with a highly-developed, professional conscience and craft pride, such as watchmakers or typographers.

It is because of this emphasis that an easily perceptible anarchist strain is to be found in so much of the literature of work. For his part, Zola was, of course, following Fourier in *Travail*; but there is surely in Fourier himself, despite the rigid order of his phalanstery, an early enunciation of certain aspects of anarchist thought. After all, he stressed that the coming Harmony was to abolish all political systems, to replace the State as we have known it by a multiplicity of smaller groupings; all the apparatus of repression, such as prisons, would then become superfluous. These are developments that Zola, too, stresses; and we have seen that Jordan regards fulfilment in work as the only constitution that society needs. Zola, it is true, had criticized the violence of anarchism in the fanatical and destructive figure of Souvarine in *Germinal*; and he continued this criticism in the later novel, *Paris*. Yet between the two there is an evolution, for in the latter book, the appeal of anarchism as an ideal is presented as being very great, and proves an attraction for the noblest figures of the novel. The rejection of violence is very clear, but it would seem that Zola is coming round to a peaceful kind of anarchism. This we sense, too, from his loathing for 'la lente pourriture parlementaire' that features so strongly in *Paris*, the world of parliamentary politics with its 'unleashing of egotistical appetites' where the differences in party labels only hide the same burning thirst for domination. There is a highly critical portrait of the socialist, Mège, (based on Guesde), whom Zola attacks for his aspiration towards a State dictatorship that would only mean a return of the old slavery under a new name.[5]

Throughout *Travail* we hear of the gradual disintegration of the governmental machine in the whole country, to be replaced by a system of more or less spontaneously co-operating communities. It is not for nothing that Jordan can call Luc, the prime mover of the community presented in the novel, an anarchist – even though Zola still shows distrust of the violent aspect of the anarchist tradition as embodied in the figure of the bomb-making, pottery craftsman, Lange. Lange, however, whose artistic integrity as an artisan is admired by Zola, eventually drops the violence and leaves his stubborn, social isolation to join the community, a community that has, indeed, evolved towards the anarchist ideal he has nourished for so long. The ultimate ideal *is*, Zola admits, the anarchist one, as we see particularly in the reflowering of the artisan tradition in his City and the growth of a system of direct exchange between producers. And just as the anarchists tended to appeal to the peasantry, so Zola is careful to include the workers on the land in his mystique of labour : the son of the idle capitalist, Boisgelin, becomes a dedicated and morally fulfilled man of the soil.

Where Zola does differ from many anarchist thinkers – and where he is more specifically Fourierist – is in the wealth and abundance of his utopia. The main stream of anarchist thought, it has often been argued, is ascetic in its peculiarly moralistic approach to human society (an approach inspired in part by Rousseau). It often contains, as Woodcock and others have pointed out, a common desire for a simplification of life, for a certain closeness to nature that may well involve a decided hostility to wealth and luxury. The great hope idealistically placed by that movement in the peasantry surely reflects a theory that they are somehow close to nature and, therefore, 'authentic'. So that although individual anarchists may appear positivistic at times, hailing techno-logical progress as Kropotkin does, it may still be said that anarchism in general has tended to pit itself against modern civilization and against that very complexity of industry which is regarded as necessary and salutary by many marxists. Hence the backward-looking element of anarchism, summarized by Joll :

> the basic assumptions of anarchism are all contrary to the develop-ment of large-scale industry and of mass-production and consump-tion. When it comes to the point, the anarchists are all agreed that in

the new society man will live in extreme simplicity and frugality and will be quite happy to do without the technical achievements of the industrial age. For this reason, much anarchist thinking seems to be based on a romantic, backward-looking vision of an idealized past society of artisans and peasants, and on a total rejection of the realities of twentieth-century social and economic organization.[6]

Proudhon, for example, comes out in *La Guerre et la paix* with a plea for poverty as distinct from wretched pauperism, a plea to be echoed later by the poet, Péguy : poverty, being the state of having just what one needs, is the free condition of man *par excellence*, that in which he lives most intensely and can best spiritualize his life.[7] Tolstoy and Morris fall into a similar pattern of response.

Tolstoy knew Proudhon — he met him in Brussels in 1861 — and there need be no doubt about the intensity of his own brand of non-violent anarchism. His distrust of all the paraphernalia of government, and not least of elections, is as strong as that of Zola. There is the memorable scene in *Anna Karenina* where Levin is shown to be totally out of his element at the elections, not even knowing for whom or what he is voting. When in distaste he leaves the hall where all the wrangling is going on, and finds himself in a room where the servants are getting on with setting out the buffet, he feels he has entered 'a purer atmosphere'. Such sordid and deceptive wrangling fulfils none of the basic needs of man, and in Tolstoy's view the whole apparatus of government, which is nothing but a hypocritical system of organized violence and repression, would inevitably disappear as an enlightened world adopts a return to the simple life of tilling the soil. Once man has realized that his 'first duty is to do his own physical labour' he will quit the towns for the country; nor, once there, will there be any need for him to establish a society as we understand it, for the natural and spontaneous association of one working man with another will suffice. Once again, a realization of the innate value of labour is the only principle of social organization that is required.

Like Tolstoy, Morris was in favour — in theory anyway — of a simplification of life : 'simplicity of life', 'simplicity everywhere' are phrases that recur in his essays and lectures. What has luxury and all that goes with it produced anyway, but a destruction of beauty in everyday objects, what has it done but to spread ugliness everywhere, even over the face of nature? It is with a certain vehemence that he rejects the view that true civilization can be thought of in terms of acquisition, of more and more luxury, 'more stuffed chairs and more cushions, and more carpets and gas.'[8] And though it never amounts to anything quite as ascetic as Tolstoy envisaged in his religious messianism, this desire for simplicity is reflected in the dream-world of *News from Nowhere*. Whether we are meant to take that world as a literal expression of Morris' socio-political ideas or not, the nostalgia is eloquent and clear, and it is surely a utopia that presents what Woodcock has described as an underlying characteristic of the anarchist tradition : 'that mental shift into a timeless world, out of progress and freed from material temptations.'[9] Morris' desire to give socialism a religious force, to found a religion of socialism, gives his moral pronouncements an absolute quality that is characteristic of anarchism; towards that end, he wrote, 'compromise is of no use, and we shall only want to have those with us who will be with us to the end.'[10] This rejection of compromise, of moral and political palliation, alienated Morris from the Fabians of the Social Democratic Federation, and it was in this spirit that he hit out at the leaders of the British trade union movement, seeing it as a potential force for real change that had come instead to a mere tinkering with the *status quo* in order to extract a little extra in the way of remuneration, shorter hours, etc., rather than dealing radically with the whole question of the nature and status of labour. Although he fell out with the anarchists in his Socialist League, Morris did admit he owed his political education to his 'anarchist friends', and was indeed even closer to their attitudes than he himself perhaps realized.[11] He remained on good terms with Kropotkin, who liked and generally respected him. George Bernard Shaw had no doubts about where Morris really stood, and he described the members of the Socialist League as 'romantic anarchists to a man . . . strong on the negative side, but regarding the State as an enemy, very much as the child regards a policeman. Morris, like all original artists and thinkers, had a good deal of this feeling too.'[12]

It is not surprising then to find in *News* that the whole apparatus of the State has been dismantled. Government, the narrator is told, was in the nineteenth-century sense simply a machinery for protecting vested interest and deluding the poor, an apparatus ultimately based on the brute force of army, navy and police. 'The government itself was but the necessary result of the careless, aimless tyranny of the times, it was but the machinery of tyranny.'[13] They are well off as to politics in this future world, for they have none, the narrator is told, and the total disintegration of the once-repressive system of parliamentary

politics is humorously suggested by the fact that the Houses of Parliament
– left standing despite their great ugliness as a memento to past folly
both architectural and political – are now no longer used for 'the
strange games they played there' but as a storage-place for manure, and
are commonly referred to as the Dung Market! Morris spoke in his own
name of his hostility to the 'wearisome shilly-shally of parliamentary
politics', and claimed that what we have lost is 'the due sympathy with
the life of the workshop, which would, if it existed, be such a whole-
some check on the humbug of party politics.'[14] As Zola and Tolstoy
thought, the best 'constitution' for society is one based *directly* on work
and its latent ethical and cultural rewards. This the narrator of *News*
quickly perceives, seeing the rediscovery of pleasure in work as a change
much more fundamental and far-reaching than any political readjustment
(though Morris is rather facile in separating the two) : 'For to speak
plainly, this change from the conditions of the older world seems to me
far greater and more important than all the other changes you have told
me about as to crime, politics, property, marriages.'[15]

If work is to be the foundation of a truly human and moral, social
order, it is essentially through the organizations of the workers themselves that this order is to be established. In Morris' story of the Great
Change in *News* that has brought all this about, it is notably the labour
organizations that are the real force, overcoming and going beyond the
inadequacies of 'State Socialism'. The fanciful tale of the Great Change
is really a projection of the author's dream of what the trade union
movement might have been without its tendency towards reform or
compromise with a system based on the degradation of human labour.
He presents this attitude in allegorical form in his romance, *The Roots
of the Mountains* : the Huns who invade and conquer the Dalesmen are
characterized as barbarians because they dislike work, enslaving their
enemies and keeping them alive for their labour. Slavery is the lot of
those who seek to temporize politically with the exploiters of labour.
Margaret Grennan has summarized the relevance of this work to the
modern world :

> No compromise with the Dusky Men of any age was Morris' insistent
> message to the workers of England, no pact with the current com-
> mercialism; and those who tried it brought a part of their troubles
> upon themselves. This principle kept Morris aloof from the 'gas and
> water' socialism of his own generation, with its acceptance of
> parliamentary reform and, therefore, its implied acceptance of

parliament itself.[16]

Morris wanted strong, labour organizations with the integrity to stay outside the palliatory meeting-ground of parliamentary politics where the vital distinction between labour and capital was in danger of being blurred. Of this distinction he once said, 'Everything that tends to mask that opposition, to confuse it, weakens the popular force and gives a new lease of life to the reaction.'[17] The words could equally well be those of the important French political philosopher, Georges Sorel.

Sorel, the man Péguy called his 'master', is a curious and changeable figure who has been regarded as the theoretician of revolutionary syndicalism, although in fact he seems to have had very little to do with the formation of that movement and exercised little influence over its members. He described revolutionary syndicalism as what resulted when the nascent, French syndicalist movement was transformed towards the end of the nineteenth century by the influx of anarchists into it. In Sorel's eyes this was important not merely because of the vital energy which this influx imparted, but also because of the injection of moral considerations into a movement which might otherwise — like trade-unionism in England — have been restricted to demands for wage increases or other exclusively material benefits. As a counter to any tendency towards political compromise, the anarchists brought to syndicalism in that period an ethical vision, that of the working class as being potentially *the* moral and creative force *par excellence*, and perhaps indeed the only one in modern society. The hint of moral asceticism that accompanied this was not without creating contradictions, of which there is no shortage in revolutionary syndicalism however attractive the aspirations of that movement may be. For revolutionary syndicalism was in a sense an attempt to come to terms with industrialism, and in theorists such as Sorel (who was himself a trained engineer) we feel at times the presence of a positivistic tradition going back to Saint-Simon; and yet this is curiously allied with a moral and romantic vision which anarchism brought with it. Unlike Morris, Sorel, for example, praises the achievements of capitalism in the field of production, following Marx and Engels in this, and the future society he envisages is a highly productive one. George Woodcock points out the inherent contradiction : 'Even efforts to encompass the industrial world by such doctrines as anarcho-syndicalism have been mingled with a certain revulsion against that world, leading to a mystic vision of the workers as moral regenerators.'[18]

If the anarchists were so attracted to revolutionary syndicalism, it was largely because of the example of federal, decentralized action embodied in the *bourses du travail* which sprang up all over France, in alliance with the syndicalist movement, from 1887 onwards. Originally conceived as labour exchanges under workers' control, the *bourses* soon became, under the secretaryship of Fernand Pelloutier, something infinitely wider. With his own anarchist leanings, Pelloutier saw the *bourses* as centres of culture, both general and professional, for the working class and eventually for the whole of society. What is especially interesting is the combination of *moral* and *professional* culture he envisaged, stressing 'the work of moral, administrative and technical education necessary if a society of proud and free men is to be viable.'[19] The 'moral capacity' of the people will be the test of its validity, he states, and their work is at the very heart of this moral capacity. Accordingly, Pelloutier planned to include within the structure of the *bourses* social museums, permanent exhibitions of the products and tools of labour.

The notion of an ethic peculiar to the worker is central to Sorel's thought. The great problem of its creation, all too often neglected by politicians and political theorists, is repeatedly evoked throughout his writings. In the *Réflexions sur la violence*, the book by which he is best known, Sorel shows great concern for what he calls 'la morale des producteurs', the new morality of the worker which is to be based precisely on his quality *as* a worker.

It was this aspect of revolutionary syndicalism that produced another contradiction; for the chief weapons of the syndicalists were, of course, the strike and sabotage, both of which, the one by a refusal to work and the other by deliberately doing bad work, hardly seemed to contribute to that ethic of work so ardently sought. Strike action was, of course, essential, and lay at the very basis of syndicalism; without it, without the concept, too, of the General Strike which Sorel erects as a potent, political myth, the workers would be powerless to do anything at all. Sabotage, however, proves a thornier problem, and one which does more definitely appear to run counter to the search for a morality of work. In his tract, *Le Sabotage*, of 1912, the syndicalist, Pouget, supports the slogan 'bad pay, bad work', advocating deliberate carelessness, work done 'à coups de sabots', malingering, etc.[20] Nor was he the only proponent of such tactics : the *bourse du travail* of Montpellier put out an article telling not only how machinery could be sabotaged, but also giving advice on by what means a joiner can superficially disguise shoddy workmanship, how a tailor can spoil clothes, how an agricultural labourer can sow seed badly and wastefully, and so on.[21] We should expect Péguy, though a friend and associate of Sorel, to abhor this, and so we find him in *Notre Jeunesse* describing sabotage as a bourgeois invention that has infected the working-class world :

> Only socialism could avoid it, avoid this contamination. It is bourgeois sabotage, the same, the only one, which by contamination descends level by level into the working-class world ... It's the working-class world gradually becoming bourgeois. Contrary to what people think, sabotage isn't innate, isn't *born* in the working-class world. It is learnt there. It is taught dogmatically, intellectually as an alien invention. It is a bourgeois invention, a political, parliamentary and essentially intellectual invention which penetrates by contamination and teaching, intellectual, from above into the working-class world.[22]

Péguy was not alone in his abhorrence : we also find the notion of sabotage being attacked by the socialist leader, Jean Jaurès, on the grounds that it is repugnant to 'the technical value of the worker', in other words it damages his integrity *as* a worker. Now Jaurès, as a parliamentary politician, was anything but well viewed by the revolutionary syndicalists; but significantly we find grave doubts about the ethical validity of sabotage coming from the pen of Sorel himself. Sorel's opinion was that syndicalism could employ any methods except those that might run the risk of depreciating in the individual worker that professional value which will, after all, be his 'titre de souveraineté' in the ideal, future world.[23]

Whilst Sorel himself was regarded with suspicion as an external 'intellectual' by some of the revolutionary syndicalists, the same doubts also appear, as we might expect, at the heart of the syndicalist movement itself. Griffuelhes, the CGT secretary during those vital and formative years for French syndicalism, 1902–9, was very worried about the ethical problems posed by sabotage, believing that the morality of 'bon travail' should be the basis of any society that syndicalism as a force might bring about. His fellow syndicalist, Alphonse Merrheim, was equally perturbed by the issue, and discussed it in terms akin to those of Sorel and Péguy, though with a greater weight of down-to-earth personal experience :

> We are present at a period of industrial development, and at the same

time, among the working class, a desire has grown up not to love work any more, through the fault of capitalism itself and of the government. You just have to know what a metallurgy workshop is like these days, a workshop for mechanical constructions; ask my comrades : we learn everything there, except to love the work we do; the work doesn't count any longer, man is nothing but a number.[24]

As the last words indicate, Merrheim shares that view which is fundamental to the literary tradition with which we are concerned, namely that there is an intimate interaction between the quality of a man's life and the quality of his work.

Two major, ideological consequences derive from the anarcho-syndicalist belief that the only basis for social change, and for the new society that lies beyond that change, is to be found in the professional organizations of the workers themselves, a belief underlined when the Congress of the CGT in 1902 expressed the faith that the *bourse du travail* will become the centre of activity of all human life. The first of these consequences is what we have seen in the work of Zola, Tolstoy and Morris : a distrust of politics in general. 'La politique, n'en faut pas!' exclaims Pouget typically, scorning the untranslatable 'ragougnasses politicardes', whilst Griffuelhes describes syndicalism as a means of action directed agains the 'corruptions politiciennes'; this corruption syndicalism is to replace by its peculiar moral force, the force capable of regenerating the world, the 'great renovator' in Griffuelhes' phrase.[25] The same distrust of parties, parliament and politics in general is also to be fundamental to the later writers in the quest for an alternative work-culture. It is certainly fundamental to Sorel and Péguy. To the latter we owe the celebrated distinction between 'mystique', the initial faith in an ideal, and 'politique', its corruption in the attempt to put it into practice : 'politique' in this period becomes in France a distinctly pejorative term. The 'charlatan parliamentary politicians' come in for a great deal of abuse at Péguy's hands, and they are criticized in particular because of their alienation from the world of work (though they often have the temerity to claim to 'represent' that world) : looking at them Péguy sees 'everywhere the same hollow pride, those stiff arms, those orator's fingers, those hands that don't know how to handle a tool.'[26] In the case of Sorel, this was amplified to a hatred of bourgeois democracy at times more reminiscent of Nietzsche than of Marx, especially in the *Réflexions sur la violence* where he evokes the flabby enervation of 'the democratic morass'.[27] He gave vent to the same anti-democratic feeling (which was to lead him to flirt for a short period with the extreme, right-wing Action Française group) in his work *Les Illusions du progrès* : attacking the newly-conceived, popular universities, he declares that if, as the bourgeois instigators of these institutions had hoped, all intelligent workers had rushed to attend them, socialism would have fallen totally into the democratic rut. And again we are brought back to that professional emphasis that is characteristic of the whole movement of revolutionary syndicalism as Sorel goes on, 'Instead of teaching the workers what they need to know for their working lives, they (i.e. the bourgeois intellectuals and philanthropists) strive instead to develop in them a lively curiosity for things found only in books written for the amusement of the bourgeoisie.'[28]

This, then, takes us on to the second ideological consequence of that movement's professional emphasis : the distrust of intellectuals. The emancipation of the workers will be achieved by the workers themselves — this was one of their recurrent watchwords, and Sorel himself, of course, fell victim to the accusation of being an intellectual outsider. He was certainly seen as such by Pouget, who for his part deliberately chose to write his most effective articles — those that appeared in his review *Le Père Peinard* — in a particularly vigorous brand of working-class slang, as if to emphasize his non-intellectual status and to imply that the workers have their own culture, their own language, and need no other.

Paradoxically, writers such as Sorel and Péguy share the same anti-intellectualism, whilst remaining undeniably intellectuals themselves! Deeply influenced by the reaction against positivism that leaves its stamp on this period, formed by the same climate that produced the revelations of Bergson with his stress on the primary of intuition, they turned in revolt against the whole intellectual tradition that Sorel saw as having been instituted in the over-facile and fundamentally bourgeois age of enlightenment. In particular the faith in science as the infallible key to universal, human values is interpreted as a false path, and even as an elaborate, class hoax. Above all, Sorel and Péguy protest against the wholesale importation of so-called scientific method into the study of man and his history. Any pretension to a 'scientific' prediction aroused their wrath, any positivistic notion of demonstrable inevitability. Sorel, taking his theory of history from Vico rather than Hegel, set out in this spirit to 'correct' marxism. His main tool in so doing — and in this he showed the irrationalist basis of his thought — was the concept of the myth. There is no rigid, social causality, no great and inflexible law of historical development, and marxism for Sorel is less valuable for the usually admired precision of Marx's analysis of economic forces than for the projection of the basically unscientific *myth* of apocalyptic revolution. It is through the immediate emotional impact of myth that the mass of workers is best mobilized towards the fulfilment of the moral aspirations peculiar to it. Myth alone, by its total, non-analysable nature, its indivisible quality, will brook no compromise nor any of the palliation which, as Morris too thought, was the danger of the mediocre present.

It is doubly significant that so many writers who exalt work should share this distrust of scientism. For not only had science led in the technical sphere to industrialism, the arch-enemy of rewarding work; in the political sphere the 'scientific' investigation of economics, which Morris found so uncongenial (parts of *Das Kapital* he admitted to finding 'stiffer going than some of Browning's poetry'!) seemed to lead away from moral and, therefore, *free* fulfilment into the realm of a mechanical determinism. These apocalyptic tendencies are surely grounded in the anarchist tradition, the romantic, semi-religious beliefs which that movement sometimes inspires under the pressure of its moral intensity. Gerald Brenan has described such characteristics among the peasants of Andalusia.[29] In the same way, did the revolutionary syndicalists not avoid all precision about the future? An early historian of the movement writes of 'those vague and ambiguous, though alluring fancies', of the 'large and glowing visions of a future society'.[30] And Sorel, contrasting the mediocrity of Social Democracy with the vitality of the anarchists, recalls the words of Proudhon on the 'decadence' of his own age : 'The only way out is through a total revolution [une révolution intégrale] in the ideas and hearts of men.'[31]

So, too, for the committed Expressionist dramatists, vision takes primacy over analysis. Hence Toller's bitter accusation in his auto-biography that the 'fetishists of economics' belittle the moral force of the people and their spontaneous impulses, remaining 'deaf to the magic of the word, blind to the power of the idea, dumb before the force of the spirit.'[32] Outside the apocalypse, in the humdrum world of political tactics, the Expressionist hero *must* feel alienated and inauthentic. It was Toller's case after the collapse of the ill-fated and idealistic, Bavarian Soviet of 1919, and it is the plight of the chief character of his play *Hoppla, wir leben!* — a play whose theme still has an actuality that is illustrated by its recent revival in Paris. An unsuccessful revolutionary returns to society after a long spell in prison, and feels lost and isolated in a world of intrigue, of parliamentary politics, of vote-catching; maybe Toller does not endorse his intransigence without reservation, but he obviously embodies in him his own problems and preferences. He, too, knew the tragedy of the fall from *mystique* to *politique*.

The same kind of disillusionment and decline seemed inevitable within the syndicalist movement itself, which in France had by 1910 begun to leave behind its anarchist-inspired phase to become more reformist in orientation, shifting the emphasis from moral aspiration to material demands of an important but non-revolutionary nature. In 1910 a declaration was made at the CGT Congress in Toulouse to the effect that 'syndicalists ought, above all, to occupy themselves with increasing wages and improving the hygienic conditions of factories, with reducing the hours of work . . .' and so on in the same vein.[33] It would be foolish and irresponsible to deny the necessity and urgency of such demands; whilst admitting this, some writers do, however, express regret over the passing of that earlier phase, and do so again from their preoccupation with the problems of work – above all, Simone Weil and Camus.

Simone Weil looked back for inspiration to the medieval guilds as others had done; but she saw their spirit as having been embodied in French syndicalism during that heroic period before the movement declined into materialism.

> As late as the beginning of this century, few things in Europe were nearer to the Middle Ages than French syndicalism, the only reflection in our country of the spirit of the corporations. The feeble remains of syndicalism are among the sparks on which it is most urgent that we blow.[34]

She speaks of the purity of syndicalism up to 1914, and in her advice to a young man entering the movement she tries to recreate something of the old spirit by couching it all in terms reminiscent of the entry into holy orders. The degeneration, she believes, has come about not only through direct money-contamination, but also through the association with political parties – and her hostility falls into what is by now a familiar pattern of response. It is perhaps not irrelevant to note that she was active in the ranks of the anarchists in the Spanish Civil War. Politics, she declares, appear to her 'une sinistre rigolade', a sinister joke.[35] Particularly is this so because no politician has had the courage and integrity, during the period of high wages, to think and say aloud that *at that very time* the working class and its aspirations were being corrupted and degraded. Like Péguy she criticizes politicians for not having worked in factories, and for not having the problems posed by this aspect of alienation in the forefront of their minds. What is the ballot-paper to a man out of work? she asks. A very poor consolation indeed.

Considering the remarkable extent to which his own thought parallels that of Weil in the same period, it is not surprising that Eric Gill looks back to the guild tradition of the Middle Ages and evokes the degradation within the trade union movement whereby money has ousted more professional concerns. And he too sees the exclusive preoccupation with higher wages as a corruption imposed by capitalism from above — 'the worship of money is a worship which the workman has learned from his superiors.' He is merely adopting the greed of the masters as *his* values; the trade union leader gets his philosophy ready-made from the people he is supposed to be fighting. This merely blinds the workman to the fact that, whatever his wages, the factory system will still be wrong.[36]

It was probably in part through the example of Simone Weil that Camus came into contact with what was left of the revolutionary, syndicalist milieu. In *L'Homme révolté* he is not only to express some admiration for the spirit of Péguy and Sorel but also to extol syndicalism in its heroic phase as being the only revolutionary movement capable of evolving a valid morality and culture. Indeed, Camus' ideological and political judgments — such as they are — are often shot through with the libertarian spirit of anarchism. It is because of this that he was so attracted to the working-class tradition of Spain, to which he devoted two plays (*Révolte dans les Asturies* and *L'État de siège*) as well as a number of articles : it was in Spain, he felt, that authoritarian communism had the least chance of winning over the workers, as it had against it the force of 'a true popular and libertarian Left and the whole of the Spanish character.'[37]

It is in the light of this affinity that we find Camus falling into the familiar pattern by his profound distrust of parliamentary speech-making which leaves him 'frightened to hear nothing with a human sound to it'; all too many speeches are mouthed whilst the most heart-breaking industrial squalor and ugliness remains unalleviated.[38] The moral intransigence that he so admired in Simone Weil was his own, too; and although in his work he sometimes writes unfairly or simplistically, or flees into a most intangible lyricism, he does represent a continuation of the moral fervour long associated with the anarchist tradition.

Arnold Wesker knows equally well that the professional politician can never show us the way out of that 'jungle of an industrial society'. The politician, he remarks in his collection of essays *Fears of Fragmentation* is 'the only man whose position in society has risen commensurate with his degree of incompetency.'[39] It is not because of this, he reflects, in terms reminiscent of Sorel in tenor if not in vigour, that there appears to be a correlation between the development of democracy and the growing acceptance of mediocrity 'at all levels of that democratic life'?[40] Not that mediocrity is inherent in the democratic ideal itself, but it does seem to go hand in hand with the direction that ideal has followed up to now — namely towards the creation of a sort of *consumer* democracy. Is it not incredible, asks Wesker, that the politician, the civil servant and the bureaucrat should so dominate our lives? Illustrative of his attitude on this score is his parable of the ideal house that Adam wanted to have built : once the builders are engaged, only wrangling ensues. The foreman struts about and calls himself Prime Minister, the tea-boy becomes Minister for Foreign Affairs; they all make grand speeches on the perennial theme of 'progress' and 'achievement' — 'and all the songs are forgotten and the stories and all that lovely living.'[41] It is this parable that Wesker bodies forth in his play *Their Very Own and Golden City*. Significantly we find that he prefaces the play with a quotation from William Morris on the subject of the unions' abandonment of their real — moral — duty through the corrupting spirit of compromise. The action of the play shows Wesker's hero trying to find a modern equivalent to the cathedrals of the Middle Ages, those edifices which have been for so many writers before the tangible symbol of collective and creative aspiration. It is, on an incomparably vaster scale, what Wesker was more modestly trying to begin with his own cultural Centre 42. Andy, the architect, receives his youthful inspiration to build a *human* city from Durham Cathedral : but despite all his ardour to create this new Jerusalem (and he quotes Blake, of course) he finds himself obstructed from every side. The spirit of political caution embodied in councillors and Party chairmen, as well as the whole economic structure, stand accused in the play of forcing a great ideal and its author into compromise. As Andy angrily says to a veteran Labour official,

> Whether you stonewall, whether you legislate, whether you lobby, argue, deceive or apply your lovely reasonable sanity, the end is the same. A cheapskate dreariness, a dull caution that kills the spirit of

all movements and betrays us all — from plumber to poet.[42]

The overall pattern of disillusion, of a fall from apocalypse to compromise, from vision to tactics strikingly underlines the anarchistic breadth of aspiration within the tradition of revolt against industrial culture. It is, of course, a utopian tradition, as distinct from so-called 'scientific' socialism. The distinction is fundamental. We have seen that a general distrust of scientific modes of thought is of great importance in this revolt, and so, too, is a lack of faith in determinism, an unwillingness to abdicate man's creative freedom vis-à-vis history. What makes them break away from the mainstream of nineteenth- and twentieth-century socialism is their refusal to accept the dogma of inevitable progress, whether in a simple and unilinear *or* in a more sophisticated, dialectical form. Marx, after all, whilst taking much of the mysticism out of Hegel's interpretation of history, still sees the *movement* of that history as all-important and as inevitably carrying us forward to a state of greater and greater technological mastery. The result of his emphasis on the importance of technological change as a precondition or an accompanying factor of revolution too easily leads (as, we have noted, in Soviet Russia) to a sort of productivity fetishism. It is significant that the first protests raised against this aspect of the new order within the USSR came from anarchists and syndicalists. Hence the role played by the ethic of work in the Kronstadt revolt against centralized bolshevism. In the bulletin *The aims for which we are fighting*, published on 9 March 1921, we find the following indictment of the regime : 'With the aid of syndicats brought under State control, they bind the worker to the machine and transform work into a new kind of slavery instead of making it pleasurable.'[43]

Socialism has become all too readily associated with a faith in science that could reduce its vital ethical basis, that could quite literally *demoralize* it. Many are the writers who have been aware of this, but few have expressed it with such down-to-earth indignation as Orwell did in *The Road to Wigan Pier*. The idea of socialism, partly because it *is* an urban creed, has come to be bound up with machine-production. In the eyes of all too many people — and the fault lies largely with the H. G. Wells type of vulgar positivist — socialism postulates a mechanized and ordered world ruled by the principle of efficiency. 'But it is precisely from that vision of the future as a sort of glittering Wells-world that sensitive minds recoil. Please note that this essentially fat-bellied version of "progress" is not an integral part of Socialist doctrine;

but it has come to be thought of as one . . .' He tells how a prominent member of the ILP once confessed 'with a sort of wistful shame — as though it were something faintly improper — that he was "fond of horses".'[44] This is no indictment of socialism itself, which for Orwell is the only way to a decent future. But it will have to be humanized; so that there is a vital function within it for those who can see through 'the swindle of progress', as a permanent conscience, an ethical force within the machine-world. To put it another way, perhaps we should heed a distinction that Péguy once drew between two kinds of socialist : the romantic, who is concerned with representation, with politics; and the classical, who is concerned with work itself. Perhaps we need rather more of the latter than we have had in the past. This means, of course, a socialism in which the ethic of rewarding work would have central importance, and in which the libertarian tradition we associate with anarchism could somehow be accommodated. In short, a new ideology, that only the still growing reaction against the industrial world can shape.

7 The mystique of creativity

In the unfree context of general depersonalization that marks the totally mechanized, Jüngerian universe, one particular human faculty or potentiality is lost which appears of infinite value to many writers, and which is intimately connected with the whole ethic-of-work question : creativity. Jünger himself does actually speak of creativity within the context of his own vision — but in what terms! The new 'creative man', he declares, will be a far cry from the old artisan type : he will not be individually differentiated from his fellows, his identity is to be submerged in the group, uniform and strictly unequivocal in all aspects of life and work, with the impersonal, metallic facial structure that will characterize that hyper-efficient world. For most writers such a vision represents the very opposite of what they understand by creativity. Their position is much more in harmony with that definition of human aspiration already given us by Jung : 'The supreme ideal of man is to fulfil himself as a creative unique individual according to his innate potentialities and within the limits of reality.' Creativity and uniqueness belong together for Jung : such is the case, too, for the anarchists and those writers who have affinities with their world-view.

For anarchists (and anarcho-syndicalists). creativity is not a quality restricted to work alone, although ideally — i.e. in valid work — it is *exemplified* there. Indeed, creativity is a quality that should inform the individual's attitude to life as a whole. This general belief embraces the typically anarchist faith in the historical initiative of the individual, the voluntarism that is such an important aspect of the anarchist philosophy, as opposed to the mechanistic concept of bourgeois

progress or equally the (vulgar-) marxist emphasis on historical determinism. So it is that Pouget writes of syndicalist direct action as 'la
force ouvrière en travail créateur', and CGT secretary, Griffuelhes,
declares with the same emphasis that 'French syndicalism is characterized by spontaneous creative action.'[1] The notions of spontaneity and
creativity merge into one. As we shall see, a more open, latter-day
marxist such as Roger Garaudy also makes a move in ideological terms
in this direction.

We know that it was against rigid, historical determinism that
Georges Sorel rebelled, and in his case, too, the stress on creativity as an
intrinsically ethical activity cannot be divorced from this very revolt.
It is this emphasis on creativity in his writings, both in terms of
historical initiative and specifically in the realm of work and production,
that saves his somewhat shadowy and fragmentary picture of the future
society from veering too close to the universe of Jünger and total
mobilization. For it is true that Sorel accepts the advances of modern
science and technology, although he refuses to equate such advances
with the myth of inevitable progress; and there is more than a hint of
unpleasant mechanical rigour in his view of the 'ideal workshop' that
science will help found.[2] However, for all his eventual flirtation with
the extreme Right, Sorel can hardly be said to anticipate the attitude
of Jünger, for to the impersonal efficiency of pure mechanical reaction
and an extreme division of labour Sorel opposes a critical and creative
outlook on behalf of the individual worker. In the *Réflexions sur la
violence* he emphasizes the creative aspect of the new proletarian
morality by comparing work to art, the latter being a key to what the
former could and should be — 'anticipation de la plus haute production'.[3]
This very phrase is admittedly ambiguous, in that it could denote either
quantitatively *or* qualitatively greater production. The element of
quality would seem to be dominant, though unlike Morris and others
Sorel sees no irremediable contradiction between the two. It is clear,
however, that he was much concerned to stress the need in *his* coming
society for the artist's gifts of invention and innovation, gifts which
every workman will be encouraged to possess as part of a new culture.
He describes 'invention' as the potential mainspring of modern industry :
it is this spirit which must replace the present inculcation of a routine
mentality. Creativity thus appears not just as an aspect of that new
culture, but as its central principle. Horowitz writes in his book,
Radicalism and the Revolt against Reason : 'The transformation of
wage labour into a primary form of aesthetic creation was for Sorel the

way in which socialism overcomes the contradiction between manual labour with its reputed servility and intellectual labour with its reputed nobility.'[4]

The concept of creativity is clearly an essential aspect of the non-ascetic ethic of work. Nonetheless, as in the ascetic approach, religious notions may well be of influence here : the act of creative work may be seen as an imitation of the act of the Creator, having thus an intimate link with the origin of all things. It is a divine act, a mimesis of the gods, and has thereby a kind of transferred, spiritual value. *Homo faber* has the divine spark in him, the creative fire that Prometheus stole from Heaven : it is not for nothing that Prometheus has been regarded as the patron of the artisan, whilst being at the same time beloved by poets such as Goethe and Shelley. Camus, too, makes much of the myth in his writings, presenting Prometheus as the rebel whose revolt has creativity as its essential concomitant.

A certain Promethean accent is perceptible in Bakunin's comments on work and creativity : 'Work is the fundamental basis of human dignity and rights. For it is only through free and intelligent work that man, becoming a creator in his turn and conquering, from the external world and his own bestiality, his humanity and his right, creates the civilized world.'[5] William Morris, for his part, draws the parallel with the divine act of creation quite explicitly, though not without humour, in a well-known and important passage of *News from Nowhere* concerning the rewards of labour in that future society. The visitor from the past asks naïvely : what could possibly be the incentive to work in a society without money, a community where apparently there *is* no reward for labour? The old sage he is interrogating is astonished at such a question, so obviously does it arise from a degraded culture and a degraded view of work as something offered for sale and for no other reason. The terms of his answer are interesting :

> 'No reward of labour? The reward of labour is *life*. Is that not enough?'
> 'But no reward for especially good labour.' quoth I.
> 'Plenty of reward,' said he — 'the reward of creation. The wages which God gets, as people might have said times agone. If you are going to ask to be paid for the pleasure of creation, which is what excellence in work means, the next we shall hear of will be a bill sent in for the begetting of children!'[6]

Good work for Morris necessarily has a creative element in it, and the moral reward, the joy of such creativity he here equates not only with God's delight in creation but also with that other basic – but this time human – creative act, procreation. The obvious implication is that work (and Morris thoroughly believed this) should reach as deep into ourselves as do procreation or childbirth, having the same crucial importance and the same ethico-cultural potential. Work then appears as a basic part of creature life, and the urge to create is as fundamental to man's fulfilment as the sexual urge. It is interesting to find Marx drawing the same parallel (though putting the emphasis on the negation of creature involvement in work under capitalism) in the early Manuscripts, where he comments on the now degraded 'relation of the worker to his own activity as an alien activity, not belonging to him; it is activity as suffering, strength as weakness, begetting as emasculating.'[7]

It was with reference to the above argument on the rewards of labour that Morris' old man in *News* invoked Fourier who in his opinion had understood the whole matter so well, even though men laughed at him. Fourier had indeed shared the same faith in creativity; and in the interacting pattern of liberated passions that is his ideal society he foresaw a great outburst of the creative spirit. Once work becomes a function of the freely expressed and indulged passions it loses all routine character and acquires a fulfilment-value. In the eyes of Zola, too, it was Fourier who had perceived with special clarity the truth on this issue; thus the thoughts of the hero of *Travail*, in the early days of his utopian plans, return to the example of that earlier dreamer : 'And again it was Fourier who was suggested, with the passions set to use, ennobled, become once more necessary and creative energies . . .'[8]

Creativity is thus for Zola, too, a part of creature life. The ideal of his creative man he embodies in the anarchist artisan, Lange, who for much of the novel lives up in a cave in the hills, emphatically 'close to nature', until eventually he is integrated into the harmonious City. In him, above all, Zola incorporates his own hatred of the parasitic and non-creative middle-men : Lange scorns all such commercial mediation and sells his own pots, though even that he does only when he is short of food. For most of the time he creates with no thought of commerce or profit in his mind, but as a free (and yet at a deeper level compulsive) exercise. 'And the rest of the time he forgot himself in potteries that weren't for sale, he spent hours contemplating them, his eyes filled with dreams, a rustic poet whose passion was to give life to things.'[9] Creativity under such circumstances is obviously its own reward. Only by a certain emancipation from the current concept of production for money and money alone can this be conceivable, though, and at this stage in the early parts of the novel such can only happen in the abnormal, individual case of the eccentric, hermit-figure living a life of elemental frugality. Only later, when Zola's utopia tends towards its apotheosis in the return to a generalized, artisan structure, can Lange come out of his cave and become one particularly gifted creator among many. The passions are liberated for free expression, and the creative urge asserts itself *not* as an ideological nicety, a mere decorative super-addition, but as an elemental part of nature. This Jordan, the inventor, has already anticipated in the same novel in his long hymn to work as a natural function, and has done so with an emphasis that is pure Zola :

> Work is life itself, life is a continual working of chemical and mechanical forces. From the first atom that stirred itself to unite with other neighbouring atoms, the great creative activity [la grande besogne créatrice] has never ceased . . . Is the whole universe not an immense workshop where unemployment is unknown, where every day what is infinitely small performs labour of vast proportions, where matter incessantly acts, produces, gives birth, from the simple ferments up to the most perfect creatures? The fields that are covered with harvests are working, the rivers running along the valleys are working, the forests in their slow growth are working, the seas whose waves roll from one continent to another are working, the worlds carried away by the rhythm of gravitation through infinite space are working. There is not a being, not a creature that can remain static in idleness . . .[10]

Here Zola is merely reiterating a theme, though now specifically in the context of work, which dominates so much of his writing and gives his novels some of their characteristic colour, their exaggeration and cosmic breadth. It is the vision of the world as a hive of universal, procreative forces, which was present in *Germinal*, most obviously in the spring-time germination at the end of that novel, or with greater intensity in a work such as *La Faute de l'abbé Mouret* where it appears in all its mystical, pantheistic and obsessive proportions. Two young people in the walled garden of Le Paradou (suggestive of the Garden of Eden) are led on to sexual union, despite all prejudices to the contrary and all their mistaken commitment to chastity, by the universal law of procreation whose presence makes itself felt to them through every aspect of the garden, where the plants embrace voluptously and even the stones are 'swollen with passion'![11]

The same theme reaches its fullest, most repetitive and altogether least digestible expression in the late novel, *Fécondité*, which together with *Travail* is one of the gospels of Zola's new religion. True to its title, the work is a hymn to fertility, first of all in terms of human procreation : Mathieu Froment, the brother of Luc in *Travail*, eventually becomes the father of a dozen children and the grandfather of innumerable others, creating his own rural community based on the faith in fertility as a revolutionary life-force. Against the 'modern' cult of sterility practiced by the bourgeoisie as a result of that class's egotism, its desire not to subdivide inheritance, a cult passed on by contamination to the labouring classes, the novelist sets the flourishing and healthy world of Mathieu and his family. Fertility becomes part of his revolutionary vision —

> And tomorrow's evolution, truth and justice — would it not be made necessary by this constant growth of the greatest number, the revolutionary fertility of the workers and the poor?[12]

Or again —

> Only by love can one give birth, can one create . . . He who will give birth, will create, is the revolutionary saviour, the maker of men for the world that is to be born.[13]

The world of the city and the bourgeoisie is evoked with an hallucinatory emphasis on the disfiguring effects of sterility and sterile pleasure, a world of sordid abortion clinics, highly dubious operations that seem to render women old overnight, 'wasted seed' and the paralysing fear of conception; all culminating in terrible personal tragedies. With this Zola contrasts the rural paradise of Mathieu and his wife, that much-apostrophized 'Goddess of fertility' who spends so much time sitting in the fields breast-feeding her progeny. She and her husband have left the world of industry and turned to farming, and the link between human procreation and the theme of the general fertility of mother earth becomes — abundantly — clear; translation would perhaps be too cruel here :

> Après le pavé brûlant de Paris, desséché par l'âpre lutte du jour, par le rut stérile et prostitué du soir, sous l'incendie des lampes électriques, quel repos amorable que ce vaste silence, cette molle clarté bleue de paradis, ce déroulement sans fin de plaines rafraîchies d'obscurité, rêvant d'enfantement dans l'attente prochaine du soleil! Et quelle

santé, quelle honnêteté, quelle félicité montait de cette nature toujours en gésine, ne s'endormant sous les rosées nocturnes que pour des réveils triomphants, rajeunie sans cesse par le torrent de vie qui ruisselle jusque dans la poussière des chemins![14]

In this novel Zola has taken up the vision of the earth he presented in the infinitely more realistic *La Terre* some fifteen years earlier; but now he carefully refines it of all the bestiality and brutality that had been such a convincing feature of the peasant world of that novel, keeping the insistence on the creative and procreative impulses as elemental aspects of life close to the soil but setting them in a utopian and harmonious milieu where health and fulfilment, rather than rapacity and brute desire, appear to dominate. Earth and woman are constantly equated, explicitly or by common imagery : both collaborate in the 'work of creation'. Mathieu's capacity as creator of children is matched and complemented by his discovery of creative work on the land, and Zola deliberately merges the two — 'And the earth and the woman would complete together the work of creation . . .' Typical of the suggestive mixture of imagery which carries this vision is the following (and again I hesitate to translate, so peculiar is the lyricism) :

C'était cette force, c'était cette puissance qui montait du domaine entier, l'œuvre de vie enfantée, créée, le travail de l'homme engrossant la terre stérile, l'accouchant des richesses nourricières, pour une humanité élargie, conquérante du monde.[15]

The final, embarrassing pages of the novel look forward to the day when other religions will be replaced by the cult, the omnipotence and the 'sovereign beauty' of the pregnant woman!

Even in the more urban context of *Travail*, we might note, the land has its vital role to play : Luc realizes that the new society must ultimately be based on a return to the fertile earth, 'the eternal nurse, the common mother'.[16] And Paul, son of the idle capitalist, rebels against the parasitic existence of his father by going in for agriculture, expressing his infatuation for the earth in terms lifted almost verbatim from *La Terre* — 'And it is superb to see the earth turned over and fecundated, right to its very entrails.'[17]

Zola's vision is, of course, obsessively and abnormally heightened, which is why it has dated so badly; nonetheless, we commonly find, in a less cosmic key, the parallel between peasant and artisan creativity on the one hand and the divine act or that fundamental part of creature life that is procreation on the other. We find it, for instance, modestly but definitely expressed in Charles-Louis Philippe's *Charles Blanchard*, that quiet, novelistic hymn to the 'vie de travail'. The fragments of the novel that we have tell the story of the bored, aimless child whose penniless mother sends him as an apprentice to his uncle, a clog-maker, and who there discovers in the narrow confines of the workshop just what life is all about. The house is full of clogs : his uncle does not make them only or even primarily for money, and will gladly carve more than he could ever sell. When there is no more room, he says, he will put them outside, he will pave the streets with them. The child watches with wonder − and the beginnings of real understanding − as the craftsman's intimate involvement in his acts of work expresses his truest and deepest motivation : an elemental struggle to create, the struggle, described in great detail and with all the tools and their functions lovingly named, between the formless material and the united art of hand and mind. It is a struggle that reaches demonic intensity in the course of the work, and appears as an intoxication − 'l'ivresse du combat' − that seems to the naïve observer to be nearing madness . . . but is really as far from madness as can be, for this is health, inspiration, fulfilment of the divine principle, and it leads to the highest form of equilibrium :

> But soon he could be seen to step back four paces. What he held in his hands was no longer the formless lump of wood that had caused him such effort. Two clogs of veined wood, making a matching pair, beautifully curved and smooth, hollowed here, arched there, with the heels well defined, were the fruits of his labour. They were as perfect as if they had come straight from the hands of the Creator. He examined them on both sides with pride, struck them one against the other; they gave a clear full sound like the ring of a fine silver coin. Once again man had carried off a great victory. Matter was vanquished, nature had to submit.[18]

Here the rewards of creativity are presented in terms of (a) mimesis of the divine, and (b) elemental intoxication, suggesting the parallel with procreation. The latter aspect is underlined by a later description which emphasizes that the clogs seem to partake of their creator's own life : 'For so long they had been the object of his movements, the companions of his hours, that it seemed they participated in his life, as if they had passed through the organs of his body, and were still warm.'[19]

A further motivation and source of pride is suggested by Philippe at the end of the long quotation above : man's conscious and intelligent victory over inanimate matter, the exhilaration of his creative struggle with nature. As a definition it is entirely at one with Marx's description of the meaning the concept 'wealth' will acquire when its bourgeois form is eventually overcome — 'It will be the complete domination of man over the natural forces, over external nature and over his own nature. It will be the full blossoming of his creative forces . . .' It is noteworthy that the controversial Roger Garaudy, who quotes this statement of Marx in his recent essay *Le Grand Tournant du socialisme*, also pays homage on the same page to the 'belle utopie' of Morris' *News from Nowhere*, invoked by Garaudy as evidence of what he calls 'the specifically human need to be a creator.'[20] Of all marxists, Garaudy has shown himself to be one of the most ready to make creativity a vital part of his philosophy. This emphasis in his writings, as we have seen in the case of Sorel or the anarchists, is surely very closely connected with his very open, humanistic brand of marxism, his desire to rid that school of thought of the rigid determinism with which it has all too often been overlaid. Some might say that there is here a kind of return to an 'original marxism', especially to the Marx of the early, philosophical manuscripts, which we have already seen to be the best source of the German writer's ideas on the potential, ethical and cultural value of work. A return, perhaps, to the spirit of that thinker before what Sartre has described as 'the nefarious meeting with Engels', resulting in a certain rigidification of an originally more flexible philosophy.[21] Far from conceding any such rigid determinism, Garaudy insists on man's creative initiative in history as well as in work. He is obviously deeply opposed to any concept of mechanistic progress, although he is more optimistic about the role of science and technical innovation than many non-marxists. Man is essentially a creative being because he is potentially free — as Marx wrote, the human character of work, as distinct from the blind, animal instinct to survive, lies in the conscious anticipation of the aim, the project, in the 'prospective moment', which is a moral faculty of which the worker is at present all too often deprived. Potential freedom in the conception of his work, potential freedom in his relationship with history — marxism, according to Garaudy, recognizes both in man.

Hence the importance in the marxist structure of values of the vital, creative aspect of work : not only is it *the* specifically human aspect of work, but also a form of pedagogy, as is art in general for Garaudy. It is a means whereby man educates himself in his capacity for moral freedom vis-à-vis life and the world generally. 'Aesthetics, in the deepest sense of a reflection on the creative act of man and on its conditions, becomes thus an essential moment in the formation of man, being a pedagogy of invention.'[22] Garaudy sees clearly that the ethic of creativity is the necessary negation of a universe of sheer, inhuman functionality. Above all, the direct, unmediated relationship between the needs of the species and the satisfaction of those needs that is characteristic of the animal world must be interrupted : only then can the worker go beyond a merely utilitarian and unfree relationship with his universe, and his activity and its product can become what Simone Weil called 'un objet de contemplation'.

> The conquest of the artistic, as of the scientific dimension of human labour calls in just the same way for a standing apart which interrupts the direct circuit between the need and the immediate object of its satisfaction. It is only then that a contemplation becomes possible, in which man sees in the object not only its content of utilitarian significance . . . but also the expression it contains of man's creative act. The aesthetic attitude begins when man, to his delight, finds in the object he has created something more than a way of satisfying a need, when he sees it as a witness to his creative act.[23]

In Garaudy's view the aim of marxism is ultimately to make this type of work available to all, which is far from being the case in our present, industrial societies, whatever political label they wear. His marxism contains an ethic that will make it possible, he hopes, for every man to become a creator. The 'new man' he looks forward to will be 'un poète de la création contre l'entropie.'[24] This will be the fulfilment of a prophecy made by Gorky to the effect that 'aesthetics will be the ethics of the future.' Garaudy is not alone among marxists in holding these views, of course — even Lenin, for all his programme of accelerated industrialization, optimistically entertained the ideal of a society made up of 'tens of millions of creators' once socialism has substituted 'work for its own sake' for 'forced work'.[25] The emphasis in Garaudy is unusual and significant, however, in the large and fundamental role he accords to creativity.

Aesthetics are to be the ethics of the future : it is striking just how many of the ethic-of-work writers place at the centre of their various pleas against the present degradation of labour arguments that turn implicitly or explicitly on aesthetic concepts and vocabulary. As well as in the obvious cases of Ruskin or Morris, the phenomenon occurs with particular clarity in the works of the socially conscious, German Expressionists. We should remember that in the vision of that Hölderlin they so admired, the modern, 'loud-roaring' world is to be condemned above all for its sterility, the absence of creativity :

> Fruitless, like the Furies, remains the toil of the poor.

For both Kaiser and Toller the notion of *Werk* is vital, and the word recurs with significant frequency. In Toller's *The Machine-Wreckers* the hero differentiates neatly between two concepts of work : *Arbeit* (the normal German word for day-to-day work) and *Werk* (usually used to denote the created object, especially in the context of art — a 'work' of art, as in English). For Toller, *Arbeit* is the equivalent of negative, neutral toil, work that is unrewarding and ultimately sterile; *Werk* , on the other hand, involves joy in creation (*Schaffenslust*) and humility in creation (*Schaffensdemut*). The spontaneous protest of the weavers has as its origin the human desire for creative activity — 'We want to create, as we created before.'[26] So, too, in the automated factory of *Man and the Masses* the workers call for the opportunity to be creative :

> Wann werden Liebe wir leben?
> Wann werden Werk wir wirken?
> Wann wird Erlösung uns?[27]
> [When shall we live love?
> When shall we perform true work?
> When shall we find redemption?]

Not only do we find in this plea the pattern of association whereby creativity is associated with love and creature life, but also the word *Werk*, being placed alongside the idea of a 'redemption' acquires resonances that go beyond the question of mere economic change, and into a semi-mystical sphere. This Toller plays on later in the same work when the heroine exclaims ecstatically, 'Das Werk — welch heiliges Wort!' ('what a holy word!')[28] There is a close parallel between this and Zola's sentiment in *Travail* where Jordan apostrophizes 'le travail sacré, travail créateur et sauveur' — holy work, creative and redemptive work.[29] In this way Zola, too, stresses the link between the creative aspect of work and its ersatz-religious role as a form of spiritual life, a redemption.

So also in the work of Kaiser : the concept *Werk* is imbued with powerful, ethical implications. In a short story called *Der Arbeiter* he tells of a worker doing automatic, unthinking work in a munitions factory. On investing money in the concern and being moved to another job he suddenly has time to think, and realizes the false direction

of his whole life : 'The work [*Werk*] in which he had laboured for years
and to which he had given up his money was no work, but an un-work
[*Unwerk*].'[30] Valid work must be creative — to be a cog in a machine
for producing engines of destruction is doubly destructive, doubly
alienated from the creative aspirations of man. The positive *Werk* on the
other hand Kaiser embodies in the harbour of Calais of his play *Die
Bürger von Calais*, and it is postulated as the highest, ethical standard
of those who have created it, an ethical standard to replace all previous,
outdated ones.

The theme of the destructive and sterile *Unwerk* is given fuller
exposition in *Gas*, of course, especially in the second part where the
factory goes over from the production of industrial gas (bad enough
already, as it has led to something like total mobilization) to the manufacture of poison gas. The real *Werk* in that play would seem to be the
child whose birth is announced at the end of part one : after the
workers have voted against the owner's scheme of regeneration, in
favour of the technological universe, that same owner turns to his
daughter, who is pregnant. Her human 'creativity' is mystically to be
the bridge to a new life and a new concept of work. The elemental,
childbirth parallel is here bodied forth in symbolism, in very much the
same way as in Zola's work. In *Travail* the work of the community
cannot be felt to be complete until the child has arrived (Luc's child,
that is); 'amour fécond', fertile love, is an essential element of the
creative community. 'On ne fonde rien sans l'enfant, il est l'œuvre
vivante.'[31] As *œuvre* is the equivalent in French of *Werk*, an interesting
parallel emerges — especially in the light of a distinction Ruskin, for
his part, drew between *opera*, happy, creative work, and *labor*, negative
work, 'that quantity of our toil which we die in.'[32] In the case of *œuvre*,
too, value is implied by the connotation of initiative and creativity it
contains; hence Zola's Jordan expresses the same idea as Kaiser — and
in closely corresponding terms — when he declares that 'jamais on
n'abandonne une œuvre', the 'work' becomes man's highest, ethical
imperative.[33] What is this but the 'new morality of the new man' that
Kaiser will proclaim in *Die Bürger von Calais*? Zola's ethical vision
contains, however, the extra dimension of a mystique of human love —
'l'œuvre ne peut commencer à etre que pour l'amour des autres', as one
of his characters piously opines — which enables him to suggest a link
between the creative impulse and the idea of community, 'cette
communauté de l'œuvre' of which he speaks in *Fécondité*.[34]

The same link between the creative spirit and the idea of community is discernible in Simone Weil's ethic of work. The two vital needs of the human soul are responsibility and initiative, the latter being the creative aspiration, the former the *social* dimension of human existence. Both needs are intertwined, however, and each is implied by the other. In the same way, the creative value contained in the term *œuvre* implies as an essential correlative the notion of community. So she emphasizes in *La Condition ouvrière* that if work is to become meaningful again, if it is to become the spiritual centre of life, not only must the workers have reason to feel that they are being creative, but this must also be linked with the sense of belonging to a community and collaborating in a collective goal : 'Workers must no longer be in ignorance of what they make, manufacturing a part without knowing where it goes; they must be given the feeling of collaborating in an *œuvre*.'[35] By adding, as Zola did, this vital social dimension to her ethic of work and creativity, Weil goes beyond the mere idealization of the artisan figure as he appeared in Philippe's *Charles Blanchard*, the isolated craftsman who obtains entire satisfaction from his own self-contained struggle to bring form out of chaos. Man cannot become truly rooted, to return to the theme of *L'Enracinement* until the acts of his daily labour appear in a genuine, social context as a form of communal creation. 'Finally, he must be able to appropriate to himself in his mind the whole *œuvre* and the collectivity of which he is a member.'[36]

Taking up here again some of Weil's ideas, Camus himself elaborates, in the context of his antipathy to historical determinism, a mystique of creativity that once more is intimately implicated in the ethic of work. On all levels, creativity is equivalent to freedom from mechanical necessity, both in terms of the production of artefacts and the creation of a truly human society. Like others before him, Camus evokes 'the drama of our age, when work, entirely at the service of production, has ceased to be creative.' It is from this point of view that he criticizes industrial socialism, for failing to restore 'la joie du créateur'.[37] Like Péguy, Camus seems to look back to an artisan past — a 'restoration' of creative work is what he, too, appears to envisage. We might note that when he refers to Péguy in the section 'Révolte et Art' of *L'Homme révolté* he is speaking precisely of the difficulties that lie in the path of true creativity in the modern age, an age of mechanistic 'faiths', of the 'bourgeois machine' with its cult of productivity and the 'revolutionary machine' with its historical determinism. In the figure of Péguy he embodies the value of a 'classicisme créateur' which seems negated by these nihilistic forces, and it is such a 'creative classicism' that he desperately hopes for in the future.[38]

The contrast between the forces of dissolution and the creative *œuvre* with its innate value was central to Péguy's indictment of the 'political' mentality and its effects : just as the parliamentarians are not concerned with work, so their influence is non-creative and even destructive, leading away from the spiritual value embodied in that very work they so disastrously neglect. 'It is we who make *œuvres* and men, peoples and races. And it is they who destroy.'[39] It is surely, then, not without a thought back to Péguy that Camus goes on, in that same section of *L'Homme révolté*, 'One of the directions of the history of today, and still more of tomorrow, is the struggle between the artists and the new conquerors, between the witnesses of creative revolution and the builders of nihilistic revolution.'[40]

Whilst Camus is certainly realistic enough to recognize the importance of adequate remuneration, his attitude to the problems posed by industrial labour is that of a moralist, and again it is the question of creativity that is the central, ethical issue — 'Work in which one can take an interest, creative work, even badly paid, does not degrade life.'[41] The only way to create a true 'civilization' and a human community out of industrial society is that which so many writers have envisaged, with varying degrees of hope and preciseness : the worker must somehow be restored to the dignity of a creator. Thus in Camus' case, too, the notion of creativity is a vital part of his vision of 'community'. 'All creation denies, in itself, the world of master and slave. The hideous society of tyrants and slaves in which we subsist will find its death and transfiguration only on the level of creation.' This is a theme he returns to again and again; in the foreword to his collection of articles, *Actuelles II*, we find him insisting once more on the role creation must fulfil in the modern, automated world, obsessed as it is by the movement of history :

> Creation, always possible, now becomes more necessary than ever . . . When the work of the worker, like that of the artist, has won some chance of fertility, then alone will nihilism have had its day, and the rebirth [*renaissance*] will take on a meaning.[42]

Significantly, Camus' ideal of work was a collective one, and thereby inseparable from the ideal of community : the artisans in *Les Muets* operate as a team (just as Camus' ideal of work in the theatre was one of team-work and co-operation).

Creativity, as an expression of aesthetic *and* moral freedom and as a notion implicit in the vision of community, is, therefore, an important aspect of Camus' theory of revolt. Hence the relevance of his section 'Révolte et Art' in the main exposition of that theory. Revolt is the moral negation of an immoral universe of inhuman necessity. Creativity, implying freedom, is an ethical imperative; so, in his way, Camus is echoing Gorky's maxim when he states that, in terms of his own theory, 'revolt is, in part, an aesthetic requirement' ('une exigence esthétique').[43]

The ideal, of course, is to abolish the distinction between work and art. In Camus' definition work becomes art when freely accepted (and presumably when there is also a measure of freedom in the means of execution), when it acquires an element of 'play'. Such play, bodied forth by skill and craftsmanship, gives the work of art. In the light of his conviction, and faced with the degradation of labour in the factories of the 1940s and 1950s, Camus concluded that intellectuals had betrayed their mission by cutting themselves off from labour, that the real 'trahison des clercs' lay in the separation between work and culture. In particular, work has been separated from art, and in this, he is not alone in thinking, lies the nucleus of the disqualification of work. It is a separation that constitutes the greatest sin of commercial and industrial civilization against man as an integral being and as a creator of values.

8 Art & work

The whole ethos of creativity central to the non-ascetic morality of work tends, as we saw in the previous chapter, to bring work ideally into the realm of 'art' — the realm, that is, reserved in our society of fragmented activities for a sublime and separate Art with an emphatically capital 'A'. The underlying assumption of the literary rebels against our civilization is surely that art and work do not originally or rightly belong to different and delimited spheres, but that on the contrary they were once indistinguishable, one and the same activity. Hence that semantic overlap in expressions such as *œuvre*, *Werk*, or 'work of art', exploited by many writers. They might argue that the perspective adopted by Huizinga in his renowned *Homo Ludens*, that highly learned exposition of the play element in culture, requires supplementing by an equal emphasis on the *work* element in culture, the *homo faber* whose predominance Huizinga does incidentally acknowledge at the beginning of his book if not in the course of his argument itself.

Taken in isolation, Huizinga's thesis would seem to suggest that culture in general — and art in particular — is largely a product of free play quite outside and independent of any impulse of necessity. 'All poetry is born of play : the sacred play of worship, the festive play of courtship, the martial play of the contest, the disputatious play of the braggadocio, mockery and invective, the nimble play of wit and readiness.'[1] He acknowledges that he defines play in the sense that Plato (who as we know had little regard for work) gave to it : 'an action accomplishing itself outside and above the necessities and seriousness of everyday life.'[2] It obviously seems to have very little to do with what we understand by work and the day-to-day problems of survival. And it is because of this determination to bring out the apparent non-necessity of cultural phenomena that Huizinga tends to see the function of the poet as remaining

> fixed in the play-sphere where it was born. Poiesis, in fact, is a play-function. It proceeds within the play-ground of the mind, in a world of its own which the mind creates for it. There things have a very different physiognomy from the one they wear in everyday life . . .[3]

The poet is, in the light of this, regarded first of all as the man possessed, and thereby taken quite outside normal experience. Huizinga cites and shares Frobenius' hostility to seeking whys and wherefores in culture, his rejection of the 'tyranny of causality' and 'antiquated utilitarianism'. He appears to subscribe to that same view of the artist as a man seized by inspiration that was taken up especially by the romantic movement — describing Frobenius' conception he writes, 'The thrill, the "being seized" by the phenomena of life and nature is condensed by reflex action, as it were, to poetic expression and art. It is difficult to describe the process of creative imagination in words that are more to the point.'[4] Clearly, play for Huizinga is no mere waste of time, for he concurs with Plato again in identifying *play* and *holiness* : the very antithesis of the ethic-of-work current's common equation of work and holiness, *laborare est orare*.

Just as the liturgy — to take one of Huizinga's examples — is essentially play, 'pointless but significant', so too is art in general for that writer. The purest play-form is music, the least obviously connected with utility of any kind; whilst the most impure are those that involve work, where the play-element is as it were compromised by the material means of expression :

> The case is quite different with the plastic arts. The very fact of their being bound to matter and to the limitations of form inherent in it, is enough to forbid them absolutely free play and deny them that flight into the ethereal spaces open to music and poetry . . . However much the plastic artist may be possessed by his creative impulse he has to work like a craftsman, serious and intent, always testing and correcting himself. His inspiration may be free and vehement when he 'conceives', but in its execution it is always subjected to the skill and proficiency of the forming hand.[5]

The play-factor, he goes on, is obstructed by the necessary element of 'handicraft, of industry, even of strenuosity', whereas music and poetry remain in the pure play-sphere. It is tempting to speculate on what Morris, as author of *The Lesser Arts*, would think of this!

Huizinga's deliberate shunning of utilitarian interpretations of culture ties up with a point he makes in his chapter 'Western civilization sub specie ludi'. From the eighteenth century onwards he perceives a tendency hostile to the Baroque (that cultural play-spirit *par excellence*); a tendency whereby 'work and production became the ideal, and then the idol of the age. All Europe donned the boiler suit.' The growth of social consciousness he regards as an intellectual aberration, utilitarianism kills the mysteries of life, banality reigns supreme. In particular there is, he claims, one terrible aberration resulting directly from a certain 'grotesque over-estimation of the economic factor' — and this is marxism. 'As a result of this luxation of our intellects the shameful misconception of Marxism could be put about and even believed, that economic forces and material interests determine the course of the world.'[6] Socialism, he goes on, like liberalism, is inimical to the play-factor in life; culture largely ceased to be 'played' in the nineteenth century, despite the 'first fine careless rapture' of romanticism. No longer was an ideal mode of life reflected in the outward forms of social intercourse. And it is significant to find Huizinga regretting the disappearance of 'the elegant gentleman of former days, resplendent in the gala dress befitting his dignity.'[7] The democratization of men's fashions is for that writer a regrettable phenomenon, and his platonic emphasis on play as the mainspring of culture, rather than work, is part and parcel of his hostility not only to marxism but to any concept of a democratic culture. The spiritual life resides essentially for him with that 'leisure class' described by Veblen at the turn of the century.[8] Is it not part of an attitude to culture that runs the danger of emasculating it of its role in society, and, cutting it off from daily work, reducing the latter to the sort of toil that Plato saw as fit only for slaves?

Swinging now to an opposite extreme, we should look, as a dialectical counterbalance, at what a very different writer has to say about the relationship between art and work. The very title of Ernst Fischer's *The Necessity of Art* points up the contrast with Huizinga's treatise : for the author of *Homo Ludens* art had value by its very non-necessity, its abstraction from normal use-value. In Fischer's view, on the other hand, the origins of art lie quite definitely in the *work* of man, in purposive action on nature. 'Art is almost as old as man. It is a form of work, and work is an activity peculiar to mankind.'[9] Art, then, is a part of the specifically human desire to change the world, and the magic it embodied at its origin was not mere gratuitous play at all, not pure disembodied 'religious experience' but a means by which man acted on his environment. 'Art in the dawn of humanity had little to do with "beauty" and nothing at all to do with any aesthetic desire : it was a magic tool or weapon of the human collective in its struggle for survival.'[10] Man as a tool-making animal learns to control nature, to have power over it through the acquired ability to choose between tools and to reproduce them — to 'make alike'. The creative consciousness of man has, then, its origin in the evolution of tools, it developed 'as a late result of the manual discovery that stones could be broken, split, sharpened, given this shape or that.'[11] This new power over nature, potentially unlimited, is one of the roots of magic and, therefore, of art. 'Making alike', the essential prerequisite of abstraction and of all conceptual thought, is itself a means of control : hence the belief common among primitive tribes that by naming an object or person they could gain mastery over it or him. In the same way, visual reproduction of, say, an animal was a means of ensuring success in the essential work of hunting.

Language itself is a product of the relationships born of work-processes : Fischer writes, 'Only in work and through work do living beings have much to say to each other. Language came into being together with tools.'[12] Language was not initially individual self-expression so much as communication, and only arose when the *need* was there. The growth of a working community is accompanied by signs for collective activity; the origins of poetry and music may then lie in the rhythms of working processes themselves. The sign, being connected with a specific activity, functioned as a stimulus and an organizing force within the collective, and it bound men together because they all gave the same meaning to it. The obvious example is the unison chant or work-song, supporting the rhythms of collective labour where close co-operation is all-important. So that even music, the very art-medium Huizinga saw as being the most 'pure' of vulgar use-value may originally be deeply implicated in the basic productive work of the community. A sign or means of expression in this way, as well as in the 'magical' function of naming or reproducing, can become a tool, a means towards man's purposive control over nature. Both the first tool-maker and the first name-giver were the founders of art, in the period preceding the division of 'culture' into fragmented functions. Fischer summarizes the point as follows :

The first organizer who synchronized the working process by means of a rhythmic chant and so increased the collective strength of man was a prophet in art. The first hunter who disguised himself as an animal and by means of this identification with his prey increased the yield of the hunt, the first stone-age man who marked a tool or a weapon by a special notch or ornament, the first chieftain who stretched an animal's skin over a lump of rock or the stump of a tree in order to attract animals of the same kind – all these were the forefathers of art.[13]

Fischer's emphasis here may appear simplistic and one-sided, perhaps, in its subordination of art to productivity; and we know that productivity – or efficiency – as a criterion is distrusted by many writers. Yet in his affirmation of the originally close unity of work and art, Fischer serves as a useful (and characteristically marxist) contrast with Huizinga's interpretation of culture.

Fragmentation had to come, of course, just as magic itself was differentiated into the 'separate' realms of science, religion and art. One of the results was the separation of art and work, more and more rigidly categorized and pigeon-holed as societies grow increasingly complex. The artist thus tended to become an isolated individuality, though always carrying with him a sense of tragic guilt at his own and society's fragmentation, the disruption of the old collective. The process by which man had affirmed his status as a *subject* by making nature an *object* for him, a place and instrument of work, becomes a potential source of anguish once the subject is cut off in any way from the community. The anguish of the artist reaches its height under the highly developed class system of capitalism. Whereas under the feudal structure the artist, like the artisan, had produced for a specific client, establishing thus a definite social relationship of a kind, the advanced form of capitalism turns everything into commodities produced for the open and anonymous market. As for production in general, so for art in particular; it, too, becomes a commodity created not for a patron but for a market of unknown consumers. The artist is 'freed' in one sense by the disappearance of patronage, but his freedom is that of a tragic solitude. So it is that art becomes an occupation that is at one and the same time 'half-romantic, half-commercial'. The phenomenon Marx described as commodity fetishism comes to apply in part to art as well, and is surely reinforced by the theory of art as pure play, as a self-justifying activity without need of external reference.[14]

Ironically, then, we might say that it is because art under capitalism was subject to the same law of commodity production as work in general that the separation between work and art was apparently finalized — with what we know to be stultifying results for both. It is in reaction against this tendency that another marxist, Garaudy, takes issue with Kant's famous definition of beauty as 'final purpose without final end'. He argues that such a notion has a doubly corrosive effect in that it 'impoverishes both the notion of labour by reducing it to the realization of strictly utilitarian and immediate ends, and that of art, which becomes a gratuitous activity and a form of play.'[15] Labour thus becomes servile whilst art is purely 'free' — a distinction that is one of the most currently accepted and most destructive aspects of our culture.

As I have expressed them, with inevitably a certain amount of over-simplification, the respective views of Huizinga and Fischer on this question represent the two poles of a possible synthesis. For, of course, play and work are by no means mutually exclusive concepts — within the act of work there *can* be (and in work at its best there *is*) room for a play-element. It is, after all, only the presence of freedom or 'play' (the two notions are closely linked) within the mechanism of necessity that allows the free expression of the workman's personality and produces that pleasure which Ruskin and others found so valuable. Perhaps, indeed, it is only through the fusion of work and play that art can be born at all.

As its association with freedom suggests, the notion of play *can* be allied with radical speculation on the values of our society. This it was already for Schiller at the end of the eighteenth century in his *Letters on the Aesthetic Education of Man* : there he presented the play-urge (*Spieltrieb*) as a means of synthesizing the urges towards sensuousness and towards form, the physical and the moral, and thus liberating man in the deepest sense and preparing him for life in a free society. Play, whose highest meaning we learn from art (hence the aesthetic education) is, therefore, for Schiller, man's means to fulfilment, to that supreme ethical state of 'lawfulness without law' of which Kant had spoken, the ideal of a non-repressive order. In Schiller's thesis Marcuse has seen the basis of 'a new mode of civilization', a far-reaching cultural revolution, 'a total revolution in the mode of perception and feeling.' Carrying as he does to an extreme conclusion that aversion for the repressive protestant ethic of work we have already noted, Marcuse turns eagerly to the ideal of play as taught by aesthetic beauty :

Once it has really gained ascendancy as a principle of civilization, the play impulse would literally transform the reality. Nature, the objective world, would then be experienced primarily neither as dominating man (as in primitive society) nor as being dominated by man (as in the established civilization), but rather as an object of 'contemplation'.[16]

The transformation of work into play — through the lesson of art — is then the key to a new and exciting form of life, and a new freedom.

The idea is far-reaching, and sounds exciting indeed — but it is very abstract in formulation, both in Schiller and Marcuse. In the former's argument this leads to dangerous parallels : Schiller quotes the Greeks as the most harmonious and aesthetic of all peoples, emphasizing that they exempted *their* gods from all seriousness and all work, transferring into Olympus their ideal for earthly existence.[17] But this shrugging off of the problem of work was, as we know, the result of a civilization based on slavery that relegated the status of work to its most debased level. Schiller appears to ignore this point. For an infinitely more concrete approach to the whole vital problem of the relation between work, play and art, we could do worse than turn again to William Morris and his ideal of a truly popular culture.

Morris was inspired again by Ruskin, who was convinced that the origin of the visual arts lay in manual work — 'A true artist is only a beautiful development of tailor or carpenter.'[18] Art can cover the spectrum from the simplest crafts to the sublimest sculpture : and it is a continuous, uninterrupted spectrum. The current split between art and labour Morris saw to be at the heart of the degradation produced by commercial society; and looking back as usual to the medieval craftsman as a contrast with our own age, he declared, 'Time was when everybody that made anything made a work of art besides a useful piece of goods, and it gave them pleasure to make it . . . The work which is the result of the division of labour, whatever else it can do, cannot produce art.'[19] As a consequence of that very division, art has, alas for our civilization, become the prerogative of the isolated and original creator-artist, who stands divorced from the everyday world of 'normal' men. What is perhaps Morris' most trenchant statement of this basic problem is embodied in his essay *The Lesser Arts*, published in *Hopes and Fears for Art*. The so-called 'lesser arts' interested Morris particularly, of course — he saw that especially the decorative arts had been debased by the modern separation between them on the one hand and so-called 'high art' on the other. The separation was ultimately damaging to both, driving the 'high' artist into cold isolation and aloofness and making his products external to the lives of men, 'dull adjuncts to unmeaning pomp, or ingenious toys for a few rich and idle men.'[20] The lesser arts, on the contrary, become trivial and mechanical, subject to the least and most transient whim of fashion. The only hope for our culture lies in the return to some kind of popular art (a development which Morris knew could only come about through radical, social and political change, through the overcoming of that capitalism that had done more than anything else to destroy the popular arts). The re-fusion of art and labour is the necessary antidote to the degradation of work in the present age, so that people might have pleasure in what they *must use*, and pleasure in what they *must make*. To be sure, there is work that is unutterably dull, especially today; but how much dullness could be mitigated!

> but now only let the arts which we are talking of beautify our labour, and be widely spread, intelligent, well understood both by the maker and user, let them grow in one word *popular*, and there will be pretty much an end of dull work and its wearing slavery; and no man will any longer have an excuse for talking about the curse of labour, no man will any longer have an excuse for avoiding the blessing of labour. I believe there is nothing that will aid the world's progress so much as the attainment of this.[21]

Far from being separate domains, art and labour belong together, and only an unnatural state of affairs has thrust them asunder; their true and potential unity Morris summarized tellingly in his celebrated definition — 'That thing which I understand by real art is the expression by man of his pleasure in labour.'[22] It is a measure of our civilization and the way it has treated *homo faber* that few people would now spontaneously think of art — or work — in this way. On the contrary, art is put on a pedestal where few can reach it, leaving what is for the most part elaborately transmitted rubbish as a poor replacement for a popular culture. And let us not be misled by the name of so-called 'pop art' which in fact is anything but popular. Warhol's soup cans are a glossy symptom of the profound alienation of art, and not of its integration. As Norman Birnbaum has put it, 'Pop art, a bastard offspring of the modern movement, makes no pretence of transcending the fragmentation and senselessness of perception in industrial culture. Pop art entails a simultaneous satiric rejection of popular culture and high culture.'[23] We have gone the way Morris feared we would, and against which he committed his whole life in the cause of what he called 'the Democracy of Art'. By that he did not just mean providing everyone with the means (education, for example) of appreciating art, so they could look up at what was on the pedestal with greater understanding and finesse. Not that at all; for Morris the aim of democratizing art goes much further, and involves making all workers into artists and creators, involves taking art from its exalted position and restoring its original affiliation with labour; it is equivalent, in short, to 'the ennobling of daily and common work'. For him, too, aesthetics was the ethics of the future.[24]

Entirely in harmony with Morris' general theory of art and its status is his thoroughly unromantic distrust of the whole concept of 'inspiration', a concept still widely prevalent today, and part indeed of our separation of the artist as a special and unique phenomenon with extra-natural modes of thought and feeling. It is part of the current adulation of the 'genius', in short, and ever since the Renaissance and the individualism it brought with it our culture has been much obsessed with the genius, especially in the culminating form of the isolated *artiste damné* of late romanticism. Such a figure stands at the opposite pole to the vision of community and integrated art, and it is in the light of this that Morris declared in *The Revival of Handicrafts* that there were *too many* geniuses around! On another occasion he stated with equal bluntness, 'That talk of inspiration is sheer nonsense, I may tell you that flat. There is no such thing. It's a mere matter of craftsmanship.'[25] He was talking of poetry, and maybe the remark is best understood with reference to his own verse, where more than anywhere else he reveals his limitations. For Morris was no Rimbaud, his prolifically produced poetry is lacking in density, and for much of the time one feels it *was* very much a craft to him, one whose rules could readily be studied and learned just as he learned handwriting as a fine art. Henry James was not far wrong when he claimed that poetry was a 'sub-trade' for Morris. His theory and practice of equating poetry and the crafts were, it seems, fine for the crafts, not so good for poetry!

This raises a serious question. If a balanced view of the ideal relationship between work and art entails on the one hand freeing work as far as possible from the rule of mechanical efficiency, whilst on the other hand seeing art in its potential relationship with purposive social activity, then we must acknowledge that this is a delicate balance indeed, and should beware of swinging to the philistine extreme of confining art to a narrowly utilitarian sphere. No-one could deny the impoverishment that would result from restricting art to the decorative arts and crafts, or from applying too rigorously or unimaginatively the criterion of social usefulness. If we take such an important, cultural movement as surrealism, for example : in one sense it appears as a form of gratuitous activity, narcissistic play within the individual world of dreams and fantasy, and, therefore, as far from the world of work and social utility as could be. And yet was it not also, at its best, a movement that aimed to reconstruct society in the image of its new discoveries about human relationships and desires, to produce a more harmonious and joyous community? So that even surrealism might be described as socially purposive in its own revolutionary way? But then it is true that the surrealists did not regard their activity as 'high art' or 'museum art', nor did they subscribe to the hallowed idea of the isolated, individual genius. One of the basic beliefs of that movement was that *all* men are potentially artists, poets — the true poet, as Éluard wrote, being simply 'he who inspires, rather than he who is inspired.' Surrealism, too, championed a form of 'aesthetic education', in the long-term interests of every one of us. For all men dream, all are potentially creative and free to body forth the rich patterns of desire within them. This is why for André Breton surrealism was, in a memorable phrase, 'the communism of genius'.

The example of music might also serve to warn us against a certain oversimplification we sometimes find in Morris; significantly it is a form of artistic expression for which he showed comparatively little interest. Whatever the social *origins* of music, it is clearly difficult to see most music today as obviously useful in any narrow sense. The ideal of bringing closer together again the realms of art and work should not tempt us to reject out of hand all manifestations of 'high art', or to apply a crass utilitarianism that runs counter to that very concept of creativity as a value in itself which we have evoked. Morris, no doubt, was polemically overstating his position when he provocatively declared, as the key to a future culture, 'Poetry goes with the hand-arts, I think, and like them has now become unreal : the arts have got to die, what is left of them, before they can be born again.'[26]

For Eric Gill, too, Art with a capital 'A' must disappear if a real culture is to be found. What are artists today, he writes in his essay on Ruskin, but eccentrics digging about in their own individual souls, with their eyes on the museum as their ultimate aim — 'That is what modern art works are for. The museum is their home.'[27] Work is no longer, as it should be, the means to culture. In this age when the ordinary needs of life are catered for by the elaborate machinery of commercial production, culture is regarded as a product and activity of leisure, something the BBC is there to provide. The result is, of course, an impoverishment, a sham culture and an enervated art. Gill saw that culture is a mere sham if it is reduced — as it so often is — to a mere facade, 'a sort of Gothic front put on an iron building — like the Tower Bridge — or a classical front put on a steel frame . . . Culture, if it is to be a real thing and a holy thing, must be the product of what we actually do for a living — not something added, like sugar on a pill.'[28]

Like Morris, Gill shows a high regard for what he calls the 'common arts', which have flourished, he claims, only in societies where 'business' was to some extent repressed or restricted, and where the premium was, therefore, on skill, not profit, such as Persia, Assyria, Egypt, or medieval Europe. And he dates the decay of true art in Europe (knowing full well that he is swimming against the tide of general opinion) from the Renaissance and the rise of the merchant class. What has ensued is first of all a divorce of personality from the everyday work of producing the necessities of life, and secondly an exaggerated importance placed on those arts which are not yet mechanized — the 'museum art' of today. It is only in 'slave architectures' (like that of the present day) that sculpture is *extra*, and, therefore, in a sense external to the building, and not a product of the natural exuberance of the workman. Unfortunately — and this is a grave reservation — we must note that some of those societies whose culture and art Gill admired were themselves highly repressive slave-civilizations.

Above all, Gill emulates Morris in reacting against the romantic concept of the isolated genius-artist : we are all artists. Constantly in his *Essays* he harks back to the phrase : 'the artist is not a special kind of man, but every man is a special kind of artist.' His distrust of the familiar view of art as something entirely divorced from work and concerned only with some kind of spontaneous self-expression is akin to Morris' feelings about 'inspiration'. There is, he claims in *Art in Education*, too much emphasis, especially in the art education of our schools, on self-expression. Not that there is no self-expression in art at all — obviously there is, and obviously it is important; but it is surely wrong to start from there, and not from the work-angle of art, from the craft that has to be learned before any truly formed self-expression can result. Self-expression is a by-product, rather than the be-all and end-all of artistic activity, it is 'only the accident, the inevitable accident and

accompaniment of all human work normally accomplished.' Standing
very much against the direction of modern, educational methods, Gill
argues that our teachers of art, by emphasizing this value of self-
expression, are wrong to make children self-conscious about their
activities (just as the introverted consciousness of being a self-expressive
individuality is the hallmark of the alienated, romantic artist, the genius
figure). What we must do is to teach our children the craft of drawing,
the craft of painting and, with due humility and perspective, to call such
occupations drawing and painting, not Art. 'Art much be abolished — it
must, it must, it must.'[29] This will not, of course, abolish self-expression,
which is after all an indispensable aspect of the fulfilling nature of true
work : it simply puts it into its proper perspective, and prevents it
becoming the sole aim of the alienated individual.

Not that Gill saw the changes that had to be brought about as residing
purely in the sphere of education. Artists must forget their isolation,
their 'specialness' and refinement and see that the future of art is linked
with the political aspiration for a different kind of society — they must
join the revolutionary workers, and with them strive to destroy the
present state of things.[30]

In a less apparently belligerent way, Arnold Wesker also sees art and
the whole question of a popular culture as being at the heart of the
struggle for a better society. The abjectness of what has replaced such
culture in the commercial, mass-media age is summed up by the awful
song 'I'll wait for you in the Heavens blue' that so appeals to the mother
in *Roots*. Such is the result of the tragic separation between work and
art. Art is elsewhere, for the privileged few. To restore it to the people
is a vital aspect of the desire to overcome fragmentation; hence Wesker's
own experiment with Centre 42, arising from Resolution 42 at the
1960 trades union congress, which recognized the importance of the
arts in the life of the community and expressed a wish to encourage the
participation of union members in all forms of cultural activity. This
was a rather less radical formulation than the old revolutionary-
syndicalist idea of creating an indigenous, working-class culture. Art,
Wesker thought, could have a regenerating role in society, and this he
implied when he stated that the essential struggle of the day is a
political one : not, though, of party against party (the old, destructive
and soulless wrangling that prevented the building of Adam's house) but
of the artist against the politician. That is one way of breaking the
incredible domination of the latter over our lives, together with his
henchmen, the civil servants and the bureaucrats. Such domination is

once again a feature of our lack of a working, living culture. When he
talks of the artist having this function as the enemy of political
wrangling he is clearly thinking of the artist who like himself has realized
that he must break out of the romantic individualism to which he is
invited by our society. This is why in *Fears of Fragmentation* he himself
constantly refers to playwriting as his 'craft', just as Morris did with
poetry, Gill with drawing and painting. Again and again we find statements such as : 'as an artist I can do no more than ply my craft . . .'[31]

In some arts, of course, it is easier to see a craft element than in
others. Least of all in literature, which makes Wesker's deliberate
emphasis especially significant; one way out for ethic-of-work writers
has been, as we know, to associate themselves with the actual crafts of
printing. Over and above this, however, the art of the theatre has never
lost a certain craft-affiliation due to the close involvement of carpenters,
painters, electricians in the actual business of putting on a play. It is not
uncommon to use the word 'craft' in relation to the literary arts in
order to denote the mastery and use of techniques, implying the parallel
with the acquisition of a trade in the more everyday world of work.
Hence, for example, the emphasis in the title of Percy Lubbock's famous
analysis of narrative techniques in the novel, *The Craft of Fiction.*

It is, though, easier to see the craft element and thereby the link
with work in the plastic arts, and especially in the often strenuous activity
of the sculptor. Gill points out that here, even despite the marked
isolation of the 'great artist' syndrome, physical labour is still honoured.
The artist must use his hands to work, even though he may no longer
grind the pigments or carve the stone himself. The link between the
traditional sculptor and the craft of stone-mason is obviously very
strong, and the same degree of sheer physical labour was often involved,
with allied if heightened skills. Now, with other materials often being
used as the basis of sculpture, an affiliation has grown up with different
work-trades, notably with metal-casting and most recently with welding,
that essential craft for many a modern sculptor. We have, then, the case
of the American sculptor, David Smith, who, though at times he defended
the notion of 'pure aesthetics', nevertheless felt a definite fellowship
with working men, having himself worked as logger, oilman and welder.
'Before I knew what art was I was an ironmonger,' he once declared, and
he continued to regard his studio as a factory and to belong to his craft
union, the United Steelworkers of America. He also hated museums,
and believed in a 'workingman's society in the future, and in that society
I hope to find a place.'[32] He was much preoccupied with the problem of

finding some sort of equilibrium between (for want of a better word) 'inspiration' and the physical labour inherent in a strenuous art-form, the problem of keeping 'physical labour in balance'. As a writer, Camus had a complementary preoccupation : even in his sedentary art-form he sought the same kind of balance with physical exertion, preferring to work standing at his desk rather than sitting, needing as he said to 'se dépenser', to exert himself and, presumably, maintain some union with the experience of labour.

For a true culture, however, the movement must be a two-way, reciprocal one. Not only must artists see themselves as workmen, but, infinitely more difficult in the modern conditions of labour, the worker must at least have the *opportunity* of seeing himself as an artist; not in his do-it-yourself leisure only, but ideally in his work itself. Art must no longer be regarded exclusively as a fruit of so-called 'free time', but that freedom (or play) which art implies must be imported into work, transforming its nature. Only then will art no longer belong to a select clique, only then will creative activity become an integral part of the community. Every man, as Wesker's Andy Cobham thought in *Their Very Own and Golden City*, should have a cathedral in his back garden — and not for weekend pottering only!

The same ideal was clearly that of Zola, and nowhere is this more evident than in the apotheosis of *Travail*. The integration into the City of Lange, the craftsman-artist, is symptomatic of a great change, whereby all men are becoming artists and where Morris' ideal of the democratic fusion of art and work even in the production of everyday objects is finally fulfilled. Hence in the last lyrical pages of the novel :

> Then arose the artists, a wider augmented beauty, become an immense universal blossoming where all could adorn and perfume themselves. There were no modest products, everyday objects, household utensils where art did not open out in charming fancies, in the form, the colour, the very expression.[33]

Lange had begun to show the way towards this new and yet old concept of art; now 'legions of artists arose, an artist was born in every industrial worker, the work in all the trades was now inseparable from the inner beauty, the great and simple beauty of the lived work of art [*l'œuvre vécue*] adapted to the service it was to perform.' Houses are now decorated with Lange's designs, beautifying the lives of the people; from the 'gros doigts d'ouvrier génial' of Lange a vital art and beauty have arisen, an authentically popular culture, 'an admirable art coming

from the people and returning to the people, all the original popular
force and grace.'[34] Lange has found his natural ground for creation in
the City of liberated work. Nor is he tempted at any stage to turn away
from the production of the smallest and humblest, the most useful
things – even apparently banal, kitchen articles are endowed with 'the
glorious charm of art.' A whole pleiade of artists have followed his
example, bringing thought and beauty even into 'the pots housewives
use for preserves and jams'![35] As in Morris' dreams, the aesthetic and
the utilitarian here merge together, art becomes an aspect of everyday
life – including the kitchen – and the museum is no longer the centre
of culture.

Fourier had once dreamed that the work of the kitchen in particular
would cease to be drudgery when cooking itself is raised to the level of
the highest art, with competitions for the best *pâtés* etc. In general
terms, the end of *Travail* owes everything to Fourier – the liberation
of the passions leads to receptivity to art as well as to the flowering
of creative impulses in all men. In Fourier's Harmony there were, let
us remember, to be thirty-seven million poets equal to Homer, thirty-
seven million playwrights of the status of Molière, and so on! His view
of work in Harmony as, in Riasanovsky's term, 'a web of passionately
pursued hobbies' welds a close link between utility and play, between
work and art.[36]

For ideally *homo faber* and *homo ludens* should not be separate
individuals or separate activities of the same individual. In such
separation lies fragmentation, anguish and a profound injustice. To fuse
back into one whole both labour and art, the work-element and the
play-element, should surely be one aim of social change. Admittedly
one of the most difficult. Work must no longer be placed in the
degrading category of sheer, unmitigated necessity and unfreedom
whilst 'play' and its concomitant freedom are restricted to non-
utilitarian, leisure pursuits. Garaudy neatly synthesizes the two aspects
of human activity in his idea of a 'double usefulness' :

> Art, the child of labour, is not necessarily something separate from
> the latter, and still less opposed to it. On the contrary it expresses
> the full significance of the object produced by labour; it expresses
> what I may call the 'double reading' of that meaning, since the
> object offers man a 'double usefulness' : its immediate, economic
> usefulness in as much as it is a product which is capable of satisfying
> a definite need, and its more generally 'human' (I would say

'spiritual') need . . .[37]

Art is potentially the fusion of play and work, of necessity and freedom, as Schiller saw; we are still grievously in need of an aesthetic education, but one that does not skip over the problem of day-to-day work, its nature and status. Culture must be the whole man, not just part of a man; it cannot, if it is to be really *alive*, exclude eight hours of his daily life. The general hostility that writers show towards fragmentation, the desire to weld the pieces back together, clearly presupposes an ideal of some kind of integral existence, preceding or lying beyond our pigeon-holed activities of today.

9 Towards organic living

There is no doubt that the notion of organic man, of integral existence is indeed a central preoccupation in the revolt against industrial culture, and is implicit in all that anti-mechanistic concern for roots we have examined. The organicist emphasis is one whose vogue we may trace from romanticism, from the idea of the identity of all things to be found in Novalis or Coleridge, in that typically romantic concept of the unity of opposites. We find it in Blake's opposition between 'Living Form' and 'Mathematic Form' and in Carlyle's notion of the organic that he inherited largely from Goethe and the German romantics. Hatred of the machine and the plea for organic modes of life naturally go together, and so it is in many writers; but we can carry the argument further. J. C. Sherburne rightly begins his stimulating study of Ruskin by pointing out the organic nature of that writer's thought, his ability to see all things in relation. The same, we may add is true of others, of Péguy for instance, or Morris. What is noticeable is that any of these can begin an essay on any topic and turn it quite naturally into any other subject that lies within the circle of their preoccupations. They manifestly see all aspects of life as interlinked and gravitating always around the same, central issues. In general, this lends extraordinary force to their organicist vision.

That aspect of organicist thought that concerns us most directly here falls into two main emphases that are intertwined in the work of many writers. First of all, the ideal of integrated, non-fragmented life for the individual, in which work can make further contact with certain basic or elemental realities; and secondly, the ideal of a true community and a true culture, whether projected into the future or placed in the past. The former ideal must have been at the back of Marx's mind when he wrote of the effects of industrial fragmentation :

> Even the division of labour in society at large entails some crippling both of mind and body. Since, however, the manufacturing period carries this social division of the branches of labour much further, and in addition, thanks to its particular method of the division of labour, cuts at the very roots of the individual's life, it is in this period that industrial pathology (to which manufacture gives the impetus) becomes conspicuous.[1]

And he is touching on the second aspect when he remarks that one far-reaching cause of fragmentation lies in the cleavage between town and country that is largely a product of industrial civilization. Engels has much to say on the dissolution of organic community in his study of the Manchester working class : urban industrial conditions herd men together as never before, in an unprecedented, physical promiscuity, but, in fact, such men are merely juxtaposed in crowded isolation, they are a collection of individuals and emphatically not a community. 'The dissolution of mankind into monads, of which each one has a separate principle, the world of atoms, is here carried out to its utmost extreme.'[2] The disappearance of community means necessarily the disappearance of popular culture : hence the regret expressed by a writer such as Péguy, evoking in typical vein the once-rooted culture of that 'past' of his : it will never be known, he writes, how far the balance of soul of that people went, for 'such finesse, such a profound culture will never recur again.'[3]

The Expressionist desire for *Gemeinschaft*, true community, as distinct from that merely political unit *Gesellschaft* is paralleled by William Morris' plea for 'fellowship' in *The Dream of John Ball*; and both ideas presuppose the possibility of an organic society and an organic culture.

Few writers have spoken more sensitively of this ideal than Simone Weil. She presents *enracinement* as the most vital need of the human spirit, and to be rooted in a historical continuum implies for her to be rooted in a living community. 'A human being has roots by his real, active and natural participation in the life of a collectivity that keeps alive certain treasures of the past and certain premonitions of the future.'[4] It is dangerous, she claims, for societies to be turned exclusively towards the future : the future is what we give, what we contribute, but to give we must first possess, and according to Weil we have nothing else, no other life or 'sap' but that we have inherited from the past and which we have assimilated, digested and recreated for ourselves. The past is our vitality. It is in such terms that she speculates on the nature of certain developments in post-revolutionary Russia : are they a further instance of *déracinement*, or are they in fact 'the profound life of the people, welling up out of the depth of ages, having remained underground, almost intact?'[5] For her, this was a vital question that must be asked of any social change. Not that she is hostile to change as such; but she does insist that a human community is not just an arbitrary institution but a growing organism, comparable for the author of *L'Enracinement* to a field of growing corn. Just as the corn-field is food for physical man, so the collectivity, be it family, homeland or whatever, is ideally of value as rooted nourishment for the human spirit.

Such a community would, of course, be a working community, and at the most instinctual level man can only be integrated into it if the collective life and work are founded on established and 'natural' rhythms. With this the sociologist, Friedmann, concurs, and the notion of integration through rhythms is an essential part of his exposition of organic life in the *milieu naturel*, some aspects of which we have had cause to look at already. The natural work-environment is characterized by a close interpenetration of man and nature : there the worker, rather than struggling against nature, works with it and is penetrated by its rhythms, which have been his from birth onwards. Friedmann refers us to the artisanal Middle Ages, where what machines there are are still activated by human energy (the potter's wheel) or by the power of natural, elemental phenomena such as wind or river — 'rhythm is everywhere in daily life, and plays an incomparable role.'[6] Some cultures have shown more consciousness of the importance of rhythms than our own : hence the principle of Hatha Yoga, that any activity not in harmony with one's 'vital personal rhythm' can give rise to grave disturbances of the organism. In the natural milieu the rhythms of work — part biological, part sociological — were truly human, having evolved out of centuries of craft traditions : 'Thus all the life of man, in the natural environment, and in particular the whole of his professional existence, is, at it were, internally woven from rhythms, slowly formed and fixed, circulating from generation to generation in the society of which they are so intimately a part.'[7] Each craft had its own rhythms, passed on often with the consecration of prior secrecy and the sense of a special 'revelation'; whereas those who worked on the land experienced in their labour a close relationship with the seasonal rhythms and cycles of the natural world. This organic 'oneness with nature' has been eloquently described by Jean Giono, as we may see from his exaltation of elemental life close to the soil in *L'Eau vive* :

> Whenever one approaches a man of the earth, there is in his gaze, in his gestures, in the slow movement of his step, the undulation of his shoulders, a magnetic force that strikes you right in the hollow of the chest. Everything is precise about them, Everything is commensurate with the present moment. Everything resides in gaze, gesture and movement. That is because the man who is before you hunts, fishes, ploughs, cultivates the trees, cuts the corn, waters the grass, sweats beneath the sun, toils in the earth, walks with head bowed in the wind. It is ultimately and quite simply because he lives his normal life, the life for which he and we are born. A dark force rises from the earth, fills such men and teaches them. The weight of the sky is there on their shoulders with its equilibrium. Rain, wind and storm sing in their ears the sacred teachings. Around them, the intertwining rivers and streams measure the rhythm of their step.[8]

Given this rhythmic integration, we should not be surprised if men who lived in this traditional way had a different experience of the human reality of *time*, for the attitude to time changes as a civilization changes. Clocks, it seems, were rare in Europe up to the end of the sixteenth century, and time was measured rather by reference to natural phenomena, to the flight or song of a bird, the growing of plants, etc. There is no greater contrast with this rooted situation than the uniform motion of the modern production-line, always at the behest of a type of 'work-study' that is more concerned with getting things done faster than in a more rewarding way. The production-line imposes a mechanical and totally uniform division of the working day, instead of the variable, flexible and organic rhythms of more traditional forms of labour. The industrial phenomenon of clock-watching is an evitable result and a symptom of the replacement of internal time by an external and inexorable 'clock-time'. We are time-haunted creatures, but the time that haunts us now is not our own. As Simone Weil remarked, 'There is a certain relationship with time that is suitable for inert things, and quite another for thinking creatures. We are wrong to confuse them.' That uniformity that results from the movement of clocks rather than constellations 'produces a form of time where man can neither dwell nor breathe' ['un temps inhabitable à l'homme, irrespirable'].[9] There is, she claims, such a thing as a natural rhythm of work, but in the industrial world one only ever suspects its existence if the mechanical routines somehow break down, as they did in the factory occupations of 1936. In these sit-ins and work-ins she saw what seemed at times a return to a natural and organic relationship with work and, therefore, with life. It was something that gave her hope in her passionate concern to establish a true and authentically human community.

Evidently, to move to such a community from the present denaturalized state of uprootedness would represent, were it possible, nothing short of a cultural revolution; something like that 'integral revolution' proposed by Proudhon in a letter to Michelet, something that goes beyond institutional change : 'The only way out is by an integral revolution in men's ideas and hearts.'[10] One essential element of this great change is that reintegration which so many have looked forward to, whereby intellectual and worker might be welded back into one whole, complete person; when these two faculties and activities of man, which in our pseudo-culture often seem alien to each other, are united in one activity. It is the revolution that Bakunin looked forward to : 'When the man of science works and the man of work thinks, free and intelligent work will be regarded as the crowning glory of humanity, as the basis of its dignity . . . and humanity will be constituted.'[11] It was a theme, too, of Kropotkin's thought, especially in *Fields, Factories and Workshops* : the painter, for example, must experience nature as a peasant before he can begin to paint it properly; once he has done so, his response will be that of a total and integrated being. In general we may say that the anarchist revolt — like any movement that rejects the alienated condition of man in the industrial world — turns on a deep-rooted aspiration for organic life. This emerges clearly in the 'intellectual anarchism' of a writer like Herbert Read, who in his *Anarchy and Order* writes of the great changes that would have to be wrought in society before we could discover, or rather rediscover, a genuine, popular culture, a culture such as we have sacrificed to the principle of mass-production. 'There will be no integral style such as prevailed in all civilizations down to the eighteenth century until we advance beyond mechanization, to rediscover the secret of organic living.'[12] For Read, the modern artist is a tragic survivor from that 'organic living', and by that token he is potentially the pioneer of a new, recreated humanism, of that *renaissance* which Camus liked to evoke. For Camus, the creative artist (and for the time being, alas, he alone) has the key to unity, whilst society around him is bent on totality : the former is an organic principle, the latter is merely mechanical and so lifeless and inhuman. It is significant that we find Jünger in *The Worker* standing at the antithesis of our movement in this respect as in so many others. He declares and accepts that the hallowed and for him outworn distinction between organic and mechanical forces is destined to disappear for good in the coming world of total, mechanical efficiency. In the same way, the distinction between town (the technical milieu) and country (the repository of natural rhythms and organic modes of being) is condemned by Jünger as pure 'romanticism', 'as invalid as the difference between the organic and the mechanical world', and thereby doomed to obliteration.[13] Jünger's universe is a tangible representation of what Camus means by 'totality' — the subordination of life to uniform and abstract principles.

The clash between mechanical and organic is at the heart of Lawrence's vision of the world, and again we must return to his portrayal of that clash in *Women in Love*. There he builds up the antithesis with an insistent repetition such as Péguy, too, had exploited :

> It was the first great step in undoing, the first great phase of chaos, the substitution of the mechanical principle for the organic, the destruction of the organic unity, and the subordination of every organic unit to the great mechanical purpose. It was pure organic disintegration and pure mechanical organization.[14]

The system of mechanical order and repetition established by Gerald Crich implies the uprooting of the miners involved, as we know; but even though their work is largely mechanical, and though Gudrun walking past them in the evening senses something 'half-automatized' about them, they nonetheless retain from the very physical nature of their work a sense of gravity, of heavy human reality. This at least is how it strikes the intellectual Gudrun :

> Miners were already cleaned, were sitting on their heels, with their backs near the walls, talking and silent in pure physical well-being, tired, and taking physical rest. Their voices sounded out with strong intonation, and the broad intonation was curiously caressing to the blood. It seemed to envelop Gudrun in a labourer's caress, there was in the whole atmosphere a resonance of physical men, a glamorous thickness of labour and maleness, surcharged in the air.[15]

Of course, this exercise and involvement of physical being was of overwhelming importance for Lawrence, and he saw it as being threatened, undermined by scientific progress which produces an estrangement from the physical, an alienation from our own physical being. Hence the modern hatred for physical labour, which reveals that being to us intimately — or should! Such is his argument in the curious essay *Men must work and women as well*, where he evokes the 'plan of the universe laid down by the great magnates of industry like Mr Ford', a plan consisting in the interposition of mechanisms between man and nature, between man and his own physical being. This is for him the origin of the phenomenon of modern culture whereby 'for some mysterious or obvious reason, the modern woman and the modern man hate physical work.' And he goes on : 'One of the greatest changes that has taken place in man and woman is this revulsion from physical effort, physical labour and physical contact, which has taken place within the last thirty years.'[16] It is all part of the shamefaced attempt to abstract, to shuffle off the physical in work and relationships. The trend of civilization is towards ever greater separateness, thought Lawrence; separateness first of all of the different aspects and faculties of man, and of men and women among themselves. It is, once again, the death of the organic in its two principal aspects.

Of the second kind of separation, Lawrence had something to say in the original draft of *Lady Chatterley's Lover*. It is the cold intellect coupled with addiction to the mechanical, as represented by Clifford, that prevents contact and community, breeds egotism and isolation. In the light of this distrust of the intellect, the 'communism' of gamekeeper, Parkin, is seen as possibly being of value. For it is a force that goes far beyond abstractions and 'isms', as the artist, Duncan, realizes when he sees in Parkin 'a glow of soft, human power which made Duncan suddenly see democracy in a new light, man kindled to this glow of human beauty and awareness, opened glowing to another sort of contact.'[17] Perhaps, he reflects, if the present, mechanical system were smashed a new relationship between men might emerge, one that would go beyond money or the ballot-box. 'What we want is a flow of life from one to another — to release some natural flow in us that urges to be released.'[18] There is a similar sentiment in the final version of the novel, where Lawrence looks forward to the time when people will cease to be just 'cerebrating makeshifts, mechanical and intellectual experiments', and when we can perhaps at last get 'a democracy of touch, instead of a democracy of pocket.'[19] Mellors' letter at the end of the book summarizes the ideal of a living and physical community :

> They ought to learn to be naked and handsome, and to sing in a mass and dance the old group dances, and carve the stools they sit on, and embroider their own emblems. Then they wouldn't need money. And that's the only way to solve the industrial problem : train the people to be able to live, and live in handsomeness, without needing to spend.[20]

What Lawrence is suggesting in these various works, though one may have serious reservations about the implications of his anti-intellectualism and the whole nostalgia for 'the half-dreamy warmth of unawakened life', finds some (paradoxically) intellectualized echoes in Marcuse's Freudian critique of modern, industrial work and culture. Such work, he argues, by its routine and mechanical nature, tends to the almost total exclusion of libidinal relations from this important sphere of life. Alienation, the negation of the pleasure-principle in favour of a non-libidinal reality principle, means in effect that the body is de-sexualized for its working period. Thus, in Freud's analysis, the 'reproductive' world of Prometheus is incompatible with Pandora, the female principle of libidinal fulfilment who appears as a disruptive curse : 'The beauty of the woman, and the happiness she promises, are fatal in the work-world of civilization.'[21] As a result, all-embracing Eros is replaced by a narrow sexuality that characterizes our society; the vogue of pornography (sexuality at its narrowest, its most genital) could then be seen as an offshoot of the alienation of work. Instinctual gratification, being removed from the sphere of labour, takes refuge in the single realm of genital sexuality, and this implies a division within man and a fragmentation of his organic being. The libido is limited spatially to one part of the body and temporally to 'leisure' time outside work; and it is regret over this disruption that produces the nostalgia we have seen so often. It is not a nostalgia that Marcuse can accept wholesale, but he certainly sees the reason for it :

> This is the kernel of truth in the romantic contrast between the modern traveler and the wandering poet or artisan, between assembly line and handicraft, town and city, factory-produced bread and the home-made loaf, the sailboat and the outboard motor, etc. True, this romantic pre-technical world was permeated with misery, toil and filth, and these in turn were the background of all pleasure and joy. Still, there was a 'landscape', a medium of libidinal experience

which no longer exists.[22]

If we are to go beyond the present impoverishment and fragmentation of our lives, it must be towards what Marcuse calls 'an enlarged order of libidinal relations', which is community. Were that cultural revolution to take place, organic living would again become possible, the physical and the spiritual would cease to be separate spheres, and work would become part of life — 'the free development of transformed libido within transformed institutions, whilst eroticizing previously tabooed zones, time and relations, would *minimize* the manifestations of *mere* sexuality by integrating them into a far larger order, including the order of work.'[23]

Marcuse is here formulating notions glimpsed and hinted at in one way or another by many writers. In addition to Lawrence we could cite Eric Gill and his attack on the Leisure State as a heresy of a fundamentally manichean nature : 'It is the notion that matter is essentially evil and therefore work essentially degrading . . . that is the basis of our Leisure State — the release of man from his entanglement with matter.'[24] Needless to say, this 'release' is really seen as an impoverishment and an aspect of disintegration.

All this Morris had stressed before Lawrence or Gill. In his essay *How We Live and How We Might Live* (in *Signs of Change*, 1888) he pointed out forcefully that our false civilization has denied us — by its very mechanicalness — the organic experience of physical existence that is our natural right. For all living things derive vital pleasure from the exercise of energy, and good work is more than just the fruitful channelling of that energy, it is the union of body and mind. 'To feel mere life a pleasure; to enjoy the moving one's limbs and exercising one's bodily powers; to play, as it were, with sun and wind and rain; to rejoice in satisfying the due bodily appetites of a human animal without fear of degradation or sense of wrong-doing.'[25] The mechanical work of today cannot, however, give us any such pleasure or health. By way of contrast, the health, beauty and amazing youthfulness of the figures who people the utopia of *News* must no doubt be attributed to the fact that they lead integrated lives in which physical labour is given its due and honourable role, and where the cyclical rhythms of the seasons, as well as the equally natural rhythms of each working day, are spontaneously observed and followed. This instead of the iron rule of the clock, that inhuman mechanism so conspicuously absent from the minds of the happy people of this future world. Time is not an obsession for them as it is in the modern factory, although the harvest comes as ever at its due season and life organizes itself around such pivotal points of the year. In the same way, that twenty-first-century world has a timeless flavour, anarchronistic to a deliberately high degree. History is no longer seen as a becoming but as a recurrent cycle of natural phenomena; it is stripped of its headlong dynamism. It is not, indeed, a Hegelian view of history to which Morris subscribes, any more than it is one of straight-line constant progress — like Sorel or Péguy, his view is nearer to the cyclical philosophy of history of Vico. The essential development is that from 'mechanic' to 'organic' society.

No such development can take place, of course, unless work can be seen, not as a means of disintegration, but as the natural centre of a whole and integrated existence; revision of the current debased notions of work is to lead the way to a new man. This is the extent of the 'cultural revolution' proposed, based though it may be on nostalgia for the past. So Morris saw the age of the artisan as one founded on the rule of natural rhythms, and the work is produced as involving the whole man. Work is this, ideally — the complete integration of a man :

> Under this sytem of handiwork no great pressure of speed was put upon a man's work, but he was allowed to carry it through leisurely and thoughtfully; it used the whole of a man for the production of a piece of goods, and not small portions of many men; it developed the workman's whole intelligence according to his capacity, instead of concentrating his energy on one-sided dealing with a trifling piece of work.[26]

In fulfilling this integrating function, work fuses with art. It is only, as we know, through the merging of art and work that organic and integral existence can be possible, exercising *all* the faculties of man simultaneously. Such a merging, it is often thought, was once achieved by architecture, and what Morris describes as the loss of architecture in the modern age is linked by him with the transference — and it reads prophetically as an indictment of the inorganic universe of Jünger or the Futurists — the 'transference of the interest of civilized man from the development of the human and intellectual energies of the race to the development of its mechanical energies.'[27] There is such a thing as 'organic architecture', and when Morris uses the phrase it is not surprisingly in his essay on Gothic, contrasted with the rootless, inorganic equivalent of our own times, 'the horrible and restless nightmare of modern engineering.'[28] The work involved in this 'nightmare' is not the

kind to make men whole again; for wholeness is unthinkable without
the presence of art in all things, in all realms of life. Of the mechanized
labour of his age, he writes, 'And this toil degrades them into less than
men : and they will some day come to know it, and cry out to be made
men again, and art only can do it, and redeem them from this slavery.'[29]

This cry : 'to be made men again' is closely akin to that which
resounds in the work of Kaiser and other Expressionists. We have seen
how emphatic was his play *Gas* in its indictment of the fragmentation
of man in modern industrial processes. Kaiser's desperate plea throughout
is for the advent of the *Mensch*, the complete man; as his hero tries to
convince the workers, 'You are men . . . Multifariousness flowing from
you to each around you. No-one is a part . . . each individual complete
in the community . . . Gather yourselves out of dispersal − and cure
yourselves of all injury . . . become human beings [*Menschen*]!! Human
beings in unity and fullness you can be tomorrow!'[30] And later the
cause of the whole man is pleaded again − 'When will he overcome the
curse − and fulfil the new creation he destroyed : − the human being?'[31]
The problem is conceptualized in the same author's *Der kommende
Mensch* of 1922, where, like Morris, Kaiser lays great faith in art as the
means to reintegration. It is not a means that present, economic reality
can provide − quite the contrary : 'we know today that a man can
maintain himself economically with the cultivation of only one of his
innumerable possibilities.' The exaggeration of one single capacity of
man at the expense of all the others is the 'deadly sin' of the age :

> It turns against the wholeness of man and truncates universality
> into speciality. Man is simply a hand or a foot or a head − yet he
> *needs* only a head or an eye to earn his living in this age! Man is
> made of head and brain and heart and blood. The man who only
> writes and interprets poetry fails to achieve his totality just as much
> as the worker who does nothing but move his piece of machinery by
> the pressure of a limb.[32]

Clearly he believes that art as an *isolated* activity is not enough to
restore unity, but only in so far as it becomes part of life; yet at the
moment the only testimony to the synthesizing power of the fully
rounded human being is art − 'Poetry proclaims the synthesis : *Mensch*!'[33]
As for Camus, so for Kaiser − art today is the premonition of a genuine
culture, it is not *in itself* that culture. Art, work and life must first
become inseparable, synonymous. And we are very far from that.

For work must become a part of life, not an antithesis to life, or a temporary divorce from life, as it so often appears. As Zola's hero says in *Travail*, 'L'œuvre est la vie même, il faut la vivre jusqu'au bout.'[34] The apprentice workshops in that novel are designed to promote that essential aspect of the ethic of work, and the children attend them in their breaks from school, mixing work with education and life from the beginning. For 'a happy life is made up of the happy use of every hour, with the whole being set to work, using all his physical and intellectual energies to live logically, normally, for the whole of his life.'[35] It is a clear expression of Zola's faith in integral existence – and the role work must play in that existence. The habit of holding wedding celebrations, christenings, etc., in the factory of *Travail* : what is that but a vivid (if sometimes ludicrous) illustration of the desire to integrate work and life even in the most intimate moments? Simone Weil is later to write that the worker will emerge from his 'exile' from true life only when he comes to feel 'at home' in his place of work; and in this she is echoing Péguy's nostalgia for a time when there was *not* today's radical distinction between home and workshop, when man was not divided between two totally different spheres of life, two antithetical activities and sets of values.

> All men converged in this honour. A decency, and a finesse in language. A respect of the home . . . A ceremony that was, so to speak, constant. Moreover the home was still often merged with the workshop, and the honour of the home and the honour of the workshop were the same honour.[36]

This explains much of the idyllic quality of Philippe's *Charles Blanchard*, where house and workshop are one, and where the artisan's stock of carved clogs spills over into the living quarters without there being any sense of intrusion or hiatus. There is no question here of the craftsman's wife having to declare, as in the case of the industrial worker's wife whom we quoted in an earlier chapter, that she did not know what her husband did every day 'up at the plant'. Nor is there any question of that peculiarly modern form of fragmentation, commuting, which sharply cuts work and home life into entirely separate spheres. It is interesting that the historians P. Laslett and E. P. Thompson, who as we know view the Industrial Revolution in such very different ways, both agree on the alienation produced by the disappearance of the cottage and peasant economy. Laslett writes, 'Time was when the whole of life went forward in the family, in a circle of loved, familiar faces, known and fondled objects, all to human size. That time has gone for

ever. It makes us very different from our ancestors.'[37] Thompson, for
his part, stresses the role played in work at home by 'inner whims and
compulsions' as opposed to the external discipline of the factory. 'Each
stage in industrial differentiation and specialization struck also at the
family economy, disturbing customary relations between man and wife,
parents and children, and differentiating more sharply between "work"
and "life".'[38]

The modern situation is based on a complete and abnormal division
that can be inimical to the moral well-being of the worker; it can, indeed
undermine his very sense of reality. Such is the situation analysed by an
American specialist in this field, Peter Berger (*The Human Shape of
Work*), and his comments do much to validate the concern shown by
more 'literary' figures :

> The typical and statistically normal state of affairs in an industrial
> society is that people do not work where they carry on their private
> lives. The two spheres are socially and geographically separate. And
> since it is in the latter that people typically and normally locate
> their essential activities, one can say even more simply that they do
> not live where they work. 'Real life' and one's 'authentic self' are
> supposed to be centred in the private sphere. Life at work then tends
> to take on the character of pseudo-reality and pseudo-identity.[39]

It is obvious that when Berger uses the word 'normally' it is in a
purely statistical and descriptive sense, not in a moral or normative one.
For, taking the latter meaning, what could be less 'normal', less natural
than to split human activity into distinct and hermetic spheres? The
separation of work from home is part of the modern elimination of
libidinal relations from the sphere of labour. The apprehension of this
truth is central to Wesker's Trilogy : it appears in Ada's impassioned
outburst in *Chicken Soup with Barley* where she announces that she and
Dave plan to get out of London so that they can found their socialism,
live their socialism as an integrated life, as an organic unity; and this
turns on the vital subject we are considering — 'your work and your life
should be part of one existence, not something hacked about by a bus
queue and office hours. A man should see, know and love his job. Don't
you want to feel your life?'[40] The notion of the organic is evidently
important to Wesker, as we might expect of the author of *Fears of
Fragmentation*. In the final part of the Trilogy, we find that Dave's
workshop is next door to the house, and his life is, by that token, not
split in two, not fragmented. The members of his family, he senses,

must not be strangers to him, strangers to his work, and his relationship with them must be a total, inclusive one, it must involve his work-life as well. He shows his awareness of the importance of this when he analyses his reasons for moving at the beginning of the play : 'There I shall work and here, ten yards from me, where I can see and hear them, will be my family. And they will share in my work and I shall share in their lives.'[41] That is what integrated living is all about − it is, as Dave reiterates, an attempt to *live* socialism, a socialism that is classical in Péguy's sense in that it is essentially to do with work, i.e. it accords work a role in life itself, and makes it creative of relationships : 'we enjoy our work, we like ourselves.'[42]

The critic, Ronald Bryden, has emphasized, in an introduction to *Their Very Own and Golden City*, the importance of this theme of organic living, both for the work of Wesker in particular and for our civilization in general. 'Wasn't it Wesker, more than any other play-wright of his generation, who taught us how everything counts and hangs together in questions of culture, the quality of living? That the way you fry chips and make tea is connected with the sort of moral decisions you take?'[43] It is a lesson we urgently need. The way Dave and Ada bring up their son, Danny, is symptomatic of this belief : he is encouraged to see the things around him, to sense them wholly and not just take them for granted. One of their favourite games consists of making him describe things − hedges, for example − in a tangible, non-stereotyped way, in terms of colours, textures, and so on. The object is to make him really and wholly alive, and nearer to what Ernst Toller described as 'the deep springs of instinctively felt life' (which is what the weavers in *The Machine-Wreckers* complained they were deprived of in their regimented and mechanical work). Danny's parents are anxious that he should become what Ada calls 'a real human being'.[44]

It is the same plea that we have seen throughout − the plea for a total, integrated and rounded human being, the *Mensch* of Expression-ism, the organic being of Lawrence, the 'men again' of William Morris. It is a plea for the new man, who is yet really a projection of the *old* man − the pre-industrial artisan figure as fondly imagined by writers.

There are, then, two essential features of the concern for 'organic living' : one implying the integral development of the individual, his non-fragmented existence as a unique, creative and sentient human being for whom work and 'personal life' are inseparable; and the other concerned with his ideally rooted situation in an organic community. It is this latter aspiration that perhaps most clearly explains the historical nostalgia shown by so many for certain aspects of feudal society. And it is true that in some respects medieval society, for all its manifest oppressions and injustices, was more of an organic unit than anything seen since, with its reciprocity of relationships and obligations that implicated the whole human being.

Nevertheless, the tendency to look back can have its dangers, and it is when the insistence on organic community (not only in the feudal image) eclipses the notion of a full development of the personality — whereas the two aspects should be inseparable and undivided — that disturbing parallels begin to suggest themselves.

10 Dangers & contradictions

It is unfortunate that the cult of the organic — apparently so sane and attractive in many respects — can evoke more sinister spectres. And it is this that leads us necessarily to question the whole ethic-of-work revolt, and to ask : does it not involve contradictions and even grave dangers?

Nostalgia for the organic is not, alas, without an unfortunate and ominous ring it has acquired from certain political figures, movements and writers; when advocated only in terms of the collectivity without a corresponding concern for the integral life of the individual, it can give rise to the idea of the fascist corporate State. So we find that in his breakdown of the factors that characterize fascist movements and ideologies, John Weiss includes among others not only the 'idealization of "manly" (usually peasant or village) virtues', but also 'organicist conceptions of community'.[1] This is enough to make us begin to ask whether the ethic of work might not have played into the hands of fascism. Certainly it is easy for the notion of the organic society to be used to propose a rigid hierarchy of co-operative elements unequal among themselves.

Some of the evidence is disturbing indeed : Lawrence's search for the organic was to lead him on to the distasteful, all-male, fascistic ethos of *The Plumed Serpent*, where he shows how dangerous his exaltation of the instinctual can be when it is translated into political terms. Stridency and hysteria all too often await the lone prophet, and for Lawrence this meant losing sight of that counter-balancing respect for the individual as a whole and rounded person. When this happens,

Lawrence is not only at his most unacceptable in ideological terms, but also at his worst as a novelist.

Lawrence was no systematic thinker, and his views might be said to cover the spectrum from anarchism to fascism, though revolving always around his hatred of current, industrial democracy. Equality he saw as a mechanical thing and a symptom of the modern disintegration, whereas the organic view implied hierarchy. As he wrote to Bertrand Russell, 'The thing must culminate in one real head, as every organic thing must . . .'[2] There was once, he believed, a sort of 'blood connection' holding society together, binding one class to another, the peasantry to the squire. This has been broken by the modern consciousness : class-consciousness in particular, whose growth 'was only a sign that the old togetherness, the old blood-warmth has collapsed.'[3] This idea leads Lawrence along the dangerous path to a hierarchical system at times reminiscent of H. G. Wells. He was convinced that there must be 'an aristocracy of people who have wisdom', and above them a single authority — a Kaiser rather than an elected President.[4] Ironically, Lawrence does not seem to see that his hierarchy — like that of Wells — could only increase the fragmentation he so bitterly criticized, splitting apart labour and thought once and for all, and in fact producing the very situation he condemned in Gerald Crich's Jünger-world. In the largely political novel *Kangaroo* he distinguishes between the 'irresponsible' and the 'responsible', between the proletariat and the ruling class. It is true that his main character, Somers, does in that same novel hold back from the fascistic movement of the Diggers, but his sympathies lie largely with its principles. He muses on

> The mystery of lordship. The mystery of innate, natural, sacred priority. The other mystic relationship between men, which democracy and equality try to deny and obliterate. Not any arbitrary caste or birth aristocracy. But the mystic recognition of difference and innate priority, the joy of obedience and the sacred responsibility of authority.[5]

The irrationalism of this view of society then leads Lawrence into an affinity with what is perhaps the darkest side of the dark doctrine of fascism when, through Somers, he exalts the ritual of blood-sacrifice which becomes 'The ritual of supreme responsibility, and offering. Sacrifice to the dark God, and to the men in whom the dark God is manifest. Sacrifice to the strong, not to the weak. In awe, not in dribbling love. The communion in power, the assumption into glory.'[6]

The same sinister ritual is to play its part in the Mexico of *The Plumed Serpent* and the story *The Woman Who Rode Away* : there Lawrence preaches the Nietzschean lesson of submission to the strong – the strong individual, the strong race. The collectivity should be a sense of joy in power, concentrated in a hero-figure, a leader; and, most dangerous of all, this should represent a 'union in the unconsciousness'.[7] Hence the importance of ritual. And in unconsciousness there is hierarchy : 'For the mass of people knowledge *must* be symbolical, mystical, dynamic. This means you must have a higher, responsible, conscious class : and then in varying degrees the lower classes, varying in their degrees of consciousness.'[8]

This idea immediately evokes Sorel and his notion of the myth, which is also 'symbolical' and 'dynamic' knowledge – and again the irrationalism implies hierarchy, for if the majority are motivated and mobilized by myth, there is also a minority, no doubt, who create and control the myth. Both Sorel and Péguy were described as forerunners and influences by Mussolini, and not entirely without cause – though as in the case of Lawrence neither could simply be called fascist without distortion, without an unfair selection of certain of their writings to the exclusion of the rest. In Péguy's case, this would entail stressing the nationalistic and hierarchical aspects of his organicist vision whilst ignoring the concern for social justice and for the development of individual potential, the rejection of State authority and the overall distrust of industrial society. After all, was fascism not a method – a particularly brutal one – of effecting the transition to an industrialized society? Péguy, like Lawrence, could only have been horrified by the machinery of Nazism. In Sorel's case, selection was equally necessary if he was to be presented as a theoretical ally of fascism. True, he seems more readily assimilable in that he did not reject industrialism out of hand, whilst his Nietzschean cult of energy and his vehement hatred of parliamentary democracy all too easily led into dangerous spheres. It was just such aspects of this contradictory thinker that brought him to his flirtation with the extreme Right, and in particular with the Action Française movement, after he began to move away from syndicalism in 1907 : in his view the syndicalists were moving into enervating co-operation with political parties, and he needed some other platform.

The organicist theme was a central part of Action Française doctrine; and we must remember that this movement, too, looked upon itself as a revolt against decadence. Liberalism has produced only disintegration, evident in all aspects of life, and this group of the extreme Right react against it in a way that will sound all too familiar to us. This is how Eugen Weber, in his monumental history of the Action Française, describes their reaction :

> By their lights, the atomized society in which individuals appeared as free and separate entities before the law actually wrenched the individual away from such natural societies as his family, his trade, and his region, only to incorporate him in a much vaster and less natural one.[9]

Bureaucracy, a vast and impersonal system, has replaced the natural and rooted units of family, trade guild and village. The Action Française proposed instead the moral and social integration into a national whole, a corporate order based on small, artisanal patterns of ownership, and guilds not controlled by the workers themselves.

Together with another ex-syndicalist, Georges Valois, Sorel moved into the sphere of the Cercle Proudhon, a study circle in the orbit of the Action Française which Valois was later to describe as 'the first attempt at fascism'.[10] The name of the circle is particularly interesting, and demonstrates the apparent appeal of Proudhon — whom we know to be an important figure in the ethic-of-work tradition — for the extreme Right. Typical is the approval of *fascisant* F. Coty in the 1930s, and of the Vichy regime, who saw the current represented by Proudhon as an authentic 'French' socialism as opposed to 'foreign' marxism. In fact, Proudhon is all things to all men, and his name has often been pressed into service as an ally by interests whose principal enemy is marxism. Again, we find the self-avowed fascist, Drieu la Rochelle, writing in 1938, 'It matters little who invented fascism. France has a lot to do with it : the France of Sorel, of Péguy, of Barrès and Maurras, the France of Proudhon and revolutionary syndicalism.'[11] We see that not only Proudhon, Péguy and Sorel are implicated by Drieu, but the whole phenomenon of revolutionary syndicalism, and again we know that the ethic of work has its place in the sketchy theories of that movement. But is there anything inherently fascistic about it? It is true that some of its erstwhile supporters did end up in fanatically right-wing organizations; but the theory according to which extremes of Left and Right are synonymous is basically false, and revolutionary syndicalism taken as a whole is the antithesis, just as Proudhon's doctrine taken as a whole is the antithesis, of that suppression of the consciousness, influence and initiative of the workers, of those rigid and immovable hierarchies proposed by fascism. However, if there is emphatically no *identity* between fascism and revolutionary syndicalism, there is a certain parallelism, a certain similarity in the point of departure of both : in his study of the latter movement, Professor Ridley writes :

> Parallel to it ran movements of right-wing revolt, first nationalist, then fascist. Both were a reaction to the same apparent failure of democracy; they had a common object of attack : the parliamentary system. Both could be seen as the expression of a similar temperament — romantic, activist, anti-intellectual — which linked them in another object of attack : bourgeois values and bourgeois life.[12]

It must be emphasized, though, that the aims beyond this revolt are fundamentally dissimilar; and fascism, though it often used notions derived from left-wing socialisms, tended to do so as bait to ensure the necessary acquiescence in the corporate State of an element of the working class. The bait, of course, was often successful. In every case where fascism has been put into practice, however, these socialist-derived aspects of the ideology have been eclipsed, inevitably leaving greater exploitation and an intensification of all the ills associated with work in industrial society. The universe of Jünger's *Worker* gives the best indication of what such regimes tend towards in practice. In other words, whatever lip-service fascisms may pay to notions such as the organic society and the dignity of work, their revolt against bourgeois liberalism leads in a direction that can mean only the negation of these notions.

In this context it is interesting — and initially disturbing — to find Hitler in *Mein Kampf* playing on concepts similar to those we have met in literary figures. The organicist theme is particularly prominent : the State is to be a 'völkischer Organismus' as opposed to an 'economic organization', which is what it has become under the degradation of bourgeois democracy and its institutions, especially parliamentary government — compared at one stage to a cattle-market. The parliamentarian is painted as a figure of decadence, deprived of all integrity and heroism; and it is he who is standing in the way of an ideal and healthy social situation, that situation which would obtain if 'the centre of movement had not been vested in parliament, but in the workshop and the street.'[13] On the surface (only!) this sounds very close to revolutionary syndicalist doctrine. One of the great sins of the bourgeoisie, according to *Mein Kampf*, is the uprooting of workers, especially in large cities, leading to a loss of self-sufficiency. A great social problem has been created by the 'modern' split between the givers and takers of work; this was not the case before, especially on the land, when employer and 'hand' ate and worked together in organic unity. The result was, in those days, a certain respect for hand-work which we have now lost. A familiar theme : but here it takes on sinister and obsessive racialist overtones —

> The separation of the taker of work from the giver of work now appears to be complete in all spheres of life. Just how far in this respect the Jewish influence in the midst of our people has progressed can be seen from the lack of respect, even scorn, that is shown for manual work. That is not German. Only the frenchification of our life, which was really a jewification, changed the former respect for handiwork into a certain scorn for every kind of physical labour.[14]

All this must be changed in the Nazi State :

> Thus the national State will have to attain a fundamentally different attitude to the concept 'work'. It will have to break, even if centuries of education are necessary, with the nonsense whereby physical labour is despised.[15]

Playing on the appeal of syndicalism, Hitler goes on to exalt the possible role of unions, stating that the strength of the State should be based partly on a 'richtige Gewerkschaftsbewegung', a true trades union movement, which would involve not only a protection of interests but also an education. But then he reveals the immense gap between the real aims of National Socialism and those of the revolutionary syndicalists by claiming that the *Gewerkschaft* is not by its nature an organ of class struggle : such it has become only through the 'pernicious' influence of marxism.[16] The cult of the organic leads in all forms of fascism to an emasculation of syndicalism.

Theoretically, the ethic-of-work syndrome is present in the pages of *Mein Kampf*, but it is clearly exploited with considerable dishonesty for the sake of the widest possible appeal among the working population. The grim reality behind it all — and the bitterest irony of this exploitation of the ethic of work — lies in the Nazi labour camps and their slogan : Freedom through work!

The immense and revolting confidence trick this implies is reflected in other fascistic movements, in La Rocque's French *Croix de Feu*, for instance, based on the usual notion of class harmony and on 'a total respect for work in all its forms' (as La Rocque wrote in *Le Flambeau* in 1934.) It is reflected, too, in the cult of the rooted and hard-working

peasant manifest in the *Francisme* movement, which has been called
'the most truly fascist of French fascisms', and whose leader Marcel
Bucard spoke in Peguy-like tones of his own origins : 'I come from
what one calls the peasant *plèbe*. Wherever I have struggled, I have
remained faithful to its rude and ardent spirit. Outside all parties, I
push the ploughshare with robust labourers.' (*Le Franciste*, 1934)[17]
Or, to take a further example, and one in which the 'organic' theme
appears in close juxtaposition with a certain, traditional work-ethos,
Paul Marion of the extreme right-wing *Parti Populaire Français* wrote
in the organ of that movement, *L'Émancipation nationale*,

> Joan of Arc wasn't just the saint and heroine of the homeland, she
> was a symbol, too.
> The symbol of France at the beginning of the fifteenth century,
> essentially provincial and peasant . . .

> Our fathers, the artisans and peasants of those days, proud of their
> hard-won freedoms, solid on their feet and their feet planted firmly
> in their land . . .[18]

The cult of the peasant Joan of Arc (who had been Péguy's favourite
saint) was pushed to a paroxysm under the collaborationist government
of Vichy, together with the idea of a return to the land which came to
involve certain familiar aspects of the nostalgic ethic of work. The
broad appeal of Pétain in 1940 has significance for us — he was greeted
at first not only as a father-figure but as an alternative to parliamentary
politicians. Even those who should have known better fell into this
response : typical is the veteran writer Daniel Halévy, once an associate
of Péguy, who declared, 'It was not the skilful, advantageous voice of
the professional politician, that voice we all knew too well . . .'[19]
   Vichy set itself up, in terms of moral education, as a return to
traditional virtues and a reversal of the modern process of national
enervation and degradation — a reversal to be carried out by returning
to the roots of organic life, to the earth — 'la terre, elle, ne ment pas',
the earth cannot lie (unlike the parliamentary politicians), so that the
return to the land is presented by Pétain as a rediscovery of truth.[20]
France will 'regain all her strength by resuming contact with the earth' :
she should never have stopped being an agricultural nation. Let us not
be deceived, though; for however sincere Pétain's moralism may have
been (and there are grave doubts about that, too) objectively he was
merely fulfilling Hitler's plan for the construction of Europe : the
desire to return to a pre-industrial situation in France then appears,

willy nilly, as another gross confidence trick, for the whole ethos played into the hands of the Nazi occupiers who planned to use France as the 'market garden' of nazified Europe, whilst industry and power were to be concentrated in Germany itself. This helps explain why the regional writers of France, and especially those who had emphasized in their writings the 'eternal' virtues of the peasant and of life and work on the land, tended to be regarded as 'collaborationist' in spirit. Giono, having been imprisoned at the outbreak of the war for antimilitarism and suspected communist sympathies, found himself in trouble again in 1945 under the accusation of being a Vichy-ite! The accusation was unfair, in the light of Giono's humanism; but the concordance of peasant cult and Vichy ideology was unfortunate to say the least.

Pétain went further in his ethic-of-work propaganda : the eternal values of labour are to replace the lies on which our civilization has of late been based —

> One of the great innovations of Christianity was to teach man to accept freely the necessity of work, and to attribute to the most humble work a spiritual value. We aspire with all our soul to restore that value, which ultimately rests on the sense of duty and respect of the human person.[21]

In particular he stresses that there must be a return to the 'purest' and 'most authentic' forms of labour : to peasant patterns of work, of course, but also to artisan professions as expressions of skill and responsibility, of freedom in work. In an article in the *Revue des deux mondes* that appeared on 15 September 1940, he compares this ethic he is seeking to propagate with what he flatteringly describes as the National Socialist idea of the primacy of work and its essential reality vis-à-vis the 'fiction of monetary signs'. It is, he maintains, however, part of the classical heritage of France; and he quotes in support of this claim La Fontaine's fable *Le Laboureur et ses enfants* with its pious moral : 'work is a treasure'. This, claims Pétain, is a truth we have since forgotten, and which it is vital we should rediscover.[22]

It is all as misleading, of course, as Hitler's version of the ethic of work (if we can grace it with that title). To suppress the reality of class conflict is the real aim in both cases, and to do it by stifling the political aspirations and consciousness of the working masses, by teaching them to be content with their subservient lot in a 'natural' and 'moral' order. Pétain writes typically that the causes of the class struggle can be eliminated only if the proletariat, at present suffering by its isolation, 'can rediscover in a work-community the conditions of a worthy and free life together with reasons for living and hoping.'[23] There is too much empty verbiage in this ethos, and we are left with a sense of sham, as in the regime's motto : *Travail, Famille, Patrie.* The reality that lay behind the 'Travail' aspect of this was soon to be revealed by Laval : 'The institution of work camps must be envisaged.' Freedom through work indeed!

One aspect of the revolt against modern civilization that we have seen to be a recurrent theme is a distrust of the intellect, or, to be more accurate, of intellectualism. We know that 'intellectual' can become a pejorative term under the pen of a Péguy or a Sorel, and that for Lawrence or Tolstoy intellectualism represents a stunting of the organic personality. However, excessive anti-intellectualism has its dangers, and again recurs as a factor in certain varieties of fascism, whether in Jünger's cult of the elemental or the Spanish extreme Right's slogan during the Civil War : 'Down with intelligence, long live death!'

Nor is our survey of those aspects of the ethic-of-work tradition that are reproduced in fascistic ideologies complete. For we must add to the others that very cult of the medieval period which we have seen to be so recurrent. John Weiss has remarked, as have others, on the concurrence of neo-feudalism and fascism in the general framework of a hostility to liberal culture. He cites the example of a German literary circle at the turn of the century, marked by elitism and a faith in the medieval and the organic — in short, 'a radical right in feudal guise'.[24] As a socialist, Morris placed himself in strange and contradictory company in his medievalism : in the nineteenth century the ultra-conservative Young England movement also made much of the medieval example, whilst the Tory Disraeli declared, 'The principle of the feudal system was the noblest principle, the grandest, the most magnificent or benevolent that was ever conceived by sage or ever practised by patriot.'[25] In the same way, the fundamentally reactionary, Distributist movement of Belloc and Chesterton early in our own century drew much of its character from its medievalist bias.

There are areas of confusion between 'Right' and 'Left', of course, and there is no *a priori* reason why the concern for a culture founded on work should exist on the Left rather than the Right. After all, a number of the figures we have evoked in previous chapters are themselves politically ambiguous, to say the least. Others, like Morris, are definitely of the Left. Now Morris, it is true, does fall into the sometimes facile temptation of idealizing the past — for the medieval worker was not really so free in his work, the areas of improvisation were much more limited than he suggests, and the factors of oppression, including the reality of forced, press-gang labour, are too much glossed over in his exposition of the period. Yet he does try to put the past into perspective and to place the as yet unattained goal of social and political liberation squarely in a socialist future, a future to be based on the workers' acquisition of control over their own destinies and activities — and not the abdication of that creative control and initiative to others, to a leader-figure or any kind of static hierarchy inspired by the feudal system. Clearly, there is no need for the ethic of work to be fascistic in import, there is no inevitability about it : only isolated aspects tend to crop up in fascist ideologies, though they do so with a frequency that might suggest contradictions in the tradition we are examining. What we can say is that there is a potential danger in the ethic of work — that danger of its possible exploitation we have seen so amply illustrated. This said, let us remember that most of the writers involved are temperamentally as far from fascism as could be, whether in the manner of Zola, of Tolstoy, or of Weil and Camus (both of whom were involved in the struggle against fascism in concrete situations).

Some of them do, it is true, show nostalgia for stable, unchanging hierarchical systems. Of Péguy we expect this nostalgia : here he is in *L'Argent* defining the special dignity of the *métier*, the craft — 'it was putting yourself in your place in a workshop. It was, in a laborious City, quietly putting yourself in the place of work that awaited you.'[26] This does seem to lead away from the critical desire to question the bases of existing society and social organization — in the same way that Levin in *Anna Karenina*, faced with the peasant-women at work, 'drowned in the sea of their joyful common toil', is deeply impressed by their uncritical attitude to the work :

> God had given them the day and the strength, and both the day and the strength had been devoted to labour which had brought its own reward. For whom they had laboured and what the fruits of their labour would be was an extraneous and unimportant affair.[27]

Fundamentally the same presuppositions, and the same quietism they imply, are also to be found in Simone Weil, especially in her later writings. In *L'Enracinement* she speaks of hierarchy as a vital need of the human soul : 'A true hierarchy has the effect of bringing each man to settle morally in the place he occupies.'[28] Each to his place — this is the (feudal-inspired) doctrine she teaches, with her hatred of social mobility; so that for her the *army* is the image of the only kind of equality she can envisage. To obey is also a need of the soul . . . Disturbingly, the same argument was used in *Mein Kampf*, just as it is also frequently found in expositions of Action Francaise doctrine. Carlyle had earlier taken this moral value of obedience a little further, to exalt the spirit of sacrifice; from the midst of his protestant ethic he blandly exhorts the worker : 'My brother, the brave man has to *give* his life away.'[29] Hitler, a century later, was to enthuse over the 'high idealism' of the worker or peasant who toils without being able to attain for himself happiness or prosperity, sacrificing himself, whether he realizes it or not, for the community!

So, too, the position of women in the ethic of work tends to be fixed in the very limited and sometimes self-sacrificing role of the home-maker – exaltation of the family as an organic unit encourages this. Philippe, Lawrence and even at times Morris stress the ethical value of conscientious, careful housework, and Lawrence (unlike Zola) would deny women the aid of domestic labour-saving devices in the name of their spiritual well-being! Women had, in any case, an essentially subservient role as far as he was concerned.[30]

The appeal to a stable system is reflected in Simone Weil's distrust of any revolutionary change. She does not envisage abolishing the *patronat* – the employers – as such, but restoring them to a 'natural' position in society, whereby they would accept 'the modest limits of their natural function.' An uncomfortably similar argument had its place in F. Coty's reactionary ideology, where he distinguished between two types of capitalism (in just the same terms Péguy used to distinguish the 'classical' socialist from the 'romantic') :

> There are two opposed types of capitalism : the good and the bad; the honest, founded on work, and the pillaging, founded on speculation . . .; that whose beneficent and fertile activity is exposed in the light of day, in factories, farms, industries and trade . . . and that which acts in the dark, by fraud.'[31]

Even Zola, as we know, had to base his utopia on the beneficent and paternalistic *patron*-figure.

In the light of these parallels, it is perhaps not surprising if the ethic of work has been dismissed wholesale as an elaborate confidence trick perpetrated in the interests of those who profit from the labour of others. Charming the call for simplicity of life may be from the pen of a Tolstoy or a Morris, but the exploitative possibilities in the exaltation of poverty as a moral state are equally clear, whether in Proudhon's claims for the redemptive value of poverty as a natural condition, Péguy's distinction between *misère* (utter poverty, which is bad) and *pauvreté* (relative poverty, which is not necessarily bad, as hierarchy and lack of equality do not exclude fraternity), or Eric Gill's plea for poverty as 'the rational attitude towards material things', so that, if a rebirth of spiritual values is to come about, England must become poor and needy again![32]

One man who was sensitive to the dangers implied in this ethos, seeing it as a possible tool of social quietism and exploitation, was Marx's son-in-law, Paul Lafargue, who in the studies collected under the title *The Right to be Lazy* vehemently arraigns the ethic of work as a bourgeois mystification. A mystification propagated by those who are fundamentally opposed to change and who wish to 'keep the workers in their place' — whilst getting the most out of them at the same time. Lafargue is really criticizing with fierce irony the call for the 'right to work', which he regards as a sad aberration among the working class and an ideological cloak for slavery. He speaks of the strange delusion that possesses that class in capitalist nations, a delusion that has dragged in its train all the individual and social woes that have tortured humanity for the last two centuries :

> This delusion is the love of work, the furious passion for work, pushed even to the exhaustion of the vital force of the individual and his progeny. Instead of opposing this mental aberration, the priests, the economists and the moralists have cast a sacred halo over work. Blind and finite men, they have wished to be wiser than their God; weak and contemptible men, they have presumed to rehabilitate what their God has cursed . . .

The proletariat, he continues, has betrayed its best interests and its historical mission by allowing itself to be 'perverted by the dogma of work. Rude and terrible has been its punishment.' In utter contrast to Tolstoy, Hardy or Giono, Lafargue scorns what he calls the 'bovine' life of the peasant; agricultural work he sees as servile toil. Surely leisure is basically more rewarding and healthy; again in sharp contradiction of the ethic of work, Lafargue associates labour with degeneracy, and glibly compares the beauty of a thoroughbred, 'idle' horse in Rothschild's stables with a clumsy, Norman farm-horse. He even goes on to equate the impact of work with that of disease : look at the noble savages, he says, look at the sheer native beauty of man in those happy countries — like Spain — where economic prejudices have still not rooted out the natural hatred of labour :

> Look at the noble savages whom the missionaries of trade and the traders of religion have not yet corrupted with Christianity, syphilis and the dogma of work, and then look at our miserable slaves of machines.

The last words are significant : unlike Morris, Péguy and others, Lafargue is thinking of work specifically in terms of the industrial proletariat, and not of the declining class of artisans to whom he does not even refer in this ironic treatise.[33]

A similar criticism of the same 'bourgeois mystification' arose from within the revolutionary-syndicalist movement itself, and in particular from the pen of that successful pamphleteer, Pouget. Once again, Pouget is writing in terms of the capitalist organization of labour in the specifically industrial situation, and his exasperation is closely comparable to that of Lafargue. All would be well in the capitalist heaven, he remarks wryly, if the workers were politically unconscious slaves; in order to produce this effect, a morality has been evolved by the bourgeois class and imposed on those it employs, a morality from which it derives the useful virtues of devotion to the employers' interests, assiduity at the most fastidious and least remunerative tasks, the 'idiotic scruples' that create the 'good worker', and in short all the 'ideological and sentimental chains that rivet the employee to the carcan of capital, better and more surely than wrought iron links.'[34] The apotheosis of this charade, this confidence trick, is the exploitation of human vanity by presenting medals to the best slaves, those who have distinguished themselves by their resignation and the suppleness of their backbone. The criticism is reminiscent of the marvellously ironic episode in Flaubert's *Madame Bovary* where, at the *commices agricoles* the wretched, brutalized, agricultural labourer, Catherine Leroux, proudly hobbles up to receive *her* medal for fifty-four years of unstinted toil, hypocritically applauded by all.

Here we can see the importance of distinguishing between the two ethics of work : the 'protestant' one which says that work (as it exists) is a moral duty and therefore a good, upholding and reinforcing the *status quo*; and another, aspiring to a different kind of work, which as we know means a different kind of society. The one can be an instrument of exploitation, the other cannot, for it stands for values that are the opposite of all exploitation. Confusion of the two areas is flirting with danger — so, for instance, Marcuse castigates and deplores the tendency in post-Freudian, psychoanalytic theory to 'glorify repressive productivity as human self-realization'. For Marcuse, 'to link performances on assembly-lines, in offices and shops with instinctual needs is to glorify dehumanization as pleasure.'[35]

The kind of accusation made by Pouget or Lafargue does not in fact apply to the whole ethic of work spectrum by any means, although a writer like Péguy does lay himself open to such criticism by his stubborn refusal to analyse his own concepts. It is more certainly not true of Zola or Morris. The French writer scorns, through the mouth of the farmer, Feuillat, in *Travail*, those who tell the peasants to love the land while they are still working it for others who exploit them; and he presents in a bitterly satirical light the unproductive, middle-man figure who at the beginning of that same novel complains, in the face of working-class agitation, that 'there are no good workers any more.'[36] Morris was equally aware of the danger of being classed with those forces that were likely to use the 'good worker' ethos in the interests of the employers. In *Useful Work versus Useless Toil* he explicitly states his distrust of the happy labourer syndrome as manipulated by the supporters of the present system, and he adds, 'Now we have seen that the semi-theological dogma that all labour, under any circumstances, is a blessing to the labourer, is hypocritical and false.' His own position is a sane and balanced one, and he shows that he has his feet planted more firmly in reality than, say, Péguy. Not all work is good in itself, he stresses, especially not in our society; indeed, 'there is some labour which is so far from being a blessing that it is a curse; and it would be better for the community and for the worker if the latter were to fold his hands and refuse to work.'[37] Romantic dreamer Morris may have been at times, but he was no fool for all that.

Attacks such as those we have seen against the morality of work appear a good deal more valid when we take a case such as that of Carlyle, who with his fear of Chartism and the whole nascent movement of working-class protest was quick to insist that there are deeper laws binding men than the cash-nexus — 'obligations sacred as Man's life itself' as he puts it in *Past and Present*. Only those who carry on working, come what may, can learn these laws and participate in them. 'Heroic' souls will realize that the wages of their noble work lie in Heaven, and not in bank-notes. The main thing as far as Carlyle is concerned is that the worker shouldn't complain, that he shouldn't ask for more or in any way question the system :

The only happiness a brave man ever troubled himself with asking much about was happiness enough to get his work done. Not 'I can't eat!' but 'I can't work!' that was the burden of all wise complaining among men. It is, after all, the one unhappiness of a man, that he cannot work; that he cannot get his destiny as a man fulfilled.[38]

He even takes this to the extent of maintaining that it is nothing to die of hunger if you do so 'with honest tools in your hand', and much completed labour around you! Liberty for Carlyle means only the freedom to find out, or to be forced to find out 'the right path, and to walk thereon. To learn, or to be taught, what work he was actually able for; and then by permission, persuasion, and even compulsion, to set about doing of the same!' An industrial artistocracy is what Carlyle says we need, a hierarchical system of order to put an end to the present chaos, a 'Chivalry of Work' with laws and fixed rules as the kingpin of society. Speculating on the distant possibility of workers participating in the running of industry, he is more than sceptical of such an eventuality : 'Despotism is essential in most enterprises,' he concludes.[39]

The very rigidity of the society Carlyle proposes is a reflection of the absence of creativity from his ethos of work and, therefore, of life generally. Ruskin for his part stressed creativity as we know, and this made his ethic fundamentally different from that of Carlyle. Yet we find that Ruskin, especially in his later years, refused to follow the principle of creativity through to its full conclusion, and consequently he, too, fell into proposals for society that were of a feudal rigidity. *Unto this Last* and *Fors Clavigera* present the vision of an extremely hierarchical society modelled on the master-servant structure to a degree where paternalism is eclipsed by strict authoritarianism — 'The essential thing for all creatures is to be made to do right; how they are made to do it — by pleasant promises . . . or the whip — is comparatively immaterial.'[40] The organism Ruskin proposes is a static and closed one, not a developing and open one, it is based on 'the impossibility of equality among men; the good which arises from their inequality; . . . the honourableness of every man who is worthily filling his appointed place in society, however humble; the proper relations of poor and rich, governor and governed . . .'[41] In his Guild of Saint George, Ruskin was to be the supreme Master, wielding undivided authority. There would be no liberty in the Guild, but only 'instant obedience to known law, and appointed persons'; no equality either, but 'recognition of every betterness that we can find, and reprobation of worseness.'[42]

His increasingly hysterical hatred of the modern world led him even to the defence of slavery.

Politically, then, Ruskin falls into the same repressive pattern as Carlyle because he fails to carry his vital emphasis on creativity in labour over into the political sphere. He makes a great value of initiative and invention in a man's work, but then refuses him the exercise of those same faculties in the political organization of his life. It is a serious contradiction, and marks the breakdown of Ruskin's organicist vision by fragmenting man's ethical nature, giving him different and opposed principles for different areas of his life, The contrast with William Morris could not be clearer, for Morris is ready to apply the criterion of creativity, as we have seen, to the whole of human experience, and instead of rejecting democracy he gives us a democratic ideal of great depth, one in which initiative and responsible freedom are the ruling factors of both the social and the political spheres.

One criticism, though, that might appear to apply to Morris just as well as to Ruskin is that the ethic of work is a fond invention of well-to-do, middle-class intellectuals with something of a guilt complex concerning their position in society. H. G. Wells, who had no ethic of work, rejects the whole subject in just this way : speaking of the belief that all would one day partake in labour and enjoy it, he wrote, 'It needed the Olympian unworldliness of an irresponsible rich man of the shareholding type, a Ruskin or Morris playing at life, to imagine as much.'[43] Wells is facile, as so often, but there is a suspicion of truth in his sarcasm. Ruskin's experiments in road-building at Hinksey, which, as Wells remarked, proved the least contagious of all pursuits, are partly explicable in these terms. And let us remember that further contradiction whereby the articles turned out by Morris' company could only be afforded by the wealthy; could, in fact, only be manufactured at considerable cost. Hence the attack made at the end of the nineteenth century by the sociologist, Thorstein Veblen, in his *Theory of the Leisure Class*; in his view, both Ruskin and Morris exalt the defective at the expense of the serviceable and the efficient, theirs is a 'propaganda of crudity and wasted effort'. The point he makes is that the products of this propaganda only appeal to the rich and snobbish, for whom the criterion of 'conspicuous waste' is an essential part of their leisure-class outlook. The books produced by the Kelmscott Press inevitably appeared in expensive and limited editions, and their appeal lay more in their scarcity and their guaranteed sense of 'waste' than in their dubious serviceability.[44]

Be that as it may, though, the ethic of work is a good deal more than just a leisure-class mystification, as we can sense if we pause over the example of Robert Tressell and his popular socialist classic *The Ragged-Trousered Philanthropists*. Now Tressell was himself a working man — a decorator — first of all, and only took up writing afterwards. In his novel he shows great concern for the maintenance, even — things have gone so far — the rediscovery of pleasure and fulfilment in work well done. Clearly the concern for the moral and cultural value of work, as Tressell movingly if sometimes clumsily demonstrates, is not simply something dreamed up by idle intellectuals. A serious reservation must be made, however, and Tressell shows the same balance we have observed in Morris and Zola when he warns that the painters and decorators who people his novel are not dupes : 'They had no conception of that lofty ideal of "work for work's sake" which is so popular with the people who do nothing.'[45] Having made that point, though, he then moves far away from the position represented by *The Right to be Lazy*, and in a down-to-earth key tends rather to reflect the preoccupations of a Morris or a Wesker. Some of the most telling sections of the book concern Tressell's regret (so clearly based on personal experience) over the loss of craftsmanship in the modern world, 'for there had arisen a new generation which cared nothing about craftsmanship or art, and everything for cheapness or profit.'[46] The whole system of competition and profit is shown to be inimical to high standards of work, to real professional conscience. One new employee of the decorating firm is reprimanded for being too conscientious at the job, for doing it properly instead of 'scamping' and rushing it; the supervisor finds he spends far too long preparing the wood before painting it, even to the extent of buying his own glass-paper! Much preferred is the 'work' of an unskilled and cheaper labourer who gets through his task in half the time, painting incidentally half the windows as well as the frames. Tressell makes us feel his own disgust at this degradation :

> The paint was of a dark drab colour and the surface of the newly painted doors bore a strong resemblance to corduroy cloth, and from the bottom corners of nearly every panel there was trickling down a large tear, as if the doors were weeping for the degenerate condition of the decorative arts. But these tears caused no throb of pity in the bosom of Misery (the supervisor) : neither did the corduroy-like surface of the work grate upon his feelings. He perceived them not. He saw only that there was a Lot of Work done

and his soul was filled with rapture as he reflected that the man who had accomplished all this was paid only fivepence an hour.[47]

Only very occasionally is a workman as fortunate as Tressell's hero, Owen (described as 'an exceptionally good workman'), who is given a piece of creative work to do : he is asked to decorate a room in Moorish style, and we are given a great deal of loving detail of this ambitious task. It is work that Owen can mix with his life, thus achieving briefly some sort of integrated existence – he takes the plans home with him, to the great distrust of foreman and supervisor. Typically, alas, the work is done for a rich philistine with no artistic feeling whatsoever; but despite that, Owen can still feel himself lucky, for deep down *all* the men would have liked to take time and pains 'because all those who are capable of doing good work find pleasure and happiness in doing it, and have pride in it when done.' Unfortunately the economic system as it is gives incentive only to 'hurry and scamp and slobber and botch'.[48] Owen, at least, can still find a disciple for his doctrine of conscientious work in the apprentice, Bert, to whom he can give no better Christmas present than his old set of graining combs that Bert has been longing for. It is, however, only within the perspective of an authentically socialist future that rewarding work for all can be envisaged : it will be carried out, in Tressell's utopian vision, not on the commission of wealthy philistines, nor under an industrial system of maximum haste for maximum profit, but so that all can benefit from it in a world without money. Whatever gold there is will not be used for barter but beaten into gold leaf and used for the embellishment of public buildings and the houses of ordinary people.

In general we can say that the ethic of work may present dangers and lay itself open to valid criticism only when it is divorced from the complementary concern for social justice, for initiative and choice on behalf of the workman himself – not only in his work, but, wider, in his political role, to which his creativity must also extend. Only with this emphasis can the area of ambiguity evoked by the reflection of ethic-of-work ideas in ideologies of the extreme Right be cleared up and eliminated.

Not that, even so, the 'movement' can be absolved of all contradictions or of the sense of despair that goes hand in hand with those contradictions. We see the pessimism of Kaiser or Toller; the ideals of Wesker forced into compromise. In some cases there is a danger of sheer absurdity in facile primitivism, whether it be Lawrence on the menace of electric cookers or Weil deploring the entry of radio and films into the villages. It is perhaps too easy to brush off all progress as 'the poison of the age'!

Obviously, if these writers appear doomed to contradiction, to airy utopia or to despair, it is because the realization of their dream of a valid work-community would in most cases involve something never yet seen in the world — a radical change in, and perhaps even a reversal of, the technical dynamism of our society. No revolution has yet led in that direction.

11 The future of work

Although the search for a morality of work involves elements of despair, wild idealism or possibly blind and even fanatical devotion to a fondly imagined past, it has still created a concerted, ethical indictment of our civilization of inestimable value; and it has thrown up some invaluable criteria by which a culture − in the very widest sense − can be judged. This much we have seen so far. But in addition it has also managed to give, on the basis of those ethical principles, some more than merely interesting suggestions on how work in our world can possibly be humanized again, and culture revitalized. It is these suggestions we must now consider.

As a preliminary, let us ask someone who is considered an expert in the field : what are the psychological needs that cry out to be fulfilled? Friedmann summarizes them as follows :

> First of all, work, considered globally, must be made up of a body of tasks that remain under the complete control of the operator : tasks which are consequently defined and co-ordinated according to his *initiative*, his *will*, and which, by definition, keep a certain quality of *flexibility*; tasks which possess in his eyes a certain *finality* (which he understands and dominates) and are directed towards a completion that remains under his control, towards an aim that may be more or less distant, but which must remain within his field of vision and action; tasks which as a result call into play his *responsibility* and constitute a *challenge*, perpetually renewed and surmounted . . .[1]

Such fulfilment would surely constitute at its highest a love of work. Even within the industrial situation where we find ourselves, this is no mere idle dreaming. Many sociologists and industrial psychologists have concerned themselves with the problem of restoring value to human work, not least in America, where the situation has in many ways been most acute. Thus, for instance, Professor Herzberg has applied the concept of 'psychological growth' to the world of work, to argue that what men seek from their activity is not simply a passive happiness, but a means of increasing their experience and understanding, of 'growing' (whereas so much automated work tends to diminish them). The requirements of such growth, involving such elements as creativity and the perception of new relationships between things, would seem to be largely covered by Friedmann's exposition of the satisfactory work-situation above. But what do the largely literary figures with whom we have been concerned have to suggest? Have they in fact fulfilled a role by infusing life and the wide appeal of immediacy into the more arid and abstract speculation of the social scientists?

However powerful and vivid the indictment of a world that has degraded work, what we all too often find when it comes down to the question of what should be done is that the answer is despairing or non-existent, or made up of a vague and wordy optimism such as Camus, with all his ill-defined talk of a 'renaissance' came to cultivate. (It is that aspect of Camus that makes so much of his *L'Homme révolté* embarrassingly unsatisfactory.) And meanwhile the spirit of Zola sits waiting for a Fourierist factory owner to chance along, complete with an impossibly contagious scheme for the renewal of society and the most sophisticated machinery to create energy that can ultimately be dispensed to the workers' own homes so that they can create . . . we are not quite sure what! How would Zola's utopians – the basic impossibility of the situation apart – acquire the love of work which that writer repeatedly states to be the moral basis of his community (though which it hardly seems to need in practical terms, given the perfection of machinery)? We know that it is education from early childhood that is all-important : no sooner do children start to read and write than they have tools put into their hands, developing their muscles and skills as they develop their grammar. Work takes on the character of recreation : at break-time they are only too pleased to rush over to the workshop where they plane wood, file metal, while others – both boys and girls – learn how to use sewing machines and weaving looms. Later, when they leave school, this same Fourierist principle finds its extension in the practice of diversity in work — no-one is to spend more than two hours at any one task without moving on to something else, switching from physical labour to industrial art, general culture or administrative duties. All men are to partake of all these fields : Zola's key to psychological growth is diversity, and to this we must add participation in the affairs of the City, in the running of the community; and in this latter respect he reaches beyond the suggestions of most sociologists or psychologists. On the other hand, Zola has his own kind of vagueness : he can appear to reach further because his vision is utopian, but he fails to be at all specific about what actual work is carried out in this future and highly automated society, and this contrasts uncomfortably with the close, plastic evocations of the acts of work before the ideal community was ever set up. This area of vagueness is the measure of Zola's failure, which is the failure of utopia.

One 'realistic' option open to writers is, of course, to assume defeat — if it is fair to describe it as such — under the inevitable onslaught of technological progress. Typical of this 'solution' is that of Toller at the final point of his reflections on the problem of work in industrial society : as machines are not to be undone, perhaps man will at least be able to fulfil his deep moral and psychological need for rewarding work in his increasing leisure time.[2] It is noteworthy that a latter-day sociologist such as Friedmann can come to the same rather resigned conclusion. He considers it romantic idealism to dream of reversing or even arresting the technical development of our society, though he still hopes for something very different from the technological totalitarianism of Ernst Jünger's world. He prefers to associate himself with those who place their hope in augmented leisure activities — 'Some observers even foresee, in the society of the future, the flowering of a "new man" of the artisan type, devoted to the patient and creative fashioning of materials with the aid of manual tools, a new *homo faber* resurrected by leisure.'[3] He does go on to stress, though, that a great, unprecedented and highly delicate effort of mass culture is needed to make this sort of fulfilment available to all — and we know that the signs are hardly propitious on present evidence, whatever occasional *bricolage* may interrupt the seances of television-watching.

By no means all authorities accept the resignation implicit in this theory that leisure-pursuits, extra-work activities, may become a substitute for the rewards that work, at its best, can bring. Hence Herzberg and his colleagues :

An individual living in such a world is debarred from seeking real satisfactions in his work. Interpersonal relationships outside work are overloaded; the hobby often becomes a substitute for the job. But the hobby cannot give the complete sense of growth, the sense of striving towards a meaningful goal, that can be found in one's life work. A carpenter's workshop in the basement and a neatly groomed backyard are no substitute for the direct relationship between work and the fulfilment of the individual's needs . . . Thus we reject the pessimism that views the future as one in which work will become increasingly meaningless to most people and in which the pursuits of leisure will become the most important end of society. We cannot help but feel that the greatest fulfilment of man is to be found in activities that are meaningfully related to his own needs as well as those of society.[4]

If we now look back to William Morris, we find that his whole ethico-cultural outlook led him to adopt a similar standpoint, and to hope for something other than the reduction of working time to a minimum. It is true that in *How We Live and How We Might Live* he does say that if one day there were *real* labour-saving machines (and not just machines that create more toil by increasing competition and the furious desire to produce more consumer goods in a vicious circle of mechanical servitude) these might allow men to do their 'best work' in what might be regarded as leisure time. The important point is, though, that Morris still regards what is done in this 'non-industrial' time left to man by the perfection of machinery as *work*, that is as purposive activity carried out in a social context for a socially useful purpose. It is not to be thought of as the short-term, largely self-centred and gratuitous occupations we call hobbies, which lack two essential characteristics of good work : consistent finality and a genuine social dimension. Morris' horror at the idea of the Leisure-State becomes clearer from his argument in *The Art of the People*, where of the future of work he asks,

> Shall all we can do with it be to shorten the hours of that toil to the utmost, that the hours of leisure may be long beyond what men used to hope for? and what shall we then do with the leisure, if we say that all toil is irksome? Shall we sleep it away? — Yes, and never wake up again, I should hope, in that case.[5]

The only hope for a future society is in daily labour as a moral value, and Morris' hope is substantially this : when the principle of competition is eliminated by the advent of his brand of socialism, then technological advance will be deprived of much of its present dynamism, which is but the dynamism of profit; the volume of consumer goods will then fall, leading to a limited and even decreasing need for machinery. The rediscovery of delight in the voluntary expenditure of energy could also lead to a limitation on the use of machinery in agriculture – why, men will realize, should such pleasure be given up to the jaws of a machine? And this applies to really rough work – any healthy man worth the name would get pleasure from doing a certain amount of such labour, as long as it is clearly useful and as long as it is voluntary and not continuous : by the first two characteristics the work acquires an ethico-social justification, and by the third is ensured that the man occupied on it can move to other work of a different nature, thus fulfilling the familiar principle of variety or diversity.[6]

One form of variety Morris liked to dream of was that enjoyed by the medieval journeyman – first of all as a geographical diversity produced by the workman's travelling, preferably abroad as well as throughout his own country. This eminently fulfils the principle of psychological growth by making the job a veritable education in the widest and most organic sense, a forming of the whole man as well as the perfection of his skills. It is a formula that Morris would like to see resurrected in the future. And as the new, unexploited workman of the future would have greater opportunities for learning, his work-culture, acquired on the journeying pattern, could be much broader; so that a cobbler might go to Rome to make shoes for three months or so, and bring back with him new ideas of building from that city, which he could help introduce into his home country . . .[7]

It all sounds hopelessly romantic and idealistic, of course, especially in the context of today's increasing specialization of techniques and the ever greater bureaucratic complexity of almost every country in the world, both of which militate against the sort of flexibility Morris envisages here (though we shall see that nostalgia for the journeyman principle is to inspire a writer nearer our own time). Beyond this particular point, however, what is difficult to swallow in Morris' optimistic vision of the future is the whole idea of men moving away from machines to revert to earlier forms of work, even within the frame-work of the 'post-revolutionary' social structure where he postulates this profound change. It is against the faith in this kind of reversion that Orwell argues with grim lucidity in his depressing *The Road to Wigan Pier*. At the same time he is sceptical of the theory of fulfilment through creative leisure; suppose the much-vaunted mission of the machine were realized, so that the automatized working day could be cut to a minimum —

> The citizen of Utopia, we are told, coming home from his daily two hours of turning a handle in the tomato-canning factory, will deliberately revert to a more primitive way of life and solace his creative instincts with a bit of fretwork, pottery-glazing, or handloom-weaving. And why is this picture an absurdity — as it is, of course? Because of a principle that is not always recognized, though always acted upon : that so long as the machine is *there*, one is under an obligation to use it. No one draws water from the well when he can turn on the tap . . . Hence the absurdity of that picture of Utopians saving their souls with fretwork. In a world where everything could be done by machinery, everything would be done by machinery. Deliberately to revert to primitive methods, to use archaic tools, to put silly little difficulties in your own way, would be a piece of dilettantism, of pretty-pretty arty and craftiness. It would be like solemnly sitting down to eat your dinner with stone implements. Revert to handwork in a machine age, and you are back in Ye Olde Tea Shoppe or the tudor villa with the sham beams tacked to the walls.[8]

Such is Orwell's realistic but gloomy conclusion — gloomy, because he, too, believes firmly that the tendency of mechanical progress is 'to frustrate the human need for effort and creation.'

Even if we accept the reality of mechanical progress, and see its continuation as inevitable, this does not necessarily invalidate all Morris' speculation about the future, or reduce it to mere wishful dreaming from beginning to end. For he is not fanciful enough to imagine that the machine would wither away completely : some industry is bound to be left, and the idea is that we should all do a stint in it from time to time. What, then, of the period that people spend within this context of industry — how can it be made other than a sheer — if temporary — loss of life, and, therefore, ruinous to that ideal of integrated and organic living? Some of Morris' most interesting suggestions are on this relatively practical and down-to-earth question. Their most cogent exposition is in *A Factory As It Might Be*, where he deals first of all with the 'aesthetic' aspect : the buildings, quite contrary to normal, utilitarian practice, should be beautiful 'with their own beauty of simplicity as workshops.'[9] Factories should be set in gardens, to be tended by the workers themselves, which would serve both to give them a pride in their place of work and to give them contact with the earth and its natural processes and rhythms, to enroot them, in the vocabulary of Simone Weil (who herself is to propose giving industrial and other workers plots of land where they can grow some of their own food). The factory will also — taking further Pelloutier's ideal for his *bourses du travail* — contain a library, a school, places for study, etc., making it something of a community focal point. The place of work thus becomes a place of education and culture as well, and this juxtaposition or rather this fusion of functions is of inestimable, moral value. Children — as in Zola's utopia — will be introduced to manual work during their book-learning; their intellectual and technical education will be carried on simultaneously, so that, Morris comments hopefully, the child will be as eager to handle the shuttle as the young gent of his own day was to grab his gun and go off hunting.

This, however, is not the full extent of the educative value of the future factory : just as Pelloutier envisaged exhibitions of the techniques, tools and products of labour in the *bourses*, so Morris sees the factory itself as a means of teaching the community in general how work is carried out, how goods are made — something not really feasible under the secrecy of the competitive system. This in turn could only lead to a greater pride in the work, which becomes truly a part of the life of the community, and a greater moral standing for labour in general.

But, further, the factory could supply another educational want by showing the general public how its goods are made. Competition being dead and buried, no new process, no detail of improvements in machinery would be hidden from the first enquirer; the knowledge which might thus be imparted would foster a general interest in work, and in the realities of life, which would surely tend to elevate labour and create a standard of excellence in manufacture, which in its turn would breed a strong motive towards exertion in the workers.[10]

'A strong motive towards exertion in the workers' — when isolated, the sentiment and almost the phraseology might seem at a casual glance to resemble those of certain schools of industrial psychology that are mainly concerned with discovering for employers and managers of labour the most effective means of extracting the maximum amount of work with the least disruption, and all, of course, within the broad context of the *status quo*. Not so Morris, needless to say (even though he was himself, on a small scale, an employer of labour and head of a workshop registered under the Companies Act!). He is speaking of what can be only after integral socialism has been introduced, and competition banished, so that work can have the moral quality of finality in that it is carried out directly for the community; this in turn allows the place of work, in the way sketched out above, to be totally integrated into that community and to play its due role in organic living. And all this, let us remember, without any of that 'fretwork' nonsense that is to exasperate Orwell!

Morris is particularly anxious to point out that he is thinking in what we might describe as quite un-Zolaesque terms : the whim of one 'rich and philanthropic manufacturer', however deep and sincere his philanthropy, can never suffice to create the factory he hopes for. It is not something that can be achieved in isolation, for it presupposes not simply new concepts of work and education and the mutual inter-penetration of the two, but also a whole new morality, a new notion of *community* that can only be the product of profound, far-reaching, social change. It must be integral, not partial. So even that beautiful, external appearance of the factory cannot be the product of paternal-istic initiative, however aesthetically enlightened, for 'even the external beauty in industrial concerns mut be the work of society and not of individuals.'[11]

It is this constant appeal for a fundamental change in the social structure that is absent from the theses of Simone Weil, despite her search for roots and despite the passionate appeals for a number of adventurous modifications in the existing organization of labour. Revolution as it has been understood is not the answer for her; indeed she feels, like the Georg Kaiser of *Gas*, that any move towards industrial socialism without a transformation of work itself and the 'relationship of forces' in industry can even lead to an intensified subordination in the worker by building up a complex, technical, economic and bureau-cratic organization. There are, she claims, two different things that go under the name of revolution : one (as yet unfulfilled) consists in transforming society so that all the workers can acquire roots; the other, and the more common, consists in spreading uprootedness to the whole of society so that all may equally partake of it! As long as production is founded on passive obedience, then workers will continue to obey passively, whether the structure be called 'capitalist' or 'socialist'. Not that obedience in itself offends her — quite the contrary. Accepted hierarchy, willing subordination does not seem to her the sign of an unjust society, but, at its best, of a healthy and organic one; and this best is achieved when the hierarchy is based on an awareness of the dignity of those who obey, and on the psychological (or spiritual) growth of all. When orders attribute responsibility to the man who receives them, when they stretch him by demanding virtues — courage, will, consciousness, intelligence — from him, implying thereby a high degree of mutual trust and confidence between the giver and taker of orders, then even though a degree of arbitrary power (she admits) must inevitably remain in the hands of the *chef*, 'subordination is a fine and honourable thing.'[12] An awareness of obligations, she states at the beginning of *L'Enracinement*, is more important than the concept of rights : a right is only effective by the obligation it presupposes in an organic relationship, and it remains relative and subordinate to that obligation.[13]

The result of this emphasis in Weil's thought is that she does not basically challenge the capitalist system itself; she simply urges that the bosses should remember their 'true' function, forgotten in an age of materialism. In a sense, and despite first appearances, this makes her vision fundamentally *more* utopian than Morris' — for how can she hope to abolish that materialism she abhors whilst remaining within the economic framework which created and imposed it? She is in fact reduced to the vague aspiration for an enlightened paternalism, and it was with this ideal in view that she at one time optimistically communicated with the head of an industrial concern.

Despite this basic utopianism, positive and valuable ideas there are when she turns to the actual problems of work in an industrial setting, and how it can be made more human. She has a point when she affirms the need for such speculation :

> The problem of the most desirable *régime* in industrial enterprises is one of the most important, and perhaps *the* most important for the working-class movement. It is all the more amazing then that it has never been posed. To my knowledge it has not been studied by the theoreticians of the socialist movement, neither Marx nor his disciples have devoted a treatise to it, and Proudhon gives only a few hints on the subject. The theoreticians were perhaps badly placed to deal with the matter, for lack of ever having themselves been among the cogs of a factory.[14]

Fundamental to her preoccupation is again the notion of 'growth', which she prefers to call by a more traditional term, 'education' — in the widest possible sense, of course. 'To my mind, work should tend, as far as materially possible, to constitute an education.'[15] This for her is the only possible means of overcoming the deprivation implied by the division of labour. The work situation must be a learning situation, a source of enrichment; this presupposes a total view of what is being produced, together with the techniques involved and the reasons for that production. On the most obvious level, the workers must be informed : she wrote in *La Condition ouvrière* that one of her main concerns was with the search for a true method of vulgarizing knowledge and information, a way of making them accessible without debasing or falsifying them. She was also anxious to encourage the setting up of study circles within factories, which could organize trips round the whole plant with technical explanations and condensed but intelligent 'bulletins de vulgarisation' for the workers. Only in this way could the fragmentation of the labour-process be mitigated, and that process become meaningful again; the worker would no longer be an individual and isolated cog in a machine of which he has no overall understanding.

Her most ambitious ideas for industrial change are set out in *L'Enracinement* — but again we have to note that although they presuppose a very different attitude towards society than prevails at present, they are not explicitly founded on a basic restructuring of that society, so that for all their appeal and potential fertility they have a decidedly utopian flavour. Mere institutional or juridical changes cannot solve the problems of the working-class condition : this, she claims, Marx knew himself, though he was loath to admit it. Moreover that class itself has lost sight of the answer to its problems, its imagination tainted by the acquisitive materialism of the age to the point where it no longer even realizes the nature of its very real and unacceptable misery. What really must be changed is an organization that prevents the workers from participating intellectually and emotionally in the whole work of the enterprise that employs them.

'Participation' is her ideal — more sincerely meant, no doubt, than in the handy, Gaullist sop to thwart working-class aspirations in 1968. For Simone Weil, it is a vital aspect of the whole plan for the re-enrootment of the class, a plan in which she elaborates the 'organic' theme to the extent of demanding — not just for the individual, as is to be the case of Wesker's Dave, but for the whole of society — an end to 'the complete separation of working life and family life.'[16] Such reintegration can only be conceivable through a decline in large factories, which could eventually disappear at least as far as most industries are concerned. A large enterprise would then consist of an assembly shop linked to a number of small workshops, dispersed over one particular region. All workers, who would not be as narrowly specialized as those of today, would go by rota to do a stint in the assembly shop, so that all would acquire a view of the final purpose of the tasks involved in production. Ideally, the period spent by a worker in the central assembly-plant would constitute a kind of holiday, a *fête* in the life of the individual.

Children would be welcomed into the workshops, where they would be encouraged to help their fathers as a game; they would play in the place of work, thus leaving the two notions forever fused for them so that 'work would be lit with poetry for the whole of their lives by this childish wonderment.'[17] This would be best achieved in those cases where, by an ultimate decentralization, the father could work at home, following his own work-rhythms, his own and, therefore, essentially human relationship with time.

The machines, she suggests, should belong to the small workshops and not to the central concern, and the worker might with permission acquire his own machine, whilst still working within the framework of what might be a very large company : in this way, Simone Weil tries to reconcile the artisan values that she, like so many others, looks back to, and her realization that some social developments are irreversible, that some large-scale enterprises have become indispensable. She has also something to say about the nature of those machines, which must equally undergo transformation if their existence is to be harmonized with the same artisan values. Any change in class relationships, she claims on the authority of Marx, must be accompanied by a change in techniques and especially in machines : the new machines must allow the possibility of fine adjustment by the operator, and must have multiple functions instead of carrying out one totally automatic operation. In other words, the machine should become the technological age's equivalent of the artisan's tools, the modern prolongation of those tools instead of their negation.

Weil's aim throughout such speculation is to urge a revaluation by seeing the working life in terms of its greatest ethical potential, its greatest possible power of enrichment and 'growth' for the individual. It is nothing short of the ambition to re-instate work as the centre of culture. She is acutely aware of the imperfections of our present ener-vated and largely irrelevant culture, mainly reserved as it is for middle-class intellectuals and functionaries — themselves fragmented beings. Culture badly needs transmitting to the people, for the good of culture as well as of the people. She puts her finger on a disturbing and vicious circle that is unfortunately just as true today as when she was writing : 'culture is an instrument wielded by teachers in order to produce teachers, who in their turn will produce teachers.'[18] In her view, this is a gross perversion and an impoverishment, a short-circuit that deviates culture from its roots and its meaning. Science and letters belong by rights most closely to the working people, for they have the most acute and most direct experience both of techniques and of the human condition.

How, then, can culture be revitalized, and brought back to its source in work? A number of challenging suggestions are offered. First of all, 'intellectuals' ('a terrible name, but as they are today they don't deserve a better one,' she wrote bitterly) could be allowed as honorary members of syndicates; all students should have to go as workers in factories for longish periods. Education in general must be changed radically : in particular, the workers' education must be related to their lives, and not cast in the classical, cartesian mould whose false and empty 'universality' can only alienate them. For instance, science could be taught in terms of the techniques they are involved with, or for the agricultural worker in terms of the cycle of nature. With such a concept enrooted in them, work would take on a whole new significance, and would be 'enveloped in poetry'. But above all, the most important change would come in the organization of work itself, to make it the vital element of a living culture, to make it an education. Such a change is that whereby men in the factory would 'work' in the traditional sense for only half the day, and would for the other half attend lectures of a technical nature allied to their own skills or — equally essential — learn about and discuss the role their products have in social life, in the community, thus conferring at last on their labour a genuine sense of finality. More general culture would be available, with a 'working-class university' linked with each major assembly-shop. 'The task of the "popular school" is to give work greater dignity by infusing it with thought, and not to make the worker a compartmentalized being who sometimes works and sometimes thinks.'[19]

Like Morris, she is led by her nostalgia for the work-patterns of the Middle Ages to resuscitate the ideal of the medieval 'tour' : such journeying should once again be facilitated, she argues, for it constitutes an enriching education that is integral to the work-situation. It also allows the worker fully to indulge his desire for variety before accepting a rooted (though still not monotonous) situation : 'When the young worker, sated and gorged with variety, comes to think of settling down, he would be ready for enrootment. A wife, children, a garden giving him a large part of his food, work that links him to a concern he likes, of which he is proud, and which is for him a window opened on the world : that would be enough for the earthly happiness of a human being.'[20]

'A window opened on the world' : the phrase vividly expresses the hope Simone Weil placed in work as an educative force and as the cultural centre of existence in her enrooted society. But fascinating as the ideas may be — and they have not lost any of their urgency today — it remains true that she can offer no suggestion of the process of transformation by which such an apparently desirable situation can be brought about. Her limitation lies in the refusal to place her radical, ethical and cultural ideas in a correspondingly radical, *political* context. The furthest she is prepared to go (and in view of how much she wants to achieve it seems hopelessly inadquate) is some sort of return to individual capitalism, involving the abolition of joint-stock companies, which would allow greater scope for the kind of paternalism on which her scheme is based. It is in this context that she proposes that workers should be able not only to buy their own machines, but also to acquire a workshop with a few employees under them, and that a credit system should be set up to allow those with a vocation to become heads of concerns.

There is still a striking modernity and relevance, though, in her urgent, impassioned plea, in these days when so many have come to realize how dubious some aspects of culture are, and how a more integral civilization and culture must have at its heart a revaluation of work itself. Psychologists such as Herzberg have pointed out forcefully that such a revaluation cannot be achieved merely in terms of remuneration or the improvement of physical working conditions — for these simply have the status of 'hygiene factors' in the American professor's phrase. In the same way that attainment of real mental health is not equivalent to the mere avoidance of mental illness (as all too many have wrongly assumed), so the hygiene factors only contribute to the reduction of discomfort, without by themselves increasing fulfilment; for fulfilment and health must be centred in the work itself. 'A "hygienic" environment prevents discontent with a job, but such an environment cannot lead the individual beyond a minimal adjustment consisting of the absence of dissatisfaction. A positive "happiness" seems to require some attainment of psychological growth.'[21] Hygiene factors are not 'motivators' : according to Herzberg's surveys, even when conditions are fairly good such factors are usually low down on the list when men are asked what they positively seek from their job. Salary and physical working conditions may be dominant elements of job dissatisfaction when they are felt to be inadequate, but are rarely major factors of active job satisfaction. Such satisfaction touches instead on criteria beyond the merely hygienic, on the need for creativity and responsibility.

Such views are not so different from the more literary exposition we have followed, however different the language and terminology may be. The arguments of some industrial psychologists and sociologists do sound considerably less human at times, and one is easily led to suspect that such speculation is often much more designed to perpetuate the present order of things than to change it : the concern of *some* specialists has, it would seem, been to find a means of persuading workers to accept what are still basically alienating tasks. That is, they seem to be out to fit the man to the job, and not to achieve the potentially much more radical aim of fitting the job to the man (which ultimately means transforming the whole organization of work). The maintenance or increase of *efficiency* has often been the main aim, and it lies behind such innovations as the American 'counseling' system, based on the work of Elton Mayo : 'counselors' are installed in comfortably furnished rooms within the factory, and are at the disposal of employees with problems concerning their work. Their function is to listen — they have no active role within the concern and never intervene, above all, never give advice, despite their title. Clearly, they represent an advanced technique of personnel management, a safety valve for the *status quo*, whereby the anxious worker 'purges' his frustration and leaves in a more integratable state of mind. Georges Friedmann is justly suspicious of this kind of 'integration', so different from that envisaged by the ethic-of-work tradition : 'But is this "harmony" not obtained at the expense of the personality of the workers . . . is conseling interested in men, or only in the human factor of productivity?'[22]

The call made by Morris and Weil for new machines and techniques of production also finds its echo in observers of the modern industrial scene, observers such as Friedmann again : and in this field he, too, shows a measure of optimism in the hope for a radical transformation of the moral and psychological status of work even within the framework of mass-production :

The appearance of special machines, substituting cyclical for linear succession, the multiplication of teams working together, the regrouping of operations in universal machines, the new architecture of workshops, offer on a technical plane the potentiality, the initial impetus of a new polytechnism and consequently of an intellectual revaluation of work.[23]

In practice, changes in production lines are not uncommon today. More and more, workers are allowed to assemble a whole product by the use of cyclical systems, and this has been found at least as efficient as the linear method. Here is the point, though : the criterion is still efficiency, as it must be as long as a competitive system prevails. This puts a severe and crippling limitation on the extent to which an alternative work-culture can be realized.

Beyond such minor changes lies the need for a wider participation in the whole process of production, for the worker's own control (within a collective framework) of his work, its techniques and its destination. It is a radical and far-reaching need — and it seems unlikely that piece-meal adjustment of the present situation under the label of job satisfaction can go very far towards fulfilling it.

Perhaps hope could come from a more complete automation, whereby we could see the end of operations in which the worker is just an accessory of an as yet imperfect machine which demands from him monotonous, repeated gestures. Maybe indeed, hope may be found in the further development of the technical civilization. It is certainly the view of Garaudy, who bases his committed optimism on the development of cybernetics, whereby the operator might eventually exercise considerably more intelligence and initiative than by controlling a conventional machine, so that 'a little technical development leads us away from man, a lot brings us back to man.'[24] Present developments, however, can only make us sceptical about this kind of 'cybernetic optimism'. There is absolutely no guarantee that such an evolution will not lead to an even greater degree of alienation, though it is true that there are others, equally determined to be 'progressive' who share the same faith. Henri Arvon in his *Philosophie du travail* expresses the belief that machines will be substituted for men in so far as men were previously condemned to automatic work; the worker will thus be released from the circuit of blind, mechanical forces, so that he can control them from above and 'direct them towards harmonious ends'. Ultimately the machine should allow man to specialize in the human sphere. Man ceases to be a slave, and becomes a supervisor; technical development 'bears in its flanks the promise of a better world, widened and enriched by human effort ... A metacosmos is superimposed on the cosmos to constitute a universe in which the human spirit merges with the natural order.'[25] The possibility is envisaged, then, of a reintegration of man with nature thanks to the perfection of technology; one aspect of alienation in work might then be overcome without the need for a romantic 'return to nature'.

Substantially Marcuse has the same hope. Although he rejects the whole anti-ethos of affluent productivity, he does not equate his revolt with a commitment to simplicity or to 'nature'; instead, he conceives of liberation in the form of 'a higher stage of human development, based on the achievements of the technological society.'[26] We are reaching the stage where all necessary production can be automated to the extent that obligatory labour-time could be minimal – 'From this point on, technical progress would transcend the realm of necessity, where it served as the instrument of domination and exploitation which thereby limited its rationality; technology would become subject to the free play of faculties in the struggle for the purification of nature and of society.'[27] Automation could thus revolutionize the whole of society :

> The reification of human labor power, driven to perfection, would shatter the reified form by cutting the chain that ties the individual to the machinery – the mechanism through which his own labor enslaves him. Complete automation in the realm of necessity would open the dimension of free time as the one in which man's private *and* societal existence would constitute itself. This would be the historical transcendence towards a new civilization.[28]

An as yet 'uncharted realm of freedom beyond necessity' awaits us through the triumph of technology, when what work there is will, because of its very freedom (it would presumably be freely chosen and freely executed), naturally tend to have a libidinal content, to gratify the instincts. Life in general would acquire an aesthetic character – the character of *play* in its highest form.

The sweeping optimism of Marcuse's theory is not, however, easy to accept wholesale. 'Uncharted' this realm is indeed, and no amount of subtle, abstract argument (Marcuse can be remarkably abstract in his predictions) can convince us that his confidence is well-founded. Does he see no danger in the kind of centralization of the productive apparatus he outlines? Is it not just as likely to lead to a profound disorientation and alienation? The question remains very much open : are we heading for a new liberation of our essentially human faculties in work, or for the untold alienations of technocratic totalitarianism as presaged in the inhuman 'worker-universe' of Ernst Jünger? No amount of optimism should blind us to the danger of the latter, and it is for playing their part in awakening our consciousness and vigilance to this fundamental problem that we must be grateful to the writers of the tradition we have examined. Some specialists, such as the psychotechnician, Otto Lipmann, have gone so far in the opposite direction as to suggest that a kind of 'salvation' for the industrial worker may lie in making the gestures of work as monotonous and mindless as possible, whilst assuring the physical comfort of the worker at his post. The theory is that this would allow him to carry out his work unconsciously, so that he could think about other things at the same time.[29] Obviously this development would be counter to the search for an ethic of work, amounting, on the contrary, to a complete despiritualization of work — with the danger of leaving man without an adequate, ethical centre.

This danger is by no means an abstract one. The whole future of both culture and democracy is at stake. Culture, because when separated from work it becomes gratuitous and socially divisive, a luxury for the happy few. Democracy, because the undermining of creativity in industrial work must inevitably have a corresponding influence on life as a whole, not least on political life. To strip a man of all responsibility in his work is to encourage a lack of responsibility in the whole of his life, it is to promote apathy and thereby to put more and more in jeopardy the real basis of democratic society. To strip him of creativity in his job is to invite a passive attitude towards history, and, therefore, towards the formation of his own life and his own society. To take away that sense of finality in work that hardly seems able to survive the extreme division of labour and the competitive consumer industry of our civilization only contributes to make man less of a member of a meaningful community — worst of all, it undermines the very notion of community as an ethical entity with a common sense of purpose. This invitation to passivity, non-creativity, acceptance and lack of respon- sibility creates precisely the pre-conditions for fascism. The gradual erosion of those qualities associated with work at its best — qualities of critical acumen, initiative, purposiveness — could with the aid of propaganda, which flourishes precisely in the absence of such qualities, have more far-reaching dangers for society that we commonly care to

imagine. It would appear that Morris was — as so often— remarkably
clear-sighted when he equated the popular arts (embodying the qualities
of work at its best) and democracy.

It is in this context that we must read Camus' insistence on the need
for a renaissance of creativity. The vagueness of its formulation should
not hide its real urgency. And the same applies to the whole tradition
of protest and aspiration represented by the search for an ethic of
rewarding work in the industrial world. Vague, utopian, contradictory,
unrealistic, romantic — all this at times it may be. But the protest is of
inestimable value for our life and culture, and in what we can learn from
these writers may lie a salvation or an enrichment. The truth of this may
well begin to dawn, in the far-reaching re-thinking of our whole way of
life that energy crises — which are almost certain to affect the economic
fabric of most industrialized countries — are already beginning to
provoke. Such idealistic visions as Morris' *News from Nowhere* may
appear sterile at first, mere unrealistic sentimentality and wishful
thinking : but maybe it is wrong to overstress the objective factors of
a need for change at the expense of the subjective. Without the vision,
would men ever be moved to apply themselves with the necessary
passion to the objective problems at all? And what is politics without
an ethical centre of gravity? Herbert Read has argued movingly if a
little unfashionably for the importance of the utopian tradition. It has,
he claims, been the inspiration of political philosophy, providing a
'poetic undercurrent which has kept that science intellectually alive.'
And he adds a quotation from Cassirer's *Essay on Man* with which we
could well end :

> The great mission of the Utopia is to make room for the possible as
> opposed to a passive acquiescence in the present actual state of
> affairs. It is symbolic thought which overcomes the natural inertia
> of man and endows him with a new ability, the ability constantly to
> reshape his human universe.[30]

Notes

Notes to Chapter 1

1 R. Garaudy, *Marxism in the Twentieth Century* (London, Collins, 1970), p.97.

2 G. Orwell, *The Road to Wigan Pier* (Harmondsworth, Penguin, 1962), p.173.

3 B. Jowett (ed.), *The Dialogues of Plato*, 3rd ed. (London, Oxford University Press, 1924), Vol. III, p.194.

4 Quoted by A. Tilgher, *Work – What it has meant to Men through the Ages* (London, Harrap, 1931), p.5.

5 Quoted by D. Scott, *The Psychology of Work* (London, Duckworth, 1970), pp.34–5.

6 G. Friedmann, *Où va le travail humain?* (Paris, Gallimard, 1963), p.342.

7 S. Freud, *The Complete Psychological Works* (London, Hogarth, 1935–71), Vol. XXI, p.8.

8 F. Herzberg, B. Mausner, B. Snyderman, *The Motivation to Work* (New York, Wiley and Sons, 1959), p.131.

9 Quoted by G. Friedmann, op. cit., pp.344–5.

10 D. Scott, op.cit., p.98.

11 G. Friedmann, op.cit., p.44.

12 K. Marx, *Capital* (London, Dent, 1957), pp.379–80.

13 ibid., p.355.

14 ibid., p.385.

15 G. Friedmann, op. cit., p.118.

16 Quoted by E. Chinoy, 'Manning the Machines – The Assembly-line Worker' in P. Berger (ed.), *The Human Shape of Work* (New York, Macmillan, 1964), p.66.

17 A. Smith, *The Wealth of Nations* (London, Oxford University Press, 1904), Vol. II, p.417.

18 H. Arvon, *La Philosophie du travail* (Paris, Presses Universitaires de France, 1964), p.25.

19 K. Marx, *Economic and Philosophic Manuscripts of 1844* (New York, International Publishers, 1964), pp.113–14.

20 G. Orwell, op. cit., p.180.

21 H. Read, *Anarchy and Order* (London, Faber and Faber, 1954), p.69.

22 P. Laslett, *The World we have lost* (London, Methuen, 1965), pp.3, 7, 45.

23 F. Herzberg, B. Mausner, B. Snyderman, op. cit., p.121.

24 E. P. Thompson, *The Making of the English Working Class* (London, Gollancz, 1963), p.211.

25 ibid., p.446.
26 ibid., p.552.

Notes to Chapter 2

1 J. -J. Rousseau, *Rêveries du promeneur solitaire* (Manchester University Press, 1964), p.77.
2 F. Hölderlin, *Sämtliche Werke* (Stuttgart, Kohlhammer, 1953), Bd. 2, p.114.
3 Quoted by H. Marcuse, *Eros and Civilization* (London, Sphere Books, 1972), p.135.
4 W. Blake, *Complete Writings* (London, Oxford University Press, 1969), p.337.
5 ibid., p.625.
6 ibid., p.636.
7 T. Carlyle, *Critical and Miscellaneous Essays* (London, Chapman and Hall, 1899), Vol. II, pp.59, 63.
8 ibid., p.74.
9 K. Marx, F. Engels, *The Communist Manifesto* (Harmondsworth, Penguin, 1967), p.82.
10 E. P. Thompson, op. cit., p.360.
11 Quoted by J. C. Sherburne, *John Ruskin, or the Ambiguities of Abundance* (Cambridge, Massachusetts, Harvard University Press, 1972), p.50.
12 K. Marx, *Economic and Philosophic Manuscripts*, p.111.
13 ibid., p.110.
14 K. Marx, *Capital*, p.381.
15 K. Marx, *Economic and Philosophic Manuscripts*, p.111.
16 K. Marx, *Capital*, p.51.
17 C. Dickens, *Hard Times* (London, Chapman and Hall, 1903), p.31.
18 J. Ruskin, *The Works* (London, George Allen, 1903–9), Vol. XVI, p.338.
19 J. Ruskin, op. cit., Vol. X, p.193.
20 ibid., p.195.
21 ibid., Vol. VIII, pp.219–20.
22 D. H. Lawrence, *Lady Chatterley's Lover* (London, Heinemann, 1960), p.143.
23 ibid., p.109.
24 ibid., p.15.
25 D. H. Lawrence, *The First Lady Chatterley* (London, Heinemann, 1972), p.151.
26 D. H. Lawrence, *Women in Love* (London, Heinemann, 1954), p.414.
27 ibid., p.218.
28 ibid., p.223.
29 ibid., p.361.
30 ibid., p.347.
31 E. Toller, *Eine Jugend in Deutschland* (Amsterdam, Querido, 1933), p.84.
32 G. Kaiser, *Stücke, Erzählungen, Aufsätze, Gedichte* (Cologne, Kiepenheuer and Witsch, 1966), p.201.
33 E. Toller, *Masse Mensch* (Potsdam, Kiepenheuer, 1922), p.70.
34 E. Toller, *Die Maschinenstürmer* (Leipzig, Tal, 1922), pp.45, 74.
35 E. Toller, *Quer durch : Reisebilder und Reden* (Berlin, Kiepenheuer, 1930), p.26.
36 L. -F. Céline, *Voyage au bout de la nuit* (Paris, Gallimard, 1952), pp.232–4.
37 H. G. Wells, *First Men on the Moon, The Works* (London, Fisher Unwin, 1924–27), Vol. VI, pp.236–7.
38 ibid., p.239.
39 ibid., pp.237, 240.
40 ibid., p.241.
41 H. G. Wells, op. cit., Vol. IX, pp.138, 91.
42 F. Herzberg, *Work and the Nature of Man* (London, Staples Press, 1968), p.39.

Notes to Chapter 3

1 R. H. Tawney, *Religion and the Rise of Capitalism* (London, Murray, 1926), p.92.
2 A. Tilgher, op. cit., pp.59–60.
3 E. P. Thompson, op. cit., p.362.
4 N. V. Riasanovsky, *The Teaching of Charles Fourier* (Berkeley, University of California Press, 1969), p.76.
5 ibid., pp.231–2.
6 H. Marcuse, *Eros and Civilization*, p.154.
7 S. Freud, op. cit., p.80.
8 H. Marcuse, *Eros and Civilization*, p.70. *
9 ibid., p.42.

10 T. Carlyle, *Past and Present, The Works of Carlyle* (London, Chapman and Hall, 1897), Vol. X, p.202.
11 ibid., p.198.
12 ibid., p.159.
13 ibid., p.141.
14 ibid., p.153.
15 ibid., p.196.
16 ibid., p.298.
17 Quoted by P. Henderson, *William Morris. His Life, Work and Friends* (London, Thames and Hudson, 1967), p.14.
18 J. Ruskin, op. cit., Vol. X, pp.193–4.
19 ibid., p.201.
20 ibid., Vol. VIII, p.218.
21 ibid., Vol. XXVIII, p.211.
22 W. Morris, *The Collected Works* (London, Longmans Green, 1910–15), Vol. XXII, p.42.
23 M. Morris, *William Morris, Artist, Writer, Socialist* (Oxford, Blackwell, 1936), Vol. I, p.276.
24 A. von Helmholtz-Phelan, *The Social Philosophy of William Morris* (Durham, Duke University Press, 1927), pp.34–5.
25 W. Morris, op. cit., Vol. XXII, p.9.
26 M. Morris, op. cit., Vol. I, pp.282–3.
27 W. Morris, op. cit., Vol. XXIII, p.90.
28 ibid., Vol. XVI, p.31.
29 ibid., Vol. XXIV, p.384.
30 ibid., Vol. XXII, p.33.
31 ibid., Vol. XVI, p.91.
32 É. Zola, *Paris* (Paris, Fasquelle, 1954), p.187.
33 É. Zola, *Travail* (Paris, Fasquelle, 1957), p.173.
34 ibid., p.49.
35 ibid., p.59.
36 ibid., p.44.
37 ibid., p.54.
38 ibid., p.160.
39 ibid., p.196.
40 ibid., pp.596, 643.
41 L. N. Tolstoy, *What Then Must We Do?* (London, Oxford University Press, 1950), p.327.
42 Quoted by R. Rees, *Simone Weil. A Sketch for a Portrait* (London, Oxford University Press, 1966), p.18.

43 E. Gill, *Essays* (London, Cape, 1947), p.67.
44 A. Malraux, *La Condition humaine* (Paris, Gallimard, 1946), p.269.
45 G. Friedmann, op. cit., p.350.
46 E. Toller, *Quer durch*, pp.121–4.

Notes to Chapter 4

1 T. Carlyle, *Past and Present*, p.277.
2 G. Eliot, *Adam Bede* (London, Dent, 1966), p.207.
3 ibid., p.13.
4 ibid., p.113.
5 ibid., p.205.
6 ibid., p.313.
7 I. Howe, *Thomas Hardy* (London, Weidenfeld and Nicolson, 1968), p.19.
8 M. Williams, *Thomas Hardy and Rural England* (London, Macmilian, 1972), p.124.
9 T. Hardy, *Far from the Madding Crowd* (London, Macmillan, 1904), p.167.
10 T. Hardy, *The Woodlanders* (London, Macmillan, 1903), p.76.
11 T. Hardy, *Tess of the D'Urbervilles* (London, Macmillan, 1903), pp.421–2.
12 T. Hardy, *Jude the Obscure* (London, Macmillan, 1906), pp.6–7.
13 ibid., p.100.
14 ibid., p.117.
15 ibid., pp.384–5.
16 M. Williams, op. cit., p.190.
17 G. Perris (ed.), *The Life and Teaching of Leo Tolstoy* (London, Grant Richards, 1901), p.114.
18 ibid., p.128.
19 Quoted by G. R. Noyes, *Tolstoy* (New York, Dover Publications, 1968), p.216.
20 E. J. Simmons, *Leo Tolstoy* (New York, Vintage Books, 1960), Vol. II, p.62.
21 C. -L. Philippe, *Charles Blanchard* (Paris, Gallimard, 1924), p.223.
22 L. N. Tolstoy, *The Cossacks* (London, Scott, 1888), p.259.
23 L. N. Tolstoy, *Anna Karenina* (London, Oxford University Press, 1949), p.40.

24 ibid., p.313.
25 ibid., p.286.
26 ibid., p.292.
27 C. Péguy, *Œuvres en prose 1909–1914* (Paris, Gallimard, 1961), p.593.
28 ibid., p.1104.
29 ibid., p.1105.
30 ibid., p.1106.
31 ibid., p.594.
32 S. Weil, *La Condition ouvrière* (Paris, Gallimard, 1951), p.261.
33 S. Weil, *L'Enracinement* (Paris, Gallimard, 1949), p.49.
34 ibid., p.73.
35 ibid., p.87.
36 S. Weil, *La Condition ouvrière*, p.158.
37 S. Weil, *L'Enracinement*, p.99.
38 A. Camus, *Carnets* (janvier 1942 – mars 1951) (Paris, Gallimard, 1964), p.200.
39 A. Camus, *Essais* (Paris, Gallimard, 1965), pp.854–5.
40 A. Camus, *Théâtre, récits, nouvelles* (Paris, Gallimard, 1962), p.1600.
41 ibid., p.1604.
42 A. Camus, *Essais*, p.797.
43 ibid., p.842.
44 J. Giono, *Rondeur des jours* (Paris, Gallimard, 1969), p.173.
45 A. Solzhenitsyn, *The First Circle* (London, Collins, 1969), p.74.
46 ibid., p.206.
47 ibid., p.183.
48 ibid., p.169.
49 A. Solzhenitsyn, 'Letter to the Soviet Leaders' (*The Sunday Times*, 3 March 1974).
50 A. Wesker, *The Wesker Trilogy* (London, Cape, 1960), p.42.
51 A. Wesker, *The Kitchen* (London, Cape, 1961), p.53.
52 ibid., p.78.
53 A. Wesker, *The Wesker Trilogy*, pp.165–6.
54 A. Wesker, *The Four Seasons* (London, Cape, 1966), p.59.
55 A. Wesker, *The Wesker Trilogy*, p.196.

Notes to Chapter 5

1 E. Gill, op. cit., p.16.
2 W. Morris, op. cit., Vol. XXIII, p.24.
3 E. Toller, *Masse Mensch*, p.31.
4 E. Toller, *Die Maschinenstürmer*, p.43.
5 W. Morris, op. cit., Vol. XXIII, p.87.
6 ibid., p.161.
7 ibid., Vol. XVI, p.71.
8 ibid., Vol. XXII, p.38.
9 É. Zola, *Travail*, p.379.
10 ibid., pp.477–80.
11 ibid., pp.580–1.
12 ibid., p.545.
13 W. Morris, op. cit., Vol. XXII, p.340.
14 E. Jünger, *Der Arbeiter. Herrschaft und Gestalt, Werke* (Stuttgart, Klett, 1964), Bd. VI, p.250.
15 H. Marcuse, *Eros and Civilization*, p.23.
16 E. Jünger, op. cit., p.56.
17 ibid., p.61.
18 ibid., pp.260, 270.
19 ibid., p.103.
20 ibid., p. 214.
21 ibid., p.83.
22 ibid., p.97.
23 ibid., p.74.
24 ibid., p.108.
25 ibid., pp.116–17.
26 ibid., p.118.
27 ibid., p.111.
28 ibid., p.232.
29 U. Apollonio (ed.), *Futurist Manifestos* (London, Thames and Hudson, 1973), p.21.
30 ibid., p.22.
31 ibid., p.85.
32 ibid., pp.22, 97.
33 ibid., p.172.
34 G. Kaiser, op. cit., p.174.
35 ibid., pp.211–12.
36 ibid., p.228.
37 D. H. Lawrence, *Women in Love*, pp.220–1.
38 C. Péguy, *Œuvres en prose 1899–1908* (Paris, Gallimard, 1961), p.322.
39 G. Orwell, *The Road to Wigan Pier*, pp.178, 182.
40 J. Ruskin, op. cit., Vol. X, p.191.
41 ibid., p.192.

Notes to Chapter 6

1 H. Marcuse, *One-Dimensional Man. Studies in the Ideology of Advanced Industrial Society* (London, Routledge and Kegan Paul, 1964), p.11.
2 M. Grennan, *William Morris, Medievalist and Revolutionary* (New York, Kings Crown Press, 1954), pp.136–7.
3 J. Joll, *The Anarchists* (London, Methuen, 1969), p.67.
4 ibid., p.64.
5 É. Zola, *Paris*, p.72.
6 J. Joll, op. cit., p.277.
7 C. Péguy, *De Jean Coste, Œuvres en prose 1898–1908.*
8 W. Morris, op. cit., Vol. XXII, p.76.
9 G. Woodcock, *Anarchism* (Harmondsworth, Penguin, 1963), p.344.
10 Quoted by M. Grennan, op. cit., p.154.
11 W. Morris, op. cit., Vol. XXIII, p.278.
12 Introduction to : M. Morris, op. cit., Vol. I, p.xvi.
13 W. Morris, op. cit., Vol. XVI, p.79.
14 ibid., Vol. XXII, p.334.
15 ibid., Vol. XVI, p.92.
16 M. Grennan, op.cit., p.120.
17 ibid., p.153.
18 G. Woodcock, op.cit., p.23.
19 Quoted by G. Lefranc, *Le Mouvement syndical sous la Troisième République* (Paris, Payot, 1967), pp.60–1.
20 H. Dubief (ed.), *Le Syndicalisme révolutionnaire* (Paris, Colin, 1969), p.194.
21 J. A. Estey, *Revolutionary Syndicalism : an Exposition and a Criticism* (London, King, 1913), pp.98–9.
22 C. Péguy, *Œuvres en prose 1909–1914*, pp.601–2.
23 H. Dubief, op. cit., p.198.
24 G. Lefranc, op. cit., p.151.
25 H. Dubief, op. cit., p.70; G. Lefranc, op. cit., p.85.
26 C. Péguy, *Œuvres en prose 1909–1914*, p.1111.
27 G. Sorel, *Réflexions sur la violence* (Paris, 1930), p.118.
28 G. Sorel, *Les Illusions du progrès* (Paris, Rivière, 1947), pp.122–3.
29 G. Brenan, *The Spanish Labyrinth* (Cambridge University Press, 1960).
30 J. A. Estey, op. cit., p.125.
31 G. Sorel, *Les Illusions du progrès*, p.380.
32 E. Toller, *Eine Jugend in Deutschland*, p.10.
33 J. A. Estey, op. cit., p.202.
34 S. Weil, *L'Enracinement*, p.51.
35 S. Weil, *La Condition ouvrière*, p.16.
36 E. Gill, *Essays*, p.107.
37 A. Camus, *Essais*, p.784.
38 A. Camus, *Carnets* (mai 1935 – février 1942) (Paris, Gallimard, 1962), pp.39, 64.
39 A. Wesker, *Fears of Fragmentation* (London, Cape, 1970), p.76.
40 ibid., p.108.
41 ibid., p.74
42 A. Wesker, *Their Very Own and Golden City* (London, Cape, 1966), p.52.
43 D. Guérin (ed.), *Ni Dieu ni maître. anthologie historique du mouvement anarchiste* (Lausanne, La Cité, 196-), p.563.
44 G. Orwell, op. cit., pp.166, 176.

Notes to Chapter 7

1 G. Lefranc, op. cit., p.89.
2 G. Sorel, *Les Illusions du progrès*, p.284.
3 G. Sorel, *Réflexions sur la violence*, p.452.
4 I. L. Horowitz, *Radicalism and the Revolt against Reason* (London, Routledge, 1961), p.103.
5 D. Guérin, op. cit., p.211.
6 W. Morris, op. cit., Vol. XVI, p.91.
7 K. Marx, *Economic and Philosophic Manuscripts*, p.111.
8 É. Zola, *Travail*, p.183.
9 ibid., p.298.
10 ibid., p.195.
11 É. Zola, *Les Rougon-Macquart* (Paris, Gallimard, 1963), Vol. I, p.1408.

12 É. Zola, *Fécondité* (Paris, Fasquelle, 1957), p.17.
13 ibid., p.331.
14 'After the burning pavement of Paris, parched by the harsh struggle of day, by the sterile and prostituted rut of evening, beneath the fire of electric lamps, what adorable rest was afforded by this vast silence, this heavenly soft blue glow, this endless unfolding of plains refreshed with darkness, dreaming of procreation in the expectation of tomorrow's sun! And what health, what honesty, what bliss rose from nature in child-bed, falling asleep under the dew of night only in preparation for triumphant awakenings, ever renewed by the torrent of life that streams even in the dust of footpaths!' ibid., pp.85–6.
15 'Such was the force, the power that rose from the whole estate, the work of life born forth, created, the work of man fertilizing the sterile earth, delivering it of its nourishing riches, for an increased humanity that would conquer the world.' ibid., p.604.
16 É. Zola, *Travail*, p.120.
17 ibid., p.438.
18 C. -L. Philippe, op. cit.. p.94.
19 ibid., p.222.
20 R. Garaudy, *Le Grand Tournant du socialisme* (Paris, Gallimard, 1969), p.50.
21 J. -P. Sartre, *Situations III* (Paris, Gallimard, 1949), p.213.
22 R. Garaudy, *Le Grand Tournant du socialisme*, p.55.
23 R. Garaudy, *Marxism in the Twentieth Century*, p.178.
24 R. Garaudy, *Le Grand Tournant du socialisme*, p.57.
25 ibid., p.110.
26 E. Toller, *Die Maschinenstürmer*, pp.44, 108.
27 E. Toller, *Masse Mensch*, p.30.
28 ibid., p.49.
29 É. Zola, *Travail*, p.326.
30 G. Kaiser, op. cit., p.654.
31 É. Zola, *Travail*, p.378.
32 J. C. Sherburne, op. cit., p.130.
33 É. Zola, *Travail*, p.325.
34 É. Zola, *Fécondité*, p.216.
35 S. Weil, *La Condition ouvrière*, p.212.
36 S. Weil, *L'Enracinement*, p.20.
37 A. Camus, *Essais*, pp.620, 676.
38 ibid., p.678. See my article ' "Un classicisme créateur" : Charles Péguy and Albert Camus', *Forum for Modern Language Studies*, Vol. VIII, No. 2, April 1972.
39 C. Péguy, *Œuvres en prose 1909–1914*, p.542.
40 Camus, *Essais*, p.678.
41 ibid., p.620.
42 ibid., p.713.
43 ibid., p.659.

Notes to Chapter 8

1 J. Huizinga, *Homo Ludens. A Study of the Play-Element in Culture* (London, Routledge and Kegan Paul, 1949), p.129.
2 ibid., p.26.
3 ibid., p.119.
4 ibid., p.17.
5 ibid., p.116.
6 ibid., p.192.
7 ibid., p.193.
8 T. Veblen, *The Theory of the Leisure Class* (New York, Macmillan, 1912).
9 E. Fischer, *The Necessity of Art* (Harmondsworth, Penguin, 1963), p.15.
10 ibid., p.36.
11 ibid., p.21.
12 ibid., p.23.
13 ibid., p.33.
14 ibid., p.49.
15 R. Garaudy, *Marxism in the Twentieth Century*, p.180.
16 H. Marcuse, *Eros and Civilization*, pp.136–7.
17 J. C. F. von Schiller, *Sämtliche Werke* (Stuttgart, Cotta, 1881), Bd. XII, p.59.
18 J. C. Sherburne, op.cit., p.172.
19 Quoted by A. von Helmholtz-Phelan, op. cit., pp.42–3.
20 W. Morris, op. cit., Vol. XXII, p.4.
21 ibid., p.6.
22 ibid., p.42.

23 N. Birnbaum, *The Crisis of Industrial Society* (New York, Oxford University Press, 1969), p.163.
24 W. Morris, op. cit., Vol. XXII, p.79.
25 Quoted by P. Henderson, op. cit., p.369.
26 ibid., p.240.
27 E. Gill, op. cit., p.170.
28 ibid., p.45.
29 ibid., p.56.
30 ibid., p.55.
31 A. Wesker, *Fears of Fragmentation*, p.44.
32 D. Smith, *Sculpture and Writings* (London, Thames and Hudson, 1968), pp.50, 61.
33 É. Zola, *Travail*, p.644.
34 ibid., p.600.
35 ibid., p.601.
36 N. V. Riasanovsky, op. cit., p.242.
37 R. Garaudy, *Marxism in the Twentieth Century*, p.78.

Notes to Chapter 9

1 K. Marx, *Capital*, p.384.
2 F. Engels, *The Condition of the Working Class in England in 1844* (London, Allen and Unwin, 1892), p.24.
3 C. Péguy, *Œuvres en prose 1909–1914*, p.1103.
4 S. Weil, *L'Enracinement*, p.45.
5 ibid., p.51.
6 G. Friedmann, op. cit., p.47.
7 ibid., p.51.
8 J. Giono, *Rondeur des jours* (Paris, Gallimard, 1943), p.40.
9 S. Weil, *L'Enracinement*, p.59; *La Condition ouvrière*, p.257.
10 Quoted by G. Sorel, *Les Illusions du progrès*, p.380.
11 D. Guérin, op. cit., p.213.
12 H. Read, *Anarchy and Order* (London, Faber and Faber, 1954), p.228.
13 E. Jünger, *Der Arbeiter*, p.176.
14 D. H. Lawrence, *Women in Love*, p.223.
15 ibid., p.108.
16 D. H. Lawrence, *Assorted Articles* (London, Secker, 1930), p.131.

17 D. H. Lawrence, *The First Lady Chatterley*, p.219.
18 ibid., p.222.
19 D. H. Lawrence, *Lady Chatterley's Lover*, p.69.
20 ibid., p.277.
21 H. Marcuse, *Eros and Civilization*, p.120.
22 H. Marcuse, *One-Dimensional Man*, p.73.
23 H. Marcuse, *Eros and Civilization*, p.145.
24 E. Gill, op. cit., p.69.
25 W. Morris, op. cit., Vol. XXIII, p.17.
26 P. Henderson, op. cit., p.256.
27 M. Morris, op. cit., Vol. I, p.267.
28 ibid., p.272.
29 W. Morris, op. cit., Vol. XXII, p.66.
30 G. Kaiser, op. cit., pp.209–10.
31 ibid., p.221.
32 ibid., p.682.
33 ibid., p.681.
34 É. Zola, *Travail*, p.327.
35 ibid., p.543.
36 C. Péguy, *Œuvres en prose 1909–1914*, p.1106.
37 P. Laslett, op. cit., p.21.
38 E. P. Thompson, op. cit., p.416.
39 P. Berger, op. cit., p.217.
40 A. Wesker, *The Wesker Trilogy*, p.40.
41 ibid., p.167.
42 ibid., p.196.
43 Introduction to : A. Wesker, *Their Very Own and Golden City*, p.10.
44 A. Wesker, *The Wesker Trilogy*, p.202.

Notes to Chapter 10

1 J. Weiss, *The Fascist Tradition* (New York, Harper and Row, 1967), Editor's Introduction, p.xi.
2 D. H. Lawrence, *The Collected Letters* (London, Heinemann, 1962), Vol. I, p.355.
3 Quoted by S. Sanders, *D. H. Lawrence : The World of the Major Novels* (London, Vision Press, 1973), p.177.
4 D. H. Lawrence, *The Collected Letters*, Vol. I, p.352.

5 D. H. Lawrence, *Kangaroo* (London, Heinemann, 1955), p.105.
6 ibid., p.289.
7 D. H. Lawrence, *The Collected Letters*, Vol. I, p.402.
8 Quoted by J. R. Harrison, *The Reactionaries* (London, Gollancz, 1966), p.187.
9 E. Weber, *Action Française* (California, Stanford University Press, 1962), p.29.
10 J. Plumyène and R. Lasierra, *Les Fascismes français* (Paris, Seuil, 1963), p.32.
11 ibid., p.140.
12 F. F. Ridley, *Revolutionary Syndicalism* (London, Cambridge University Press, 1970), p.8.
13 A. Hitler, *Mein Kampf* (Munich, Franz Eher, 1933), p.118.
14 ibid., p.348.
15 ibid., p.482.
16 ibid., p.675.
17 J. Plumyène and R. Lasierra, op. cit., pp.53–60.
18 ibid., p.127.
19 ibid., p.147.
20 R. Aron, *Histoire de Vichy* (Paris, Les Productions de Paris, 1959), p.152.
21 ibid., p.156.
22 ibid., p.158.
23 ibid., p.155.
24 J. Weiss, op. cit., p.27.
25 Quoted by M. Grennan, op. cit., p.14.
26 C. Péguy, *Œuvres en prose 1909–1914*, p.1105.
27 L. N. Tolstoy, *Anna Karenina*, p.313.
28 S. Weil, *L'Enracinement*, p.23.
29 T. Carlyle, *Past and Present*, p.204.
30 D. H. Lawrence, 'Men must work and Women as well', *Assorted Articles*.
31 J. Plumyène and R. Lasierra, op. cit., p.47.
32 E. Gill, op. cit., pp.48, 63.
33 P. Lafargue, *The Right to be Lazy (and other Studies)* (Chicago, Kerr, 1907), pp.9–12.
34 H. Dubief, op. cit., p.198.
35 H. Marcuse, *Eros and Civilization*, p.155.
36 É. Zola, *Travail*, p.23.

37 W. Morris, op. cit., Vol. XXIII, p.98.
38 T. Carlyle, *Past and Present*, pp.186, 156.
39 ibid., pp.212, 220, 282.
40 J. Ruskin, *Munera Pulveris, The Works*, Vol. XVII, p.255.
41 J. C. Sherburne, op. cit., p.70.
42 J. Ruskin, *Fors Clavigera, The Works*, Vol. XXVII, p.96.
43 H. G. Wells, op. cit., Vol. IX, p.91.
44 T. Veblen, op. cit., p.162.
45 R. Tressell, *The Ragged-Trousered Philanthropists* (London, Lawrence and Wishart, 1955), p.97.
46 ibid., p.67.
47 ibid., p.140.
48 ibid., p.401.

Notes to Chapter 11

1 G. Friedmann, op. cit., p.326.
2 E. Toller, *Quer durch*, p.124.
3 G. Friedmann, op. cit., p.366.
4 F. Herzberg, B. Mausner, B. Snyderman, op. cit., pp.130, 139.
5 W. Morris, op. cit., Vol. XXII, p.33.
6 ibid., Vol. XXIII, pp.20–1.
7 ibid., pp.19–20.
8 G. Orwell, op. cit., pp.175, 176.
9 M. Morris, op. cit., Vol. II, p.132.
10 ibid., p.137.
11 ibid., p.133.
12 S. Weil, *La Condition ouvrière*, p.149.
13 S. Weil, *L'Enracinement*, p.9.
14 S. Weil, *La Condition ouvrière*, p.216.
15 ibid., p.149.
16 S. Weil, *L'Enracinement*, p.54.
17 ibid., p.59.
18 ibid., p.65.
19 ibid., pp.80, 86.
20 ibid., p.71.
21 F. Herzberg, *Work and the Nature of Man*, p.78.
22 G. Friedmann, op. cit., p.382.
23 ibid., p.259.
24 R. Garaudy, *Le Grand Tournant du socialisme*, p.23.
25 H. Arvon, op. cit., p.97.
26 H. Marcuse, *Eros and Civilization*, p.15.

27 H. Marcuse, *One-Dimensional Man*, p.16.
28 ibid., p.37.
29 G. Friedmann, op. cit., pp.212–13.
30 Quoted by H. Read, op. cit., p.12.

Bibliography

Apollonio, U. (ed.), *Futurist Manifestos*, London, Thames and Hudson, 1973.

Aron, R., *Histoire de Vichy*, Paris, Les Productions de Paris, 1959.

Arvon, H., *La Philosophie du travail*, Paris, Presses Universitaires de France, 1964.

Bellamy, E., *Looking Backward, 2000 – 1887*, London, Routledge, 1922.

Berger, P. (ed.), *The Human Shape of Work*, New York, Macmillan, 1964.

Birnbaum, N., *The Crisis of Industrial Society*, New York, Oxford University Press, 1969.

Blake, W., *Complete Writings*, London, Oxford University Press, 1969.

Brenan, G., *The Spanish Labyrinth*, London, Cambridge University Press, 1960.

Calvet, J. -Y., *La Pensée de Karl Marx*, Paris, Seuil, 1956.

Camus, A., *Carnets mai 1935 – février 1942*, Paris, Gallimard, 1962.
Carnets janvier 1942 – mars 1951, Paris, Gallimard, 1964.
Essais, Paris, Gallimard, 1965.
Théâtre, Récits, Nouvelles, Paris, Gallimard, 1962.

Carlyle, T., 'Chartism', in *Critical and Miscellaneous Essays*, Vol. IV, London, Chapman and Hall, 1899.
Past and Present, The Works of Carlyle, Vol. X, London, Chapman and Hall, 1897.
'Signs of the Times', in *Critical and Miscellaneous Essays*, Vol. II.

Céline, L. -F., *Voyage au bout de la nuit*, Paris, Gallimard, 1952.

Cole, G. D. H., *Guild Socialism Re-stated*, London, Parsons, 1921.

Dickens, C., *Hard Times*, London, Chapman and Hall, 1903.

Dubief, H., *Le Syndicalisme révolutionnaire*, Paris, Colin, 1969.

Eliot, G., *Adam Bede*, London, Dent, 1966.

Engels, F., *The Condition of the Working Class in England in 1844*, London, Allen and Unwin, 1892.

Estey, J. A., *Revolutionary Syndicalism. An Exposition and a Criticism*, London, King, 1913.

Farmer, P., *Vichy, Political Dilemma*, London, Oxford University Press, 1955.

Finley, M. I., *The Ancient Greeks*, London, Chatto and Windus, 1963.

Fischer, E., *The Necessity of Art*, Harmondsworth, Penguin, 1963.

Fourier, F. M. C., *Œuvres complètes*, Paris, Anthropos, 1967–8.

Freud, S., *Civilization and its Discontents, The Complete Psychological Works*, Vol. XXI, London, Hogarth, 1961.

Friedmann, G., *Où va le travail humain?*, Paris, Gallimard, 1963.

Garaudy, R., *Le Grand Tournant du socialisme*, Paris, Gallimard, 1969.
Marxism in the Twentieth Century, London, Collins, 1970.
Pour un Modèle français du socialisme, Paris, Gallimard, 1968.

Gill, E., *Essays*, London, Cape, 1947.

Giono, J., *Rondeur des jours*, Paris, Gallimard, 1943.
Un de Baumugnes, Paris, Grasset, 1929.

Grennan, M. R., *William Morris, Medievalist and Revolutionary*, New York, Kings Crown Press, 1945.

Guérin, D. (ed.), *Ni Dieu ni maître. Anthologie historique du mouvement anarchiste*, Lausanne, La Cité, 196-.

Hardy, T., *Far from the Madding Crowd*, London, Macmillan, 1904.
Jude the Obscure, London, Macmillan, 1906.
Tess of the D'Urbervilles, London, Macmillan, 1903.
The Woodlanders, London, Macmillan, 1903.

Harrison, J. R., *The Reactionaries*, London, Gollancz, 1966.

Helmholtz-Phelan, A. von, *The Social Philosophy of William Morris*, Durham, N. Carolina, Duke University Press, 1927.

Henderson, P., *William Morris. His Life, Work and Friends*, London, Thames and Hudson, 1967.

Herzberg, F., *Work and the Nature of Man*, London, Staples Press, 1968.

Herzberg, F., Mausner, B., Snyderman, B., *The Motivation to Work*, New York, Wiley, 1959.

Hitler, A., *Mein Kampf*, Munich, Franz Eher Nachfolger, 1933.

Hölderlin, F., *Sämtliche Werke*, Stuttgart, Kohlhammer, 1953.

Horowitz, I. L., *Radicalism and the Revolt against Reason*, London, Routledge, 1961.

Howe, I., *Thomas Hardy*, London, Weidenfeld and Nicolson, 1968.

Huizinga, J., *Homo Ludens*, London, Routledge and Kegan Paul, 1949.

Huxley, A., *Brave New World*, London, Chatto and Windus, 1971.

Illich, I. D., *Tools for Conviviality*, London, Calder and Boyars, 1973.

Joll, J., *The Anarchists*, London, Methuen, 1969.

Jowett, B. (ed.), *The Dialogues of Plato*, Vol. III, London, Oxford University Press, 1924.

Jünger, E., *Der Arbeiter, Werke*, Bd. VI, Stuttgart, Klett, 1964.

Kagarlitski, J., *The Life and Thought of H. G. Wells*, London, Sidgwick and Jackson, 1966.

Kaiser, G., *Stücke, Erzählungen, Aufsätze, Gedichte*, Cologne, Kiepenheuer and Witsch, 1966.

Kropotkin, P. A., *Fields, Factories and Workshops*, London, Nelson, 1912.

Lafargue, P., *The Right to be Lazy (and other Studies)*, Chicago, Kerr, 1907.

Laslett, P., *The World we have lost*, London, Methuen, 1965.

Lawrence, D. H., *Assorted Articles*, London, Secker, 1930.
Collected Essays, Harmondsworth, Penguin, 1950.
The Collected Letters, London, Heinemann, 1962.
Kangaroo, London, Heinemann, 1955.
The First Lady Chatterley, London, Heinemann, 1972.
Lady Chatterley's Lover, London, Heinemann, 1960.
The Plumed Serpent, London, Heinemann.
Women in Love, London, Heinemann, 1954.

Lefranc, G., *Le Mouvement syndical sous la Troisième République*, Paris, Payot, 1967.

Lucas, J. (ed.), *Literature and Politics in the Nineteenth Century*, London, Methuen, 1971.

Malraux, A., *La Condition humaine*, Paris, Gallimard, 1946.

Marcuse, H., *Eros and Civilization*, London, Sphere Books, 1972.
One-Dimensional Man, London, Routledge and Kegan Paul, 1964.

Marx, K., *Capital*, London, Dent, 1957.
Economic and Philosophic Manuscripts of 1844, New York, International Publishers, 1964.

Marx, K., and Engels, F., *The Communist Manifesto*, Harmondsworth Penguin, 1967.

Meakin, D., 'Decadence and the Devaluation of Work', *European Studies Review*, No. 1, January 1971.
' "Un classicisme créateur" : Charles Péguy and Albert Camus', *Forum for Modern Language Studies*, Vol. VIII, No. 2, April 1972.

Morris, M., *William Morris, Artist, Writer, Socialist*, Oxford, Blackwell, 1936.

Morris, W., *The Collected Works*, London, Longmans Green, 1910–15.

Noyes, G. R., *Tolstoy*, New York, Dover Publications, 1968.

Orwell, G., *The Road to Wigan Pier*, Harmondsworth, Penguin, 1962.

Péguy, C., *Œuvres en prose 1898 – 1908*, Paris, Gallimard, 1961.
Œuvres en prose 1909 – 1914, Paris, Gallimard, 1961.

Perris, G. N. (ed.), *The Life and Teaching of Leo Tolstoy*, London, Grant Richards, 1901.

Philippe, C. -L., *Charles Blanchard*, Paris, Gallimard, 1924.

Plumyène, J., and Lasierra, R., *Les Fascismes français*, Paris, Seuil, 1963.

Read, H., *Anarchy and Order*, London, Faber and Faber, 1954.

Rees, R., *Simone Weil. A Sketch for a Portrait*, London, Oxford University Press, 1966.

Riasanovsky, N. V., *The Teaching of Charles Fourier*, Berkeley, University of California Press, 1969.

Ridley, F. F., *Revolutionary Syndicalism in France*, London, Cambridge

University Press, 1970.

Rousseau, J. -J., *Rêveries du promeneur solitaire*, Manchester University Press, 1964.

Ruskin, J., *The Works*, London, George Allen, 1903–9.

Sanders, S., *D. H. Lawrence : The World of the Major Novels*, London, Vision, 1973.

Schiller, J. C. F. von, *Über die ästhetische Erziehung des Menschen*, *Sämtliche Werke*, Bd. XI, Stuttgart, Cotta, 1881.

Scott, D., *The Psychology of Work*, London, Duckworth, 1970.

Sherburne, J. C., *John Ruskin, or the Ambiguities of Abundance*, Cambridge, Massachusetts, Harvard University Press, 1972.

Singer, D., *Prelude to Revolution*, London, Cape, 1970.

Smith, D., *Sculpture and Writings*, London, Thames and Hudson, 1968.

Solzhenitsyn, A., *The First Circle*, London, Collins, 1969.

'Letter to the Soviet Leaders', *The Sunday Times*, 3 March, 1974.

Sorel, G., *Les Illusions du progrès*, Paris, Rivière, 1947.

Réflexions sur la violence, Paris, 1930.

Sussman, H. L., *Victorians and the Machine : the Literary Response to Technology*, Cambridge, Massachusetts, Harvard University Press, 1968.

Tawney, R. H., *Religion and the Rise of Capitalism*, London, Murray, 1926.

Taylor, F. W., *The Principles of Scientific Management*, New York, Harper, 1911.

Thompson, E. P., *The Making of the English Working Class*, London, Gollancz, 1963.

William Morris : From Romantic to Revolutionary, London, 1955.

Tilgher, A., *Work – What it has meant to Men through the Ages*, London, Harrap, 1931.

Toller, E., *Eine Jugend in Deutschland*, Amsterdam, Querido, 1933.

Die Maschinenstürmer, Leipzig, Tal, 1922.

Masse Mensch, Potsdam, Kiepenheuer, 1922.

Quer durch : Reisbilder und Reden, Berlin, Kiepenheuer, 1930.

Hoppla, wir leben!, Potsdam, Kiepenheuer, 1927.

Tolstoy, L. N., *Anna Karenina*, London, Oxford University Press, 1949.

The Cossacks, London, Scott, 1888.

What Then Must We Do? London, Oxford University Press, 1950.

Tressell, R., *The Ragged-Trousered Philanthropists*, London, Lawrence and Wishart, 1955.

Veblen, T., *The Theory of the Leisure Class*, New York, Macmillan, 1912.

Weber, E., *Action française*, Stanford University Press, 1962.

Weil, S., *La Condition ouvrière*, Paris, Gallimard, 1951.

L'Enracinement, Paris, Gallimard, 1949.

Weiss, J., *The Fascist Tradition*, New York, Harper and Row, 1967.

Wells, H. G., *The Works*, London, Fisher Unwin, 1924–27.

Wesker, A., *Fears of Fragmentation*, London, Cape, 1970.

The Four Seasons, London, Cape, 1966.

The Kitchen, London, Cape 1961.

Their Very Own and Golden City, London, Cape, 1966.

The Wesker Trilogy, London, Cape, 1960.

Williams, M., *Thomas Hardy and Rural England*, London, Macmillan, 1972.

Williams, R., *Culture and Society*, London, Chatto and Windus, 1958.

Woodcock, G., *Anarchism*, Harmondsworth, Penguin, 1963.

Zola, É., *Fécondité*, Paris, Fasquelle, 1957.

Paris, Paris, Fasquelle, 1954.

Les Rougon-Macquart, Paris, Gallimard, 1963.

Travail, Pairs, Fasquelle, 1957.

Index

Action Française, 109, 164-5
Agyris, C., 35
anarchism, 6, 87, 99-106, 110-14, 116
architecture, 44-7, 93, 96, 156
Aristotle, 2
Arkwright, R., 29
artisan, 8, 16, 20, 22, 28, 54, 85, 91, 101, 183, 191
Arvon, H., 195-6

Babeuf, G., 99
Bakunin, M., 100, 151
Berger, P., 159
Bergson, H., 109
Birnbaum, N., 138
Blake, W., 20-2, 147
Blueprint for Survival, 7
bourses du travail, 106, 108, 187
Brecht, B., 6
Brenan, G., 110
Bryden, R., 160
Bucard, M., 168

Calvin, J., 36
Camus, A., vii, viii, 5, 71-3, 112, 118, 128-30, 144, 151-2, 157, 182
capitalism, 22-3, 36-7, 67, 135-6
Carlyle, T., 21, 41-4, 48, 59, 70, 80, 147, 172, 175-6
Cassirer, E., 198
Céline, L.-F., 31-2
Centre 42, 142
Chaplin, C., 29

Christ, 3
Clair, R., 29
Cobbett, W., 21, 24
Cole, G. D. H., 6, 46
commodities, 23, 48
commodity fetishism, 135-6
community, 4, 22, 24, 48, 57, 127-9, 147-9, 155, 160-2, 170, 187-8, 197
conviviality, 6
Coty, F., 165, 172
'counseling', 194
Croix de Feu, 167

democracy, 14, 17, 33, 99, 113, 139, 153, 177, 197-8
Dickens, C., 24
division of labour, 10-11, 32-4, 39, 52
Drieu la Rochelle, P., 165
Durkheim, E., 9

education, 39, 48-9, 136, 141-2, 182, 187, 189-90, 192
efficiency, 9, 10, 29, 35, 58, 90, 92, 94, 96-7, 194
Eliot, G., 59-61
Éluard, P., 140
Engels, F., 15, 24, 148
environmentalism, 7, 27, 75, 93
Expressionism, 25, 29-31, 110, 126, 148, 157, 160

facism, 93, 162-71, 197
fertility, 120-2
Fischer, E., 133-6
Flaubert, G., 174
Ford, H., 29
Fourier, C., 38-41, 50-1, 100, 119, 145
Friedmann, G., 3, 8, 57, 149, 181-2, 183, 194-5
Freud, S., 3, 4, 40-1, 154
Futurism, 92-3

Garaudy, R., 1, 124-5, 136, 145-6, 195
Gill, E., 56, 81, 112, 140-2, 155, 173
Giono, J., 71, 73-4, 150, 169
Gorky, M., 125
Greek thought, 2
Grennan, M., 98-9, 104
Griffuelhes, V., 107-8
Guest, R. H., 11
Guild of Saint George, 45, 176
guilds, 9, 111-12
Guild Socialism, 6, 46

Halévy, D., 168
Hardy, T., 61-4
Hegel, G. W. F., 12. 71
Henderson, P., 45
Herzberg, F., 4-5, 15, 35, 182, 183-4, 193-4
Hitler, A., 166-7, 172
Hölderlin, F., 19, 29
Horowitz, I. L., 117-18
Howe, I., 61
Huizinga, J., 131-6
Huxley, A., 32

Illich, I. D., 6
industrial psychology, 6
Industrial Revolution, 1, 5, 11, 15-16, 24, 29

Jaurès, J., 107
job satisfaction, 6, 195
Joll, J., 99, 101
Jung, C. G., 5, 116
Jünger, E., 70, 85-96, 116, 152, 166

Kaiser, G., 29-30, 32, 93-5, 126-7, 157, 179
Kronstadt revolt, 114
Kropotkin, P. A., 49, 100, 101, 151

Lafargue, P., 173-4
La Rocque, F., Compte de, 167-8
Laslett, P., 15, 158-9
Laval, P., 170
Lawrence, D. H., 26-8, 42, 88, 95, 152-4, 162-4, 179
leisure, 1, 5, 89, 141, 154, 183-4
Lenin, V. I., 57, 125
Lipmann, O., 197
Lubbock, P., 143
Luddites, 16, 82
Luther, M., 36-7

machines, 9, 23, 80-5, 191
magic, 134-5
Malraux, A., 56-7
Marcuse, H., 19, 40-1, 98, 136-7, 154, 175, 196
Marinetti, F. T., 92-3
Marx, K., 6, 10, 12-13, 22-4, 70-1, 99, 114, 119, 124, 148
marxism, 71, 99, 101, 109-10, 117, 124-5, 133, 135
May 1968, 7
Mayo, E., 194
medievalism, 14-15, 21-2, 24-5, 36, 41, 44-8, 50, 67-8, 83ʹ, 98, 111-12, 161, 170-1, 185, 192
Merrheim, A., 107
methodism, 37-8
Morelly, 99
Morris, W., vii, viii, 6-8, 14, 34, 37, 44-50, 56, 81-5, 90, 96, 102-5, 118-19, 137-40, 147-8, 155-6, 170-1, 175, 177, 184-8, 198
music, 92, 132, 134, 140
myth, 109-10, 164

Nazism, 86, 166-7, 169

Orwell, G., 2, 13, 96, 114-15, 185-6
Owen, R., 39

Parti Populaire Français, 168
peasant cult, 168-9
Péguy, C., viii, 67-9, 95, 105, 107-9, 128-9, 147-8, 158, 164-5, 171, 173
Pelloutier, F., 106, 187
Pétain, H. P., 168-70
Philippe, C. -L., 65-6, 123, 128, 158
Plato, 2, 131-3